# TWO GENTS IN ITALY

# Two Gents in Italy

ANTHONY R. WILDMAN

Plutus Publishing Australia

*Dedicated as always to Robert, my partner in life and on this amazing journey.*
*AND*
*To all the friends new and old who made our time in Italy so special:*
*Margarita*
*Olivier*
*Jan*
*Roy*
*Siobhan and David*
*Glenn and Giovanni*
*Rocky and Brendan*
*Peter and Jaycen*
*John and Judith*
*Jim and Andrea*
*Jeremy*
*Shane*
*Tricia*
*Laura*
*Alan*
*Georgeta and Gianpaolo*
*Valentino and Adina*
*Felix and Jayne*
*Garry and Paula*
*Dorothy*
*Chris*
*Ross*
*Michael*
*Luke*
*Fiona and Sue*
*Sasha*

Copyright © 2021 by Anthony Wildman

All rights reserved. No part of this book may be reproduced in any manner whatsoever without written permission except in the case of brief quotations embodied in critical articles and reviews.

First Printing, 2021

Cover design by: Terry Abraham

# Contents

| | | |
|---|---|---|
| *Dedication* | | iv |
| 1 | Introduction | 1 |
| 2 | Time Travelling in Rome | 9 |
| 3 | Venice in Winter | 20 |
| 4 | The Merchants of Venice | 34 |
| 5 | The Venetian Lagoon | 45 |
| 6 | Food, Wine, and La Dolce Vita | 53 |
| 7 | Hunting Caravaggio | 65 |
| 8 | Opera and Shakespeare in Verona | 75 |
| 9 | A Quick Tour of the Renaissance | 87 |
| 10 | Portrait of a Piazza | 98 |
| 11 | The David(s) of Florence | 108 |
| 12 | Country life: A Farmhouse in Volterra | 116 |

| 13 | Napoleon's Island | 127 |
| 14 | Milan and Leonardo: Art and Power | 135 |
| 15 | Italy has a Riviera too | 147 |
| 16 | Surprising Turin | 159 |
| 17 | The Lakes: Italy's Playground | 169 |
| 18 | Bologna: Red, Clever and Fat | 182 |
| 19 | To Spoleto for a Festival | 193 |
| 20 | The Hill Towns of Umbria | 204 |
| 21 | Welcome to the South | 216 |
| 22 | Naples: It's Complicated | 230 |
| 23 | Palermo: Normans, the Mafia, and a Leopard | 244 |
| 24 | Afterword | 264 |

*About The Author*     266

# Chapter 1

# Introduction

The impulse for this book came out of a temporary blog that I started to write while travelling in Italy with Robert, my partner of thirty-five years. The title of the blog—*Two Gents in Italy*—was intended as an ironic riff on one of Shakespeare's less well-known early plays, *The Two Gentlemen of Verona*, and its purpose was merely to communicate something of our experiences to those of our friends who were not necessarily following our adventures on social media.

Writing the blog entries soon became one of my routines, a task that was more intellectually demanding than posting up a few pictures and accompanying commentary on Facebook, and one that I found myself enjoying more and more. The feedback was positive, and so when we returned to Australia after three years of travelling, I thought it would be fun to compile the blog entries, suitably expanded to chapter lengths, and publish them in book form. Nothing, I thought, could be simpler.

Except, of course, it wasn't. The art of writing blogs and the art of writing books are complementary skills, but it took a fair bit more work than I anticipated to turn the one into the other. I soon realised that, if the book was to have any originality at all, it would have to go beyond simply recounting the details of our travels. What was more, I struggled with finding a uniform theme around which to arrange the various things I wanted to say. In the end it took several years of on and off work to get to the point where I felt I had something I could happily publish.

What I finally came up with is a mixture of straightforward travelogue, combined with my observations about the subjects that most interested us as travellers—the art, culture, food and above all the history of the Italian peninsula. The end result is a book which readers can choose to peruse from beginning to end in the traditional fashion, or dip in and out to read individual chapters that might capture their imagination.

It is also a book written primarily for the amusement and entertainment of our friends, people who know us in some capacity. Such is the revolution that self-publishing has enabled: no longer subject to the tyranny of the economics of scale, books can be published for small audiences as easily as they can for very large ones. Naturally, like most writers, I dream of reaching the masses, and no-one would be more gratified (or surprised!) if this little book reaches beyond our personal circle, but I will be happy if our more intimate circle finds my words entertaining, edifying, or merely amusing.

*

The spark for our love affair with Italy was struck about as far away from Europe as you can get, in Hawaii in the autumn of 1990. We were living in Sydney then, and we had decided to go with a group of friends on a holiday to Hawaii, where we were all to share an apartment in Honolulu. It was always going to be a hedonistic kind of holiday, the days spent on the beach or driving around the island of Oahu, the nights consumed with dinner and inevitably ending with drinks at the popular watering hole Hamburger Mary's until the wee small hours. Australian travellers were still an exotic species then, even in Hawaii, and we were a popular little group in the bars and restaurants.

It was after one such normal day, staggering back to our apartment, that we made the acquaintance of an even more exotic traveller, a young Italian who introduced himself to us as Max, though his proper Italian name was Massimo; he was doing something of a world tour, a gap year of sorts. Max was outgoing, charming and handsome, with an infectious, impish laugh and stumbling English that was delivered in a beguiling accent. We became friends, and he subsequently came to Melbourne, where we showed him around our various sights. He then suggested that we come to Italy so that he could show us something of his country. We had never been anywhere in Europe, but the idea took hold in our minds, and about a year later we went off for a month's holiday, starting in Italy and then going on to Greece.

Max was by then living in Milan, but in our correspondence before the trip, he had told us he was going to drive down in his brand-new Audi to meet us in Florence, from whence he would take us on a grand tour of Tuscany. But when he arrived he announced that plans had changed—he had lost his driver's license due to an accumulation of speeding fines, and therefore we would have to hire a car and I would have to drive. Thus, we were introduced to what we later came to understand is a defining characteristic of the Italians—flexibility!

Max had also arrived with a huge map, which he proceeded to unfold and used to explain in great detail where we were going to go. His contribution, since he couldn't drive, was to be navigation, something I was relieved about, since the mere act of driving on the wrong side of the road in a foreign country was terrifying enough (and this, remember, was long before the wonders of satellite navigation was readily available). Max's idea of 'navigation', however, turned out to be quite different from mine, for once the map had been carefully folded up and put away, we never saw it again. Instead, we used signposts and the assistance of anyone who happened to be standing on the pavement when we found ourselves lost. Over and over again, Max would wind down the window and shout 'Scusi!' to the nearest pedestrian, followed by a stream of requests for directions; a rapid exchange in voluble Italian would ensue, accompanied by much waving of hands, and off we would go again.

But however idiosyncratic our navigational methodology, that tour of Tuscany was magical. We visited the most famous of its hill towns—Siena, San Gimignano, Volterra—paddled about in the thermal pools of Saturnia and drove around the rather hair-raising road that encircles the Argentario Peninsula. We also spent a couple of nights in a seaside resort town, Castiglione della Pescaia, where, rather hilariously, we got up on our final morning to discover that our car, which we had thought safely parked in a public carpark just around the corner from our hotel, was now right in the middle of a weekend market! This incident introduced us to the Italian sense of humour, which is always light-hearted and rather wry. Some wit had placed a big piece of cardboard on the windscreen, on which they had written '*Questa macchina in vendita!*'—or 'This car is for sale!'. In any other country, certainly in Australia, we would have been subjected to no end of abuse for being so stupid as to not understand the signs saying that today was market day, and for taking up some stallholder's allocated space. The Italians just treated the whole thing as a great joke, helped us clear off the accumulated parking tickets that had been issued by the local police, and guided us through the crowds and out of the market.

Max had to go back to work, and so we parted company in the railway station at Bologna, him to catch a connection back to Milan, and us to continue on to our first encounter with the watery marvel that is Venice. Over the thirty years since, travel has become an integral feature of our lives. We've roamed all over Australia (no small feat in itself!), much of Asia, North America, and of course Europe. And several of those expeditions took us back to various places in Italy. One particularly memorable trip was an epic journey that took us from

Lake Como in the north all the way down to Tropea, on the Calabrian coast, entirely by train; another saw us crossing the north of the country, from Milan to Venice via the lakes and Verona.

Then, in 2016, we found ourselves, through good luck and conservative financial management, in a position where we could safely take the option of leaving the workforce and 'retiring', though neither of us was quite sure what that term really meant. We mused for months about all sorts of options, and then, finally, we hit on the idea of having a year's sabbatical in Europe as a great way to ease ourselves into retirement. A kind of 'senior gap year', as Rob rather gleefully described it to everyone we met.

Having made that decision, the question of where to go exercised our minds for a while and provoked many a heated argument. Our first instinct was to create a mammoth Grand Tour, covering all the places in Europe that have been on our bucket list forever to which we hadn't yet managed to visit. But that would have meant an awful lot of moving around, and in the end neither of us fancied a full year of packing and unpacking suitcases every week or two. Our next idea was to pick just three countries, and spend a few months in each; that seemed more feasible and less challenging, but as we talked about it, we realised that we needed more than a few months to really get under the skin of any country; what was more, we thought we wanted to have an experience that simulated at least the notion of actually 'living' in a foreign country, as opposed to merely holidaying.

So it was to be just one country, and after a little more debate, Italy began to feel like a natural choice. We had been there often enough that it felt sort of familiar, yet there were great swathes of the country that we had not yet explored. A previous visit to Verona had also opened our minds to the joys of 'slow travel'. Through AirBNB, a business model that was then still in its infancy, we had found a rather marvellous little apartment located in the Palazzo Maffei, overlooking one of the city's most iconic squares, from which base we had had the opportunity to really get to know the city and its surrounding countryside. The sheer novelty of being able to stay for weeks at a time in one place, from which we could venture out in every direction, opened our minds to the possibility of a completely different way of travelling.

So, Italy it was. To finance the whole enterprise, we had decided to rent our house, which meant packing up all our possessions, putting them in storage for a year, and reducing our worldly goods down to that which would fit into a suitcase and a backpack each. We were lucky enough to get a couple of good tenants for a good rent, and the real estate agents we appointed to manage the property seemed competent enough; even so, it was something of a wrench to leave the home we have lived in for twenty years and launch ourselves off into the unknown. We both experienced moments when we wondered what on earth we had done, and whether the whole idea was a piece of monumental madness.

*

Arriving in Europe from the antipodes after the long flight around the globe is always a special, if surreal, experience. Spending over thirty hours in a metal tube hurtling along at nine hundred kilometres an hour and ten kilometres above the planet's surface is about as unnatural an experience as the human body can have. Once you have got over the excitement of departure, and the activities that always fill the first hour or two of the flight—having a drink, eating some sort of meal, enjoying the novelty of exploring the vast array of movies, television programs and music that are available to distract you, fiddling with the seat to find the most comfortable position—it feels as if you have been disconnected from the rest of humanity forever, unplugged from the terrestrial world and placed in a kind of suspended animation, from which you are extracted briefly for a stop in one of the various hubs on the so-called 'kangaroo route', before being bundled back into your cocoon and whisked off on the next sector of your journey.

And then you arrive. The last hour of the flight is the other bookend of excitement in an otherwise tedious process. The cabin bustles as breakfasts are served, passengers queue for the bathroom to make some attempt to rectify the ravages that the flight has inflicted on face and hair, inexplicable immigration paperwork is hurriedly completed, and clothing suitable for the climatic conditions that will greet us when we leave the airport is extracted from carry-on bags. The aircraft shudders and bumps as it descends through ever-heavier layers of air, and beyond the windows the earth's surface comes closer, and roads, warehouses and factories become more distinct. And then at last with a bump and a roar you are back on earth, shaking yourself with the realisation that the long journey has ended at last.

Having travelled many times to Europe, all these routines, though exciting, were nevertheless familiar when we boarded our Cathay Pacific flight in early January 2017, destination Rome. But what wasn't so familiar was the circumstances, for we had purchased only a one-way ticket, and as we disembarked it finally began to dawn on us us that we were not at the beginning not of our usual four- or five-week holiday, but instead were commencing a full year's sojourn in Italy.

But whatever trepidation we had felt over the previous months seemed irrelevant when we finally landed and, having negotiated the immigration process with our newly minted English passports ( Robert and I were both born in England, thus entitling us to what was then a very useful passport), we emerged into the dark, wet pre-dawn darkness. Having organised transport into the city before we left Australia, we were met by a driver named Marko, who in a few minutes had us out of the airport and on our way down the freeway that connects Fiumicino to Rome. By the time dawn's first light had rendered the streetlights redundant, we were in among the chaotic commuter traffic going into the city, threading our way through streets lined with apartment buildings until eventually we found our way into the Campo dei' Fiori, where the first stallholders were hard at work setting up the daily market for which the square is famous.

We had arrived.

# Chapter 2

# Time Travelling in Rome

The Campo de' Fiori got its name—'Field of Flowers'—in the Middle Ages, when it was an open flower-covered meadow, never built upon because it was somewhat prone to flooding from the Tiber. Nevertheless, the area was always a locus for trades of one kind or another, there was a flourishing horse market, and there were many inns and hotels. Eventually it acquired its present character, an irregular piazza surrounded by a jumble of four and five story apartment buildings, which since 1869 has been the site of the city's main fish and fresh food market, which had been moved from nearby Piazza Navona.

By the time we emerged from our apartment on that first morning, the market was in full swing. The locals were out in force buying their tomatoes, capsicums, lettuce, cheese, pasta and all the other day-to-day staples. Local shoppers moved among the edible sculptures of fruit and vegetables so carefully constructed by the stallholders, picking out their prospective purchases with a critical eye and prepared to do good-natured battle with the shopkeeper at any moment

The Campo undergoes several transformations during the course of the day, as we were to discover in that first couple of weeks while it was our front yard, as it were. But I'll come back to that: first, I want to stop for a minute and have a look at an arresting statue that stands in the middle of the square, a grim-faced and cowled martyr who stares defiantly in the direction of the Vatican, striking a rather sombre note in the otherwise jolly atmosphere. This is Giordano Bruno, a 16th century cleric and scholar who was a remarkable scientist and theologian. Bruno adhered to the Copernican theory that the Earth circled the Sun and not vice-versa, and he went further to pose the then rather wild notion that the stars were just distant suns, with their own planets, and that the universe itself was infinite. These ideas were challenging enough in the febrile atmosphere of the Counter-Reformation, but he also held a variety of other philosophical views that left him vulnerable to charges of heresy by the Inquisition; those charges were eventually brought, and on 17th February 1600, the philosopher was condemned to be burnt at the stake on this spot.

Bruno's statue is a reminder that, like anywhere else, Rome has a history. But it is not just any old history, for this place has experienced the grandest of highs and the deepest and most humiliating of lows. From being the literal centre of the European world, Rome suffered the indignity of being sacked by barbarian tribes from Germany, became little more than a rat-infested quarry during the Dark Ages, was held hostage by various warring factions trying to control the papacy during the medieval era, before emerging in the Renaissance with an extraordinary building program that created one of the greatest repositories of art and architecture that the world has ever seen, all dedicated to the exaltation of the Papacy and the Catholic Church.

As the centuries wore on, the city and its surrounding countryside decayed under the dead hand of clerical rule. Rome became the last hold-out against the *Risorgimento*, the movement for unification of Italy, until Pope Pius IX finally surrendered control of the city after the revolutionary forces breached the city walls at the Porta Pia on 20$^{th}$ September 1870. The new kingdom required a new capital, and where else could it be but Rome? And a new capital demanded new monuments to celebrate its status, which were duly built, such as the vast Palace of Justice and the grandiose Victor Emmanuel Monument, which the post-war Italian Republic renamed as the 'Altar of the People' (though Romans, ever quick to express their opinion with a subversive nickname, have variously called it the 'Wedding Cake' or, more scathingly, the 'Typewriter').

Alas, the optimistic new kingdom was soon corrupted by a fascist dictator who vaingloriously proclaimed the arrival of a new Roman Empire and the city became the scene of rallies, marches and rousing speeches delivered from the balcony of the venerable Palazzo Veneto. The glorious new empire's lifespan was, as it turned out, to be measured in mere decades rather than centuries, and the country was devastated by war, though thankfully Rome was spared the worst of its ravages. Post-war it became the seat of one of the most dysfunctional political systems in Europe, that somehow managed to oversee an extraordinary economic recovery which saw Italy become the third-largest economy in the Eurozone. Rome has always been at the heart of an Italian story that, though occasionally descending into farce, has for the most part been operatic in scale.

With all that history, just walking about in Rome is like travelling in time, if you look carefully and know what you are looking at. So, let's take a little walking tour of the city, so you can see what I mean. From the Campo, we'll start by walking about five hundred metres, to the site of one of the most famous scenes in Roman history. The Largo di Torre Argentina is an enclosed sunken quadrangle, perhaps twenty feet deep. Leaning over the parapet, what you see is a jumble of ancient Roman ruins, the remains of a temple complex that today is inhabited by swarms of wild cats who spend their days sunning themselves and posing for the ever-present tourists' cameras.

But this place has another significance: this was the site of the Theatre of Pompey, which occasionally served as a meeting house for the Roman Senate, and it was here, on 15$^{th}$ March, in 44 BC, that the Roman dictator Gaius Julius Caesar was assassinated. That event and its aftermath, so vividly brought to life by Shakespeare fifteen centuries later, marked the end of the early Roman republic and ushered in the system of imperial governance that was to last for five hundred years, until the empire itself fell apart. Most modern visitors are oblivious to the momentous nature of the site, and are more interested in the cats.

Another half an hour, and we move forward some two hundred years, to a time when the population of Rome exceeded a million souls, making it unquestionably the biggest city in Europe and probably the world. Walking down the Via Dei' Fori Imperiali we pass the remains of the buildings that were at the heart of the imperial capital at that time—the Capitol, now crowned by the buildings of the Campidoglio, Michelangelo's masterpiece of urban design, the ancient Forums, the markets of Trajan, and finally at the end of the street the massive bulk of the Flavian Amphitheatre, built by the imperial dynasty that followed the Caesars and better known by its nickname: the Colosseum. Beyond, we can see the mass of the Palatine Hill, with its complex of palaces (we actually get the word palace from the name of the hill, home to Rome's wealthiest citizens almost from the city's beginning).

The remains are impressive enough, but you have to go into the brilliant little museum that perches amid the remains of the imperial palace and look at the various models and exhibits to get a really good idea of just how awe-inspiring the city must have been in its heyday. What are today brown walls were once faced with white plaster that must have dazzled the eye; the blank arches were filled with statues of gods and emperors; what seems to be a sunken garden was once an imperial courtyard surrounded by arched colonnades among which thousands of servants discreetly moved to do their imperial masters' bidding; and the low broken parapet from which you can look out across the grassy expanse of the Circus Maximus was once the place where emperors sat at their leisure casting bets on the chariot races.

Nothing lasts forever, and within the walls of the Colosseum we come across an exhibit that points the way towards the next stop on our historical grand tour, a picture that recreates the amphitheatre's appearance in the early medieval period, long after the western half of the empire had finally been crushed under the weight of invasions from the north. At first, Rome's new masters did little more than squat in the lower arches of a building whose very purpose must have seemed incomprehensible to them. But by the 12th century it had been converted into a massive fortress by the Frangipani family, one of the various clans who were to spend the next several hundred years in violent competition for dominance of a city that, though decayed and depopulated, still retained its importance as the centre of the papacy.

This wasn't uncommon. All sorts of buildings were commandeered for military use during this period; not far away from the Colosseum, the remains of the Theatre of Marcellus were at one stage used as a fortress for the Orsini family, and the Aretini built the Torre delle Milizie (Militia Tower) that crowns the complex of medieval and renaissance buildings constructed on top of the remains of Trajan's Market. With all these warlords busily fortifying every half-defensible site in the city, the poor popes of the period had a hard time of it, struggling to maintain any semblance of authority over a city in which they were nominally sovereign.

It is hard to imagine today, but between the 12th and 15th centuries Rome was a squalid place. The streets that threaded between the crumbling ancient monuments and medieval tenements were muddy tracks and the unwary pedestrian had to pick his way around piles of refuse, the rubble of recent construction, and the vestigial remains of ancient buildings. Sewage was non-existent, and the place most likely stank during the heat of the summer. Much of the space within the city's walls was abandoned and given over to agriculture, the sheep and cattle grazing between the weed-infested stones that were once houses, shops and temples. As if all that wasn't enough, marauding gangs of toughs in the employ of the various competing families joined the usual thieves, cut-purses and conmen to make the everyday life of the city's population a misery.

But from this unpromising soil, there sprang eventually a new glory, thanks to the growing wealth of the papacy. The popes might have struggled to control the city and the surrounding territory that eventually became the Papal States, but their authority over the wider Catholic Church was unquestioned. And apart from those relatively brief periods when they were forced to decamp from the city and set up shop elsewhere (most famously in the southern French city of Avignon, during the Great Schism), Rome was their place of residence and the place to which all the tithes and dues collected from Europe's faithful all over Europe found their way.

The administrators of this golden stream were the cardinals, the princes of the church, to whose sticky fingers much of the church's wealth adhered. While there are many fine stories of talented and ambitious prelates rising from nothing to achieve the highest honours that the church could confer, in Rome the award of a cardinal's hat was more often awarded to the sprigs of the city's great families—the Borghese, the Barberini, the Colonna—who saw the papacy as a fiefdom, for the control of which they were prepared to go to quite extraordinary lengths. Every cardinal saw himself as a future pope, an elevation for which holiness of character was rarely sufficient: it had to be augmented by copious amounts of money and a lot of political horse-trading.

Still, as conditions became a little more settled, the cardinals and popes began to glorify their faith and themselves by building churches, chapels, and vast palazzi. This is the layer of Rome's history that is most omnipresent to the modern visitor; today you can hardly walk a hundred metres without encountering the churches, chapels and palazzi that are the legacy of this extraordinary building boom. Let's go back to the Campo Dei' Fiori, and start walking again, this time west and north, to have a look at some of the greatest examples of Renaissance architecture in Rome.

Just a few metres to the west is the pure Renaissance facade of the Palazzo Farnese, the scene of Act II of Puccini's opera *Tosca*; just beyond lies the Tiber, and an easy stroll along its banks brings you to the statue-lined Ponte Sant' Angelo, crossing which will lead you to the imposing bulk of the Castel Sant' Angelo, yet another piece of re-purposing. The original cylindrical base of the building was the mausoleum that the Roman emperor Hadrian had built for himself and his family, but the popes built a massive fortress-palace on top, linking it to the nearby Vatican Palace with a raised and fortified passageway that came in handy on several occasions when the pope had to scurry from palace to castle during periods of civil unrest.

Incidentally, the Castel Sant'Angelo is also the setting for the last dramatic act of *Tosca* (and the scene of the opera's first act, the barn-like church of Sant'Andrea della Valle, is also not far away), in which the opera's heroine, Floria Tosca, hurls herself from the upmost level of the castle, supposedly falling to her death. In reality, the worst she would have suffered would have been a sprained ankle, since the drop from the point where she is traditionally shown jumping is just ten or fifteen feet. Even so, that amusing caveat aside, the opera's dark tale of an intensely pious singer manipulated by a lecherous—but supposedly equally devout—chief of police illustrates perfectly the conflicted mores of much of Rome's history.

Crossing the river again, another short walk brings us to that most iconic of Roman spaces, the Piazza Navona. Originally a chariot-racing stadium built at the orders of the emperor Domitian, it later became a market before being transformed by Bernini into the beautiful and elegant space we see today. Surrounded by Renaissance and Baroque churches and palazzi, the long narrow space is dominated by the sculptor's mesmerising fountain commemorating the Nile, Danube, Ganges and Plate rivers, at the time the four greatest rivers known to the early modern world; guessing which sculpture represents which river is a fun little game to play. Keep walking east, and you cross the Piazza della Rotonda, one of the prettiest and most crowded in Rome, thronged with tourists waiting to shuffle into the Pantheon, the temple 'to all the gods' built by Hadrian. It was later converted to the Church of St Mary and the Martyrs, which probably ensured that it was preserved rather than used as a quarry, the fate of so many other Roman buildings. And finally, crossing the Via del Corso, we come to the most extravagant example of Baroque decoration of all, the sumptuous Trevi Fountain, a place dedicated to architectural excess.

There are many, many more examples of the impact of the Renaissance period all over Rome, palaces and chapels and churches built to the glory of God and the greater glory of the popes and their cardinals. Yet even with all this building, Rome still occupied only a fraction of the area that had once been enclosed by the ancient Roman walls. Down at the southern end of the Piazza Navona in the much under-appreciated Museum of Rome, there is a fascinating painting that purports to be a panoramic view of Rome in the middle of the 19th century. In it, we can see an urban core that covers little more than a quarter of the space enclosed by the ring of the Aurelian Walls that marked the outer boundary of the ancient city. The rest is empty grazing land, barely distinguishable from the agricultural scene that stretches away into the distance.

This was the city that, ruled by clerics and a series of deeply recalcitrant popes, held out against the tide of the unification movement, the *Risorgimento*, before finally succumbing in 1870. The following year, Rome became the capital of a united Italy, and its next great building boom began. As well as its bombastic monuments, the city acquired its modern aspect as all the land left empty by the popes was filled with acres of elegant apartment buildings in the so-called 'Liberty' style (a local version of Art-Deco) that are its dominant architectural form today.

They were built to house a population that tripled between 1870 and 1922, the year that Mussolini came to power. The inventor of Fascism had to leave his mark on the city, of course, and busied himself with a program of creating long avenues (modern visitors have him to thank for the Via dei Fori Imperiali, created, it is said, so that the dictator could have an unimpeded view of the Colosseum from his office in the Palazzo Venezia), and favouring a brutalist style of architecture that can still be seen here and there all over Italy.

Speaking of Mussolini, a somewhat longer walk taking in the grand Via Vittorio Veneto (Rome's version of the Champs Elysees) and then wandering a little way into the suburbs beyond the city's ancient walls will bring you to the curious Villa Torlonia. Standing in the middle of some rather unkempt gardens, the Villa was Mussolini's residence in Rome from 1925 until 1943; after the war it fell into disuse and has only been restored fairly recently. It is a fine neo-classical style building that hosts temporary art exhibitions as well as displaying its own considerable permanent collection. Elsewhere on the grounds there is a small theatre, and the remarkable Casina delle Civite (House of the Little Owls), a playful folly built in the style of a Swiss cabin. And hidden away underground is the bunker that Mussolini had built to protect him in the event of air-raids on Rome—never used, since the city only ever suffered a few small raids.

So you see what I mean? Just walking around Rome is like having your own personal Tardis, allowing you (with, I admit, a little imagination) to skip across the centuries and see all the layers of history that have made this remarkable city what it is today. And that, I think, is the key to falling in love with the place. Today Rome faces a new set of challenges as the city's infrastructure crumbles following a decade of austerity, and its potholed streets and polluted atmosphere can often make it seem as if the city is falling apart, but if you look beyond those surface distractions its charm is as beguiling as ever.

\*

Back in the Campo de' Fiori it is now late afternoon, and the stallholders are beginning to pack away their wares. While we have been out wandering all over the city, the morning's shoppers have been replaced by tourists who, having digested their hotel breakfasts have come to buy all sorts of food-related things to take back to their many homelands as a memory of their visit to Rome: bottles of balsamic vinegar and limoncello, little plastic sachets filled with herb and spice mixtures that can be simply and easily combined with olive oil and other ingredients to make pasta sauce, jars of preserved lemons, cheeses and olives. But by now even the tourists have had enough and it is time for the shopkeepers to perform the daily miracle of folding up all their tables and umbrellas, taking what unsold produce remains, and packing up the more durable products for storage overnight. Tomorrow morning they will start the whole process again.

Meanwhile, the restaurants that line the Campo prepare for the evening, when the piazza turns into a kind of giant outdoor pub. Even in winter, it is rather magical, as people stroll from bar to bar, or stand around in the middle of the square listening to musical performers of one kind or another. From the terraces of the restaurants, warmed by gas fired heaters, diners watch the show while they eat. This typically goes on late into the night before the last reveller stumbles drunkenly home.

The next morning, and every morning after that, we would emerge from our apartment to witness this daily miracle of organisation begin again. After a while our confidence grew and we began to shop for food from the stallholders, and poke around in the butchers' shops and *alimentari* whose shopfronts were barely visible between the various restaurants and cafes. The Campo became our shopping centre, our living room, and our dining room, as well as the base from which we commenced each daily foray.

And every day we would pass brooding Giordano Bruno to remind us that the past is always lurking nearby in the eternal city.

# Chapter 3

# Venice in Winter

'I really, really want to go to Venice in winter.'

'Do you? I can't imagine anything worse. It will be wet and horrible, and it floods...'

I should have known that my protests would fall on deaf ears. Robert had been entranced by the idea of Venice in the wintertime for many years, after reading a rather misty-eyed article in *The Age* on the subject penned by Michael Shmith, our friend of many years, and nothing would budge him, certainly not my perfectly rational dislike of being cold and wet. But after a few bouts of arguing back and forth it occurred to me that it was me who was being irrational: if we were going to be in Italy for winter, why would it matter whether we were in Rome or Venice?

No matter how you do it, arriving in Venice is one of those spectacular travel experiences that you can never forget. On one occasion we were taken by a fast water taxi that whisked us from Marco Polo Airport across the lagoon encased in a cloud of spray, before gliding into the more tranquil waters of the city's network of canals; another time, arrived standing on the deck of a cruise ship, in the softness and silence of dawn, when the city is at its most mysterious and ethereal, seemingly holding its breath before the tourist onslaught begins.

But this time we arrived on a *Frecciarossa* fast train that we had boarded in Rome three and a half hours earlier. It was early afternoon by the time we stopped at Mestre, the last station before Venice; a few minutes later, having rolled past the somewhat surreal sight of a cruise ship that had been sawn in half at the Mestre shipyards, we were crossing the long rail and road bridge that connects Venice with the mainland. Glimpses of the Venetian skyline teased us for ten minutes or so, and then, after the bustle of disembarking and negotiating our way through the train terminal, we emerged into the weak afternoon sun, onto a scene that could only be one place in the world.

I have but to close my eyes and I can see it today. In front of the station a broad forecourt runs down to the Grand Canal, along whose waters all manner of craft pass back and forth. No-nonsense *vaporetti* (water buses) glide into their berths, hurriedly discharging and collecting passengers before chugging off again; sleek *motoscaife* (water taxis) zip past in a cloud of spray, confidently piloted by young men with their caps set at a jaunty angle, smugly certain that they are the most admired denizens of the canal; and workmanlike barges, their sides scuffed, their decks piled high with cargo and their crews puffing on cigarettes.

From this watery highway, the eye is drawn across the canal, to where the dome of the church of San Simeon Piccolo interrupts the facades of the palazzi and hotels that stretch off on either side; to the left, pedestrians hurry across the Ponte degli Scalzi, urgent to catch their trains in the station behind us. The sound of churning water, the excited exclamations of tourists, the shouts of the ferrymen as they call out the destinations of the vaporetti, and the cawing of the ever-present gulls are the soundtrack to this scene, while the ozone tang of seawater provides the olfactory accompaniment. It is a unique and memorable vision, and I defy anyone not to fall in love with Venice at that moment.

Half an hour later, having successfully navigated the process of buying a ticket and boarding the right *vaporetto*, we alighted at the stop next to the Rialto Bridge and set about the process of finding our apartment. Finding an address in Venice is not a simple task, due to the idiosyncratic house numbering system that the Venetians use. You see, the city is divided into six districts, called *sestiere*, and the street numbers in each *sestiere* start at one, then wind their way through the streets until they finally reach the last number of that district. So for example a street address might be '3107 Dorsoduro', but apart from the owner, the postman is probably the only person who actually knows where it is. Even Venetians find it confusing, and so everyone spends a lot of time asking for directions!

Fortunately for us, Paola, our AirBNB host, had made it simple, telling us to meet her outside the Disney store on Campo San Bartolomeo, just a short walk from the Rialto. Disney stores are pretty easy to identify anywhere, and sure enough there she was, a short, cheerful woman with equally short grey hair who conducted us to the cosy and comfortable one-bedroom apartment overlooking a little canal that was to be our base for the next month.

*

Google 'weather for Venice in February', and you will be told that the average daily maximum temperature is a chilly nine degrees Celsius, there are about ten hours of daylight, and the rainfall averages about fifty-two millilitres. It is the latter statistic that explains why February turned out to be such a brilliant time to be in Venice, since it is in fact the equal-lowest rainfall month (equal to July, in the height of summer). So there went my first misconception: the wettest month of year is actually May. And the other feature of the Venetian geography that can make life unpleasant for tourists, the *acqua alta* high tides that inundate the squares and make moving around the city a challenge, usually occur between May and October—though they are not entirely predictable, and there was plenty of evidence that the city was prepared for one when we were there, in the form of temporary wooden walkways stacked up all over the place, ready to be deployed at a moment's notice.

So, score one to Robert. It was cold, yes, but not much colder than in Rome, notwithstanding the fact that we were much further north and close enough to the Alps to see them across the other side of the lagoon, ghostly white peaks floating above the mist. And yes, it did rain from time to time, causing us to hurriedly unfurl umbrellas and scamper across deserted piazzas in search of shelter. On other days the city was invaded by mist whose smoky tendrils lingered on the surface of the canals or hung in the clammy air of silent and mysterious alleyways, giving the place a decidedly Gothic atmosphere.

But much more often the days were sunny. Can there be any more glorious combination than bright sunlight, crisp, cold air, and the ubiquitous presence of water? On those days, every tint of colour seemed more vivid, the contours of every building seemed more sharply etched against the sky, and the sounds of the canals, the seabirds and the shouts of the boatmen, seemed more musical than on other days. After a week or so of wandering the city, bundled up in coats, hats and gloves, all my hesitations about visiting Venice in winter had been vanquished and I was forced, reluctantly, to concede that what I had thought of as Robert's rather irritating whim had turned out to be a stroke of genius.

Venice is a place that just begs to be explored on foot, since it is often the only practicable way to get from A to B, even if you do end up getting lost, which almost everyone does at least once a day. The city authorities try and help a little, by placing distinctive yellow signs that direct you towards the main tourist destinations—San Marco, the Rialto, the *Ferrovia* (train station), and so on. But that trail often runs out and you find yourself standing scratching your head in some campo or another, trying to figure out how to pick it up again. And don't think that your phone's GPS will be of any use: the narrow alleyways frequently cut you off from your celestial guide just at the very moment you need it most.

What we soon learnt was that it didn't really matter anyway; if you just keep walking, eventually you find yourself at a familiar location, or one of those helpful yellow signs pops up, and you are on your way again. And wandering among the narrow alleys is great fun; time after time we were stopped in our tracks as we crossed some little bridge, our attention arrested by an enchanting view down a canal lined with elegant palazzi, a glimpse of the busy highway of the Grand Canal, or a fine piazza dominated by a baroque church. Getting lost a kind of rite of passage for first timers in Venice, but even for seasoned visitors the serendipitous discovery of some little corner of the city as a result of a momentary loss of direction is one of the city's greatest charms.

I say 'piazza', but in fact that is the wrong word, for Venice has its own urban nomenclature, different from the rest of Italy. A city square is called a *campo* (field) because they were once open, grassy spaces before they were dug up to create freshwater cisterns and then paved over (it was a remarkably ingenious system: rainwater was collected from the gutters and channelled into the cisterns where the water could be drawn up through the wells that you see in the middle of most of the *campi*). And here's one that is a great trivia question: how many canals are there in Venice? The technically correct answer is that there are just three—the Grand Canal, the Cannaregio Canal, and the Giudecca Canal; every other stretch of water is called a *rio*, or river in the Venetian dialect, which originates from the fact that the city was first built on marshy islands dissected by little rivulets. Similarly, most of the streets are called a *calle*, rather than the more usual Italian word, *via*. Mind you, many *calle* would hardly qualify as streets at all anywhere else, mere crevices between the buildings.

Another Venetian word, *sestiere*, is, as I mentioned at the beginning of this chapter, the term for the six Venetian districts. The most famous, of course, is San Marco, where all the most famous sights are concentrated—the eponymous square, the Doge's palace, the unique Byzantine-inspired cathedral, the Rialto bridge, and the Bridge of Sighs. If you then walk down the Rivo degli Schiavone, the broad paved waterfront that affords iconic views of the church of Santa Maria della Salute on the opposite side of the Grand Canal, you come to Castello, a charming district that is home to one of Venice's delights, the public gardens. Little visited by tourists except during the Venice Biennale, when exhibitions of art from almost every country in the world are displayed in the purpose-built pavilions set just behind them, at any time of year the gardens are a great place to escape the Venetian hubbub and sit on a bench to watch the water traffic going back and forth to the Lido and elsewhere in the lagoon.

On the other side of the Grand Canal, across the Rialto Bridge, you enter another *sestiere*, San Polo, whose most famous landmark is the sprawling complex of the Rialto Market, which still functions as a produce market (though sadly it is also increasingly overrun by shops selling tourist trinkets) and is a fun place to go and try your skills at local food shopping. If you keep walking, San Polo merges seamlessly into Dorsoduro, which stands on the highest land in Venice (that's not saying very much), a pleasantly residential area dotted with small museums and art galleries.

After inevitably getting lost a few times, you come out onto the banks of the Giudecca Canal, down which cruise ships make their stately way out towards the entrance to the lagoon. Giudecca itself, on the other side of the canal, was once mostly industrial, but today is a fascinating mix of high-end hotels, drab apartment buildings, and some of Venice's most interesting private art galleries. Often overlooked by visitors to Venice, Giudecca is a brilliant place to wander, and on a sunny day its waterfront can be a blissfully peaceful place to have lunch. Last but not least, tucked up in the north-eastern corner of Venice is the *sestiere* of Cannaregio, an appealing district characterised by small markets, local shops, and small restaurants whose tables line the edge of quiet canals, the peace broken only by the sound of locals chugging by in their tinnies.

In our first week in Venice, we imposed two disciplines on ourselves. Firstly, we would explore a different *sestiere* every day; and secondly, entry into art galleries, museums, and any other tourist sight was absolutely forbidden. Since we had the great gift of lots of time, we could use it to really familiarise ourselves with this wintery, watery marvel of a city, roaming its *calles*, meandering along canal-sides, lingering in the *campi*, dropping into shops here and there, and pausing for lunch at whatever café or restaurant caught our fancy.

The French have a word for someone who strolls about: a *flâneur*. It is a term that implies a kind of fashionable idleness, as of someone who has the good fortune to have the time to wander about and observe, and it describes exactly what we were doing in those first weeks in Venice. It is a luxury too often denied to travellers who, oppressed by the exigencies of time, must hurry from monument to museum in order to see everything before they return to their normal, workaday world. Perhaps for the first time since we had arrived in Italy, we realised that we were no longer bound by such shackles and could take our time to just absorb the atmosphere.

And what we were seeing as we walked around was Venice stripped down to her bare bones, in her underwear, if you like. Though the city is never completely without tourists, even in the middle of winter, their relative absence makes the city's permanent residents and its civic routines much more obvious. That older lady over there, struggling along with her shopping bags under a dripping umbrella, could no doubt be spotted in summer doing much the same thing, but you would have to look much harder to spot her against the tide of sightseeing humanity competing for space on the *campo* that today is all hers.

In the summer, getting on a *vaporetto* is a perilous exercise, akin to launching yourself into the mosh-pit at a popular concert; at the opposite season, the locals reclaim this indispensable waterborne bus service for their own, huddling in the warm passenger cabin where they can chat with friends or read the newspaper, oblivious to the parade of architectural marvels that slip by, sights with which they have been familiar all their lives, and which have long lost their novelty value.

Other working watercraft seem more visible, too. The DHL delivery boat, piled high with boxes and cartons, follows its route up and down the central highway of the Grand Canal, darting off here and there into the bigger *rios* to drop things off. A vessel we dubbed the 'poo-boat', a bulky barge whose interior was taken up by a big silvery tank, collected sewage from the ancient plumbing systems, its gloved and grimy workmen chatting happily with bystanders on the canal bank. Yellow-painted water-ambulances foamed past, sirens screaming to demand precedence so they could get their patient to the big hospital over on the eastern side of Castello. And we once saw the black-painted hull of a hearse making its sedate way across to San Michele, the Venetian cemetery island. Like the old lady, all these boats can no doubt be seen on the canals and channels in August as well, but in February there are a lot less fast tourist motorboats and water-taxis and far fewer gondolas to disguise their presence.

It is fashionable among both Venetians and outsiders to decry the effect of mass tourism on the city, but their absence in winter tells another tale. In areas like San Marco and Dorsoduro, almost every shop you pass is devoted to selling things to passing sightseers. Windows are filled with fake Carnivale masks, equally fake Murano glassware, souvenir tea-towels, Venetian flags, and all the other gewgaws that people feel compelled to spend their money on when they are on holiday. There are enough handbags and Panama hats for sale to equip every one of the city's sixty thousand permanent inhabitants with an entire wardrobe full of each.

What is missing in the winter months is customers. Absent the tourists, all these shop windows look a little forlorn. The high-end boutiques staffed by immaculately coiffured young things must wait for summer to get a reasonable stream of prospective customers, art gallerists spend their days admiring their stock knowing there is little likelihood that any of it will come down from the walls, and the antiquarian dealers with their copies of ancient maps and precious old books trade for very limited hours each day, more in hope than with any conviction that they will have any visitors. Thus the absence of the very tourists whose presence is so often reviled in the summer months underlines just how dependant the Venetian economy is on their money.

'No-one actually lives in Venice,' a young barista told us one day, and while that is an exaggeration, it is true that the present population of central Venice is now about the same as it was a thousand years ago. Those who do live there are now residents of a museum city, and they are served in the shops and banks and supermarkets by people who commute every day from the mainland. They come down the Strada Nova from the central railway station in a great human tide every morning from their homes in Mestre or one of the other mainland towns and suburbs; they can't afford an apartment in the centre, real estate values having been bid up by property investors seeking a slice of the tourist dollar.

The tourists might be missing in action in winter, but that doesn't mean that the city is glum—far from it. Though some restaurants close, many remain open and offer a welcome, brightly lit and warm refuge on a dark and went night. It is true that the tourist virus infects the restaurant trade as much as it does every other aspect of Venetian life, and usually behind the small and cosy front part of the establishment there will be a big room, often down in a basement, where coachloads of travellers can be fed the usual menu of tourist packages in Italy—a few kinds of pasta and lots of pizza.

If you ignore the empty cavern at the back, the atmosphere of the front part can be as charming as any restaurant anywhere in Italy, and if you choose wisely, the food is often very good. I particularly remember one restaurant; a place called the Ristorante Mondo Nuovo. The food was excellent, featuring local Venetian staples such as Bigoli in Salsa (Bigoli is a kind of thick spaghetti) and Fegato alla Veneziana (calf liver and onions), and the owners were welcoming; but what really caught our attention was the murals that decorated the walls. One was a view of the Grand Canal through the trees of the public gardens in Castello, and the other was a reproduction of Giandomenico Tiepolo's rather curious fresco *Il Nuovo Mondo* ('The New World'), in which an early tourism spruiker is showing a fascinated crowd a view of the Americas through a kind of magic lantern, an instantly recognisable image the original of which we were later able to see in the Ca' Rezzonico museum. Both murals were painted by local art students, so the owner told us, presumably in exchange for a few free meals, a trade that is as old as art itself.

The streets, too, still have something of a festive atmosphere, particularly in the evenings, when all of the main streets are festooned with multicoloured fairy lights bright enough to keep back night's claws and cheer up the puffer-jacket-clad throngs making their way to restaurants and theatres, or just indulging in a bit of evening window-shopping. When you come out onto the vastness of Piazza San Marco, the seats in front of the three famous cafes are just as full as they are in summer, though the patrons are somewhat more rugged up, and the musicians perform on their brightly lit stages, pools of brightness in the gathering dark. So, far from being a dreary place, Venice in winter is a rather jolly wonderland of sights and sounds that very soon make you forget entirely the cold and rain.

Towards the end of February, that jollity goes up a notch with the approach of the Carnival season. Originally, the festival was held as a kind of last gasp of fun before the grim days of fasting for Lent began. But in Venice, it was given a new significance in 1162, when Venetians began dancing in the streets to celebrate the republic's military victory over nearby Aquilea. Things went on from there and by the eighteenth century the Carnival was famous for the riotous behaviour of citizens disguised by outrageous costumes and ever more fantastical masks.

Every joy will eventually meet its killjoy, and in the case of the Venetian Carnival it was Austrian Emperor Francis II who decided to outlaw the custom in 1797, after the city had been handed over to him by Napoleon under the treaty of Campo Formio. The festival made limited reappearances in the nineteenth century, but it wasn't until 1979 that the Carnival was officially relaunched as part of a government drive to reinvigorate tourism, so the Carnival that we know today is a relatively modern invention.

We left Venice before Carnival really got going, but we did have a taste of what was to come. It became increasingly common to see men and women, masked and elaborately dressed in eighteenth-century costume, walking the streets and posing for photos with tourists. Out on the water, we would pass highly decorated traditional gondolas who were getting ready to participate in the various parades that would be held on the canals. In fact, the first few days of Carnival are traditionally taken up with aquatic displays of one kind or another.

Most of these take place on the Cannaregio Canal, where the spectators (among whom we were numbered) crowd the canal-sides and hang over the balustrades of the bridges to watch as every district of the city is represented by boats and gondolas whose crews are decked out in costumes that range from the prosaic (simple sailors' outfits) to the downright bizarre (cowled monks, a boat full of men wearing Harpo Marx wigs, and another whose crew seemed to be in dressing gowns). By the middle of the day the canal itself resembles an LA freeway, the boats jostling each other as they make their way past the cheering and shouting throngs. At the end there was a prize given for the best boat, though which vessel had won that honour it was we couldn't tell from our perch.

Even more spectacular is the night parade that marks the official start of Carnival, when magically lit floats, accompanied by the kind of dreamy but ear-splittingly loud music that is deemed appropriate for such occasions, drift down the canal past spectators hoping to capture it all (in vain, if our experience is anything to go by) on their phone cameras. By the time it was all over and we joined the human tidal wave trying to make its way home we were almost sorry that we weren't staying for the rest of the festival.

Venice offers such a visual feast of sights and sounds that it might almost be considered to be one big artwork by itself. But of course it is also the repository of one of the greatest concentrations of art in the world, and winter is much the best time to inspect it. Once we released ourselves from our self-imposed ban on museums, we were able to waltz into virtually every major site without having to stand in a queue for more than a few minutes, and once inside we frequently had the place almost to ourselves. We could take as long as we liked admiring the frescoes in the Senate chamber of the Palace of the Doges, linger in front of the greatest works in the collection of the Accademia, be bemused by the modern art on show at the Ca' Pesaro, wonder what life was like for Peggy Guggenheim as we gazed at her extraordinarily diverse collection, and explore the history of Venice (and, incidentally, get some brilliant views of St Mark's square) in the Museo Correr, all without having to compete for space and time with thousands of others.

Unlike most Italian cities, Venice is as devoted to contemporary art as it is to the great works of the Renaissance and Baroque. So on one day you can go and see Veronese's masterpiece *The Feast in the House of Levi* at the Accademia, and the next see a remarkable collection of modern works at the Ca' Pesaro, or a temporary exhibition at the Palazzo Grassi. Not to mention the cornucopia of contemporary art presented every two years down in the *Giardini Pubblici* at the Venice Biennale.

\*

'Disneyland for grown-ups' is how some wag once dismissed Venice. Condescending and unfair though that description is, you can certainly see that its author might have had a point he visited during its infuriating summer peak, when tourists of every nationality swarm through St Mark's, march down the Riva degli Schiavone in their thousands, pausing long enough to clog the passage across the Ponte della Paglia so that they can take their selfies with the Bridge of Sighs in the background, elbow each other aside on the *vaporetti* so that they can film the passing parade of grand palazzi that line the Grand Canal, or wander disconsolately along in the tail-end of a tour group, trying to keep up with the patter pouring into their brains through a little ear-piece. A great many of these visitors are day-trippers, from cruise ships or elsewhere, intent on doing nothing more than collecting the requisite images that will demonstrate to their friends back home that, hey, they have actually been there, and probably more focused on the next meal than understanding the city's subtleties.

Mind you, even in summer all this madness is fairly easy to escape if you want to. There are plenty of interesting places and quiet spots that are more like the Venice of most people's imaginations. Walk for half an hour through Cannaregio and eventually you'll find the quiet canals overlooked by the crumbling facades of ancient palazzi where you can sit and have coffee or lunch at a genuine Italian restaurant and watch the world go by. And there is always Giudecca, almost wholly ignored by tourists, peaceful and calm and a little daggy.

Or you can visit Venice in winter.

# Chapter 4

# The Merchants of Venice

Venice was always a huckster with pretentions to grandeur. Founded by refugees fleeing the invading Huns, the city that grew up on the islands of the vast lagoon had few resources that they could exploit, but being resourceful, as refugees often are, they soon learned that they had stumbled into a strategically important location from which they could make an income through trade. The villages on their marshy islands were safe from attack, the lagoon itself was a perfect natural harbour, and being cut off from other centres of civilisation by land, they became expert shipbuilders and mariners. From these ingredients, over the centuries the Venetians built a trading empire that dominated the eastern Mediterranean and became the gateway through which the spices and silks and other goods originating in the east found their way to markets to meet an ever-growing demand for such luxuries as Europe emerged from the long vicissitudes of the so-called Dark Ages.

When you are a middleman there is always someone who wants to take a slice of your pie, and for the Venetians the parasites who preyed on the body of their commerce were the pirates of the Dalmatian coast and elsewhere. So they set about building a navy, reinforced with powerful military bases at key points on the coast and on the strategic islands of the eastern

Mediterranean—Corfu, Cyprus, Crete—which they eventually knitted together into a sea-empire that made their trade routes unassailable.

There were predators on land, too, in the region we now call the Veneto, and the Venetians developed a powerful military force that could and did subjugate a huge swathe of land to the city's west. And gradually the masters of this trading nation transformed themselves into a landed aristocracy, as wealthy merchant families acquired great tracts of land in what the Venetians called the *terraferma*. The income from this new gentility funded the grand palazzi and public buildings in their metropolitan base, and thereby created the splendours that are the basis of modern Venetian prosperity.

This essential fact about Venice—that she is and has always been a city concerned with commerce—is easily forgotten by the modern visitor. But if you walk around with your eyes open and know what you are looking for, the evidence of the city's history as a mercantile hub is everywhere. So let me take you on a little guided tour of that other Venice.

We can start from our little apartment, a rather long stone's throw from the Rialto Bridge. For centuries a wooden bridge at this point was the only way across the Grand Canal other than by gondola. Like the present structure, the old bridge was lined with shops, but the shopkeepers were careless, and it frequently burned down. Eventually the city authorities decided that a stone bridge was needed, and commissioned Antonio da Ponte to design the graceful structure we see today, which has provided tourists with an irresistible viewing point since it was completed in 1591. Cross the bridge and you enter another *sestiere*, San Polo, and tumble immediately into the vibrant and colourful Rialto Market. But before we go there, let's stop and look at a building immediately to our right, just north of the bridge.

The Fondaco dei Tedeschi was built between 1505 and 1508 to replace an earlier building that dates back to 1228. The word *fondaco* has its origins in an Arabic term for an inn-like establishment for travelling merchants, while *Tedeschi* is the Italian word for Germans. But the fondaco was never solely a hotel: it also served as a warehouse, offices, and trading hub for the substantial colony of German traders who made Venice their home. By thus confining this group of foreign merchants, the Venetian government had the best of both worlds: they could easily monitor the volume and value of trade that came and went through the fondaco's waterside wharf, from which they took a substantial cut, and at the same time they could control any influence that this dangerous group of Protestant heretics might have on the Catholic population of the city.

Today the Fondaco dei Tedeschi is, fittingly, an up-market retail complex, having been acquired by Benneton Group in 2008 after a long period serving as the headquarters for Poste Italiene. Ushered through the doors by an immaculately clad young concierge, you can have coffee or something to eat at the restaurant which occupies what would once have been the central courtyard of the fondaco. Around you, the building rises in four galleried floors, the first of which contained the merchants' offices; those above contained about 160 rooms in which the traders and their employees lived. Originally open to the sky, the courtyard has been roofed over for the comfort of modern patrons sitting and sipping their caffe latte, and a remarkable viewing platform has been erected above it which affords one of the most unusual and extraordinary perspectives on the Grand Canal in the whole city; no doubt the German merchants posted youngsters up in the same spot to keep an eye on the comings and goings in the markets and on the waters of the canal.

These modern additions are designed to make the whole structure more comfortable for the present-day visitor, but they obscure a little the original functions of the place. However, with a little exercise of the imagination it is not hard to conjure up the scene as one might have witnessed it in the sixteenth century: the bustle of cargoes being received on the ground floor, overseen by harried clerks anxiously recording the details of each shipment, the domestic servants calling to each other across the balconied spaces above, the washing hanging over the balustrades to dry, the apprentices slipping out of a side door on their day off, heading into the city in search of entertainment and mischief, and the powerful senior trader arriving more formally at the fondaco gate, accompanied by his retinue of guards and servants. All in all, a busy, noisy, cheerful sort of place.

Let us resume our tour and head across the bridge to the mercantile heart of Venice, the Rialto markets. In this series of arcaded courtyards, the city's merchants used to carry on their business of buying and selling spices from the mysterious Indies, silk from China, silver and woollen cloth from northern Europe, sugar from Muslim Cyprus, and gold from Africa. Over the centuries that Venice was Europe's clearing house for trade between east and west, it was beneath these faded colonnades that energetic Venetian merchants competed and collaborated and schemed, and either got rich or lost the lot.

'What news on the Rialto?': when Shakespeare has Shylock ask this question, he is summarising in just a few words one of the most important functions of the place: the circulation of news and rumours about ships and cargoes and prices, information that could make or break reputations and fortunes. In this sense, the Rialto is the prototype of the modern stock exchange. Even in the sixteenth century it was much imitated: Sir Thomas Gresham, for example, very consciously adopted a similar design when he built the Royal Exchange in London. Like the Rialto, his market building was meant to be both practical and at the same time an imposing symbol of the growing mercantile wealth of his city.

Much of the modern version of the Rialto has been taken over by purveyors of tourist junk, but persist and you will eventually find the fruit and vegetable markets, butchers, *pasticcerie*, and fishmongers who still provide Venetians with their daily food requirements, much as they always have done. And there are plenty of interesting restaurants in this area as well, with fine views across the canal to the Fondaco dei Tedeschi. A little shopping followed by a light lunch of spaghetti *al mare* and a glass of red at a table by the canal in the winter sunshine: what scene could be more satisfying than that?

We must, alas, forego that particular pleasure if we are to continue our exploration of Venice's mercantile past, and instead make our way through the labyrinth of back streets, heading eastwards. On the way, we will pass some of the finest art museums the city has to offer—the Ca' Rezzonico, with its focus on eighteenth century art and furniture; the Accademia, home to a huge collection of Renaissance and Baroque art; and Peggy Guggenheim's former home, filled with the pictures and sculptures she collected over a long and eventful life. But it is commerce, not art, that we are interested in today, so our destination is the triangular-shaped white building that stands just beyond the iconic church of Santa Maria della Salute.

This is the Dogana da Mare, which, when translated literally from the Italian means 'Customs by Sea'. At this point, strategically positioned at the mouth of the Grand Canal and overlooking the vast basin where incoming ships would arrive from all over the globe, cargoes were unloaded into the warehouse so that they could be assessed for customs dues, a source of considerable revenue for the city. No doubt businessmen then were as reluctant to pay taxes as they are today, and one imagines they tried all sorts of tricks to get out of it, but they probably didn't have much luck given the position of the Dogana, with commanding views from its tower across all of the possible approaches to the city.

As Venetian maritime commerce first declined and then shifted its focus elsewhere in the lagoon, its use as a customs receiving point having long ago become redundant andit fell into disrepair. In 2008 French billionaire Francois Pinault teamed up with Japanese architect Tadao Ando to restore the buildings and convert them into an art gallery. They did so with considerable sensitivity to the building's heritage, leaving exposed brickwork in the big open spaces inside and restoring the glaringly white stucco outside, while creating a brilliant space for the presentation of blockbuster art exhibitions. We saw Damien Hirst's remarkable exhibition *Treasures from the Wreck of the Unbelievable* there: whatever its artistic merits (which are much disputed) these soaring spaces were a perfect setting for his fantastical creations posing as antiquities recovered from a long-lost shipwreck.

From here, we must embark on a *vaporetto*, so it is back to the forecourt of Santa Maria della Salute to await its arrival. The name of the church, incidentally, translates as 'Saint Mary of Good Health', and it was built after the subsidence of a particularly terrible bout of bubonic plague that devastated the city in the summer of 1630. It killed over 140,000 people—more than a third of the population, which puts todays Covid travails into some perspective: imagine an illness that results in the death of 1.5 million people in Melbourne, say, and you get a sense of how destructive this particular outbreak of the plague was. Salute, as it is commonly known, was built as a kind of thank-offering for the end of the plague and is today one of the city's most emblematic landmarks.

Our *vaporetto* has arrived, and so we are off across the lagoon, past the magnificence of the Doge's palace, getting off at the Arsenale stop. Down a small canal stands the entrance gate to one of the greatest military complexes of the early modern world. Still functioning as a naval base today, the Arsenale was in its day the hub for the construction of the fleet of ships and war-galleys upon whose protection the commerce of the republic depended. Behind the turreted gates there is a big basin of water surrounded by long workshop sheds, within whose walls it was said that a fully equipped galley could be completed within a day. Trading ships were built here too, including the fabulously decorated ocean-going galleys that traded to ports as far away as Antwerp.

Interestingly, the Venetians seem to have anticipated the industrial revolution by several hundred years, creating an assembly line for ships, whereby the skeleton of the vessel was moved from one group of workers to the other to install masts, ropes, sails, cabins, exterior decoration and guns, a method adopted 450 years later by Henry Ford for the production of motor cars. By 1450 Venice had over 3,000 ships in operation, an enormous fleet by any standards, carrying and protecting cargoes the length and breadth of the Mediterranean and beyond.

The modern Arsenale is a much more peaceful place. The Italian navy still occupies part of it, and some of the workshops have been repurposed to make components for the MOSE project, the flood defence system that seems to be taking an eternity to complete. But it comes to life every other year, when many of its sheds become temporary art galleries as part of the Venice Biennale.

So far we have had quite a long day, but there is one other place we need to visit to round out our survey of the Venetian commercial history, and it is way back up in the *sestiere* of Cannaregio. That's a bit far to walk, so once again we will take another *vaporetto* up to the junction of the Cannaregio canal and walk from there.

Cannaregio is often (incorrectly) called the 'Jewish Quarter'. It gets this name because at its centre lies the peaceful and atmospheric Campo del Ghetto Nuovo. The origin of the word *ghetto* is uncertain, though several theories link it to the metal foundries that used to operate in the area before it was sealed off in 1516 and the city's seven hundred Jews were relocated there, segregated from the rest of the population. There were only two bridges connecting the ghetto to the rest of Venice, whose gates were locked at night, and strict penalties were enforced on Jews who found themselves outside the walls during the curfew hours.

Why did the republic's authorities impose such seemingly harsh conditions on the city's Jewish population? Essentially because they had to solve a dilemma. The Venetian economy was increasingly complex, and they were very much aware that Jewish moneylenders provided a service that no-one else could, since the Catholic church forbade Christians to lend money at interest. As 'infidels', the Jews were exempt from such strictures, but their presence in Venice was also a source of friction with the local clergy and the papacy. Their solution was the ghetto.

The term 'ghetto' has, of course, acquired much more sinister overtones in modern times, and justifiably so; but in 16th century Venice the development of the ghetto was in fact something of an improvement for the living conditions of the Jewish population. True, their freedom of movement was curtailed and they were subjected to many restrictions, but within the ghetto they were free to exercise their own customs and practice their religion freely at the five synagogues, a freedom that was not always permitted to other minorities living and working in Venice. In fact, the Germans were deemed to be far more dangerous and were not allowed to practice their religion at all, since their heretical Protestant ideas could easily infect the rest of the population, whereas conversion to Judaism was considered to be much less likely.

The Jews weren't the only foreigners to be corralled into a single place where their activities could be monitored and controlled. A little further up the canal, on the opposite bank, is Venice's natural history museum. Its graceful, double arched façade looks vaguely oriental, which gives a bit of a clue about the building's past, for this was originally the Fondaco Dei Turchi, the warehouse of the city's Turkish merchants. Originally built as a palazzo, in the early seventeenth century it was converted to house the Turkish community in a one-building ghetto. Though the Turkish Ottoman empire was a strategic rival and a constant military threat, the Venetians and Turks nevertheless continued to do business with each other, and Venice allowed individual Turks to live in the city (though they were not allowed to bring their wives or children). The fondaco was created in 1621 when the Venetian government acquired a large house belonging to the duke of Ferrara. They closed up the windows in all of the external walls, set guards around the perimeter—mostly to protect the residents against the emotional outbursts of the Christian population—and moved all the city's resident Turks, Albanians and Bosnians into the building. Their movements while outside the fondaco were strictly controlled, but they were nevertheless able to carry on their trade without any other hindrance and did so until it declined in importance towards the end of the sixteenth century.

As well as the Muslim minorities and the Jews, there were several other minority populations in Venice; Orthodox Greeks were probably the largest single group, along with Croatians and Albanians who had come from the Dalmatian coast following the Republic's absorption of that area into its empire. By one estimate, there were fifteen to twenty thousand foreigners living in a city whose total population was perhaps a hundred thousand, so it must have been a very lively, polyglot sort of place, particularly when you add in the spice of occasional

Moorish traders from North Africa and even on one occasion an ambassador from Japan and his retinue.

Shakespeare's melancholy merchant Antonio is, of course, straightforwardly Italian. But whether the great playwright ever visited Venice or not, he seems to have caught the Zeitgeist of the remarkable and complex place that was commercial Venice in the 16<sup>th</sup> century. Listen to Shylock's assessment of the risks and rewards of the Italian merchant's ventures:

*He hath an argosy bound for Tripolis, another to the Indies. I understand moreover upon the Rialto he hath a third at Mexico, a fourth for England, and other ventures he hath squandered abroad. But ships are but boards, sailors but men. There be land rats and water rats, water thieves and land thieves—I mean pirates—and then there is the peril of waters, winds and rocks.*

There, in a spare sixty-eight words, Shakespeare lays out the scale of the risks that an Italian merchant in Venice might take to acquire his wealth. Shylock says, considering all this, that Antonio's standing is sufficient to lend him the immense sum of three thousand ducats, even though he hates the merchant—not because he is a Christian, but because he 'lends out money gratis, and brings down the rate of usuance [usury] here with us in Venice.' The latter complaint seems to have more force with Shylock than the merely religious objection. This is just one of the ways in which Shakespeare paints a picture of the world of Venetian commerce to provides a backdrop for the central plot love and revenge.

By Shakespeare's time Antonio and his ilk had morphed into landed gentry, owning great estates in the Veneto that provided less risky and more certain sources of income that enabled them to fund the building of the great palazzi that line the Grand Canal and indulge in the sponsorship of brilliant artists, architects and musicians to glorify themselves, their republic and their god. That legacy is ever-present in Venice, and we should all be grateful to them for it. But it was built upon the foundations of the toil and risk of the city's mercantile wizards, a bunch of hucksters and likely lads who extracted advantage from the precarious sandbanks and shifting sands of their lagoon and turned it into a great commercial empire.

# Chapter 5

# The Venetian Lagoon

The Venetian backyard is its lagoon. Extending over 550 square kilometres, with an average depth of just over ten metres, this watery wonderland is almost a universe of its own. There are over thirty inhabited islands, as well as many more that are uninhabited, and for many who live on them the city of Venice seems far away, visited only on rare occasions and by necessity. For others, of course, the flow of tourists from the main Venetian islands provides a critical infusion of dollars each season, without which they would live much harder lives.

On our various visits to Venice, we always made a point of getting on a *vaporetto* and making at least one trip across the calm and sparkling waters of the lagoon to one or another of the islands. The journey itself is almost as enjoyable as the destination, as the ferry chugs its way through channels carefully marked with wooden posts that stretch away into the distance. While the locals shelter inside, as absorbed in their newspapers and phone screens as commuters anywhere, we tourists line the rails and crowd into the little semicircle of seats at the stern of the ferry, and brave the cold to enjoy the experience of the sea air, the pearl-grey light of a sky that seems to merge seamlessly with the darker grey of the water, the sound of ever-hopeful gulls, and the parade of tiny shoals and islets that the ferry passes by, sending a wash up on either side that startles the waterfowl and waders on the banks and sends them croaking into the sky, protesting at the disturbance.

The nearest islands in the lagoon are actually only a short hop away by boat. Isola San Michele, for example, is very clearly visible from anywhere on the northern side of Venice and can be reached by ferry in less than ten minutes. This is the most celebrated of several cemetery islands in the lagoon; it has hosted a monastery and served as a prison at various times in its history, but when Venice was under Napoleonic rule in 1807 it was designated as a cemetery, the ever-rational French having decided that burying people on the main Venetian islands was unsanitary.

San Michele is so crowded that many of the graves are stacked vertically into walls of the dead, a common practice in Italy, where cremation is not a popular way of disposing of the remains of loved ones, leading to space shortages in most burial grounds. Divided into neat sections, the island is big enough that you need to spend some time studying the map prominently displayed near the landing point. Once inside, it is a little eerie, enclosed as the whole island is by high walls that shut out the sights and sounds of the lagoon. There is a particularly touching section devoted to children, and a lovely church, but tourists are mostly drawn here to visit the graves of the famous folk who have died in Venice and been buried here—among the most famous are those of Ezra Pound, Sergei Diaghilev, and Igor Stravinsky.

Another small island that is easily overlooked, even though it is in plain sight from almost anywhere in Venice, is San Giorgio Maggiore. Hanging just off the tip of Giudecca, this little island's most prominent feature is the brilliantly white neoclassical facade of the Benedictine church of San Giorgio (St

George), which was designed by the great Venetian architect Andrea Palladio and built in stages between 1566 and 1610. Behind it stands a belltower which can be ascended via an elevator (a godsend to ageing knees) for a very fine view of the city, and if you go at the right (or wrong) time you are treated to an ear-splitting chorus of church bells. Most visitors don't go any further than the church and belltower, but the island also boasts some lovely gardens, from which you can look across and see what the rich people are doing at the Hotel Cipriani, just across the way on Giudecca, and an excellent private art gallery, the Fondazione Giorgio Cini, housed in the former Benedictine monastery.

These places are just morsels compared to the most-visited islands of the lagoon, of which Murano is probably the most famous and most tourist-blighted. Murano is also visible from Venice and is just a quarter of an hour away by ferry. It is actually a series of islands linked by bridges and is most famous as a centre for glassmaking. Though Venice was hardly the only place in Europe where glass was made in the medieval and early modern periods, Venetian glassmakers enjoyed the advantage of regular contact with the Byzantine empire, where the art was much more advanced. By the end of the thirteenth century, Venetian glass was highly prized and becoming an important export; in part to protect its trade secrets, and in part to mitigate the risks to the rest of the city from the glass furnaces, the entire trade was moved to Murano in 1291, and the golden age of Murano glass began.

Today, genuine Murano glassware is still highly prized, though sadly it must compete with imitations produced in Asia and Eastern Europe that have taken, it is estimated, almost half of the market. As a result, the island today employs less than a thousand people in the making of glass, though of course there are many more involved with the tourist aspects of the industry. But whether you are interested in glassware or not, Murano is still a fascinating place to visit, with several beautiful churches and any number of lovely canal-side restaurants.

All these islands (and quite a few besides) are readily accessible, but to really soak up the atmosphere of the Venetian lagoon, you have to travel a little further, to places that feel as though they really are in another world. It takes about forty minutes to get to Burano, on a track that takes you via Murano and past Lazaretto Nuovo, one of several islands that were used as leper colonies and as hospitals for plague victims. The latter part of the trip threads its way between low-lying marshy islands and the occasional rocky outcrop crowned by the ruins of a long-abandoned settlement, until eventually the brightly coloured houses of Burano come into view.

Burano is one of the most densely populated places in the lagoon, its population of 2,800 jammed into just 210,000 square metres (which, if you do the maths, works out at a shade under 13,000 people per square kilometre; by comparison there are just 630 residents per square kilometre for the whole of Venice). The place is famous for two things: the houses and the making of lace. Though very little actual lace-making goes on today, it was once a thriving centre for the production of lace that was exported all over the world. As for the houses, they are most famous because of their dazzling facades, whose colours are strictly controlled by local statute. This has made Burano an irresistible destination for artists and photographers the world over, as it is today for modern happy-snapping tourists.

One of our happiest discoveries in Venice was the little island of Mazzorbo, is linked to Burano by a wooden bridge, which once crossed takes you into an entirely different world. We might never have considered a visit, were it not for a food blogger that Robert regularly reads who posted a story about the joys of making and eating a duck *ragù* from ducks shot in the marshes around the island, and served with home-made pappardelle. Naturally we had to go and have lunch at the restaurant that she mentioned, one of the four or five that line the waterfront on Mazzorbo. Trattoria Maddalena didn't look particularly enticing from the outside, but once inside we found ourselves in one of those lovely, simple Italian restaurants that focus on just one thing: good food!

We emerged an hour or so later, an excellent meal and a few glasses of wine settling in our stomachs, clutching a small bottle of a Lambrusco reduction that had been used as a vinaigrette on our salad; Robert was so taken by it that he persuaded the restaurateur to sell us a small bottle. After a quick wander over the rest of the island (mostly covered in vineyards and orchards), we headed back across the bridge to make the short ferry hop to our next destination, one of the most fascinating and haunting places in Venice, the island of Torcello.

From the ferry stop, visitors walk along the banks of a canal that almost bisects this flat and marshy patch of land. Unkempt farmland stretches out on either side, and you begin to wonder what the attraction is, particularly if you visit, as we did, in the desolate air of winter. Then, almost on the other side of the island, you come to a little piazza, dominated by two churches and a few other buildings scattered here and there. What you are looking at is the remains of the city of Torcello, which was once an important political and trading centre, and is often referred to as Venice's 'parent island'. Estimates of the population of Torcello at its height vary from 3,000 to 20,000 people, which seems quite incredible: today there is almost nothing left of what must have been a busy and thriving commercial centre. When Torcello's harbours began to silt up, the place went into a long decline, most of the buildings were dismantled and the stone was taken away to be used as building material in Venice.

But what remains is still extraordinary. The Basilica of Santa Maria Assunta was the seat of the Bishop of Altino for more than a thousand years, and it is one of the oldest religious edifices in the Veneto; inside, visitors are awed by a fantastically vivid set of mosaics that glisten and glimmer in the filtered light that comes through the basilica's windows. Next door is the equally beautiful church of Santa Fosca, built in the circular fashion of the Greek Orthodox church, and just across the piazza, overlooking the canal, is the only remaining palazzo out of the many that once filled the town's twelve parishes, now serving as the island's museum.

The last island on our tour of the Venetian lagoon lies at its opposite end and is a complete contrast to the eerie peace of Torcello. The Lido has long been famous as the playground of Venice, a place where fashionable Venetians in the 18th and 19th centuries came in the summer to enjoy the long beaches and bathe in the sea, an activity that was widely held to have great therapeutic value. As one of the two barrier islands that separate the lagoon from the sea, the long narrow cigar of the Lido has always been important militarily, since forts placed at each end of the island could control the entry and exit of shipping into Venice, and for much of its history that was the island's only use.

Then the romantic poets discovered it, and before long the seaward side of the Lido was lined by grand hotels. Probably the most famous was the Hotel des Bains, the setting for Thomas Mann's novella *Death in Venice*, filmed so unforgettably by Lucchino Visconti. Rather sadly, the hotel closed for the last time in 2010; the plan was to convert it into luxury apartments, but to date no work has been done on the project and it remains deserted, surrounded by a tall fence that allows the passer by no more than a glimpse of the famous facade. If you want to get a sense at least of what life in such a grand hotel might have been like, you have to go a little further along the beach, where the Hotel Excelsior still retains something of that atmosphere.

These days, you don't have to stay in a grand hotel to enjoy the Lido; we found a great little place on the lagoon side, right opposite the ferry terminal, when we visited one summer during the Venice Biennale. The Hotel Belvedere is a typical Italian family-owned place, complete with creaking stairs, tiny elevator, welcoming little bar filled with comfy armchairs, and a selection of long-term residents of a certain age who showed up every morning dressed in suit and tie for breakfast on the terrace; for us it made an inexpensive alternative to staying at a hotel in central Venice.

Even at the height of summer, the Lido is much less oppressively crowded than Venice proper, and it has that wonderful carefree feel common to beach resorts everywhere. Families wander down the main street hunting for the best gelato shops in town (a project Italians undertake with the same seriousness as a Melburnian in search of the perfect coffee), the restaurants are filled to capacity with laughing, chattering patrons, and groups of good-natured youngsters move happily from bar to bar; in short, a scene that is replicated in beachside hamlets from Rostock to Noosa.

It was also on the Lido that we had our first encounter with another Italian institution: the beach club. In Australia the beaches are entirely free, and I suspect that there would be a minor riot if anyone ever attempted to charge a fee to access them. In Italy, the reverse is true; most beaches are lined with clubs where you pay a fee to enter and to have the use of sun beds and umbrellas. Most of these clubs have a cafe or restaurant of some kind, and many have all sorts of other facilities—tennis courts, volleyball courts, change rooms, and even swimming pools. Because they are so ubiquitous, the fees charged are not excessive, and they are very popular with Italian families, who come for their summer break and camp out for a week or fortnight, occupying the same spot every day in their multi-generational tribes, all of which makes for great people-watching.

Of course, even on the Lido there are so-called 'free' beaches, where there is no charge for access to the actual sand; however, you do have to pay for the use of umbrellas and sun beds, conveniences that we soon came to regard as indispensable for any visit to the beach, since we are no longer at an age where lying on a towel under a baking sun has much appeal. We found one such place and spent several pleasant half-days observing the scene and going for the occasional dip in the limpid waters of the Adriatic, before retiring in search of a meal and bed at the Belvedere.

There are many other islands in the lagoon: Chioggia, down at the mouth of the Brenta Canal, a sort of mini-Venice that in the eighteenth century was an elegant summer destination for Venetian aristocrats; the various melancholy Lazaretto islands where the sick and lame went to die; and the islands such as Sacca Sessola and San Clemente that have been converted into playgrounds for the rich.

As backyards go, the Venetian Lagoon is pretty big and full of places to play, or just to contemplate from afar the enigmatic beauty that is Venice.

## Chapter 6

# Food, Wine, and La Dolce Vita

When you live for an extended period of time in a foreign country, you discover just how many new rules you have to learn in order to do the things that you used to do without a moment's thought back home. Tourists have their own rules, of course, and for better or worse the local inhabitants of the towns and cities who are invaded by tourists each year end up playing by *their* rules rather than their own, reluctantly accommodating their needs and wants. But if you are staying in a place for more than a week or two, you have little choice but to adopt the local customs.

In no sphere of everyday life is this fact more evident than in the realm of food. Before we left Australia, we had visions of shopping in little Italian markets, bargaining with the shopkeepers to buy fresh produce, and enjoying meals in obscure cafes and restaurants where we would chat amiably to the waiters in fluent Italian while savouring the local specialities. And we did indeed do most of those things—eventually.

But first we had to learn how things worked.

Let's take the simple act of shopping. On our very first morning in Rome, we ventured out onto the Campo de' Fiori and poked and prodded our way through the stalls, faithfully trying to learn the Italian names of those vegetables that were familiar and guessing the identity of those that were not. We even managed, greatly daring, to buy a tomato or two and some lettuce. So far so good.

Then as we made our way back to our apartment, feeling rather pleased with ourselves, we spotted a marvellous looking shop right next to the entrance to our apartment building, what we would think of as a kind of smallgoods shop, selling cured meats and cheeses and the like. The neon sign above announced that this was Ruggeri's, a *salsamenteria*, whatever that meant, and, more obviously, a place you could buy *vini* and *liquori*. So of course we had to go in.

Picking out a cheese or two and some sliced meat wasn't too hard. The young men behind the counter were obviously quite used to dealing with non-Italian speaking foreigners and were very patient while we tried to explain what we wanted. But then we were left in complete confusion when, instead of asking us for payment they moved straight on to the next customer. Eventually, after a few moments of observation, we worked out that we were supposed to go over to the rather bored-looking young lady sitting in a little booth near the front of the shop whose only job was to manage the payment process, using the docket that we had been handed with our parcels.

While this system isn't used in every shop in Italy, it is very common. No-one seems to know quite why they do things this way: the only explanation we ever got was that it had something to do with fighting corruption, though it doesn't seem obvious just how making customers queue up and go through this odd two-step process helps with that. More likely it is just a kind of make-work program that has acquired the status of tradition over the years.

In Australia, food shopping usually involves a trip once or maybe twice a week to the supermarket, where, with Anglo-Saxon efficiency, we load up the trolley with everything we need and take it all back home to be stowed away in capacious refrigerators and pantries. But for Italians, food shopping is a daily activity. In crowded city centres, this is in some ways a matter of practical necessity: since everyone walks to the nearest shops or markets, they can only carry a limited quantity of goods back to their apartments. But that isn't the whole story. Italian cuisine is built on fresh ingredients, and nothing guarantees freshness like buying food that arrived in the markets or supermarkets today. Not for Italians great quantities of frozen vegetables extracted from cabinet-sized freezers (in fact most Italian apartments possess only modestly sized refrigerators of any kind).

Once upon a time a shopping expedition would have involved a series of visits to the *mercato* for fruit and vegetables, the local *alimentari* for other staples such as bread and milk and eggs, perhaps a call into the *salumeria* for sliced meats to make antipasto, and to the *macelleria* to buy meat or chicken. But like everywhere else in the world, many of the functions of these specialist shops have been subsumed into the all-purpose *supermercato*. One might with justification become dewy-eyed with nostalgia at the replacement of these traditional shops with the all-purpose supermarket concept that the Americans invented and exported to the rest of the world with such success, for us supermarkets were a godsend in our first few months in Italy. At least in a supermarket everything is packaged and priced, and with a little effort it isn't too hard to work out what you are actually buying. And when you have piled your shopping basket high, the ritual of paying is familiar and straightforward, requiring only the minimum of language skills to complete.

Although even that process does have its quirks: in an Italian supermarket you always pack your own shopping bags, and the checkout operator seems to take a fiendish delight in shovelling your purchases at you far more quickly than you can get them into your bag, a task that is invariably still incomplete when they ask for payment, in the bored but impatient tone common to checkout operators everywhere. Then, having fumbled out some cash or wrestled with a card payment machine, the race is on again for you to clear away the last of your items before the next customer's goods start hurtling towards you. It became a game to see whether we could beat them and have our bags filed before the last item was scanned: on my estimate, we were victors less than five percent of the time.

But that is only one of the ways in which Italian supermarkets are not exactly like their Australian counterparts. To begin with, they are small. Well, that is not precisely true: in Florence, for example, there is one very big supermarket, and I am sure there are plenty of big ones in the suburbs, but in the *centro storico* where we usually stayed, the supermarket chains have had to squeeze their stores into whatever irregular space is available, and the result is a kind of labyrinth that twists and winds its way around corners, and between supporting arches and pillars.

In these tiny idiosyncratic spaces, every available inch is taken up with shelves and display cases, arranged to some system fully understood only by the store employees, and sometimes not even by them. You can go hunting for muesli, for example, only to discover that instead of being with all the other breakfast cereals it is in the *biologico* section, reserved for organic produce. Logical enough in some ways, but it was an Italian kind of logic, not quite the same as our Anglo-Saxon variety. Still, we took some comfort from the fact that we weren't the only people who were confused by such things: *'dove?'* ('where?') is a word one hears constantly from Italian shoppers in supermarkets as customers interrogate the staff.

If you go into a supermarket in Germany, one of the things you immediately notice is that every one of them has a huge selection of two things: beer and sausages. In Italy, the equivalent products are wine and pasta. No matter how small the actual space that the shop occupies, there will always be room for a wall of wine, almost all of it bottled, though that Aussie invention the wine-cask is beginning to make its appearance. After a while we also realised that, while you can get wine originating from all over the Italian peninsula, there was also a subtle emphasis on local regional wines, which were always given a little more shelf space and prominence.

Pasta, similarly, always has a big section of its own. There are literally hundreds of different types of pasta, and it sometimes seems as if every one of them is represented on Italian supermarket shelves. If you think the displays of pasta available in Australian supermarkets are comprehensive, I promise you that you are seeing only a fraction of the possibilities. And ranged alongside them are all the different kinds of sauce to go with them, tomato-based *passata*, pesto made with basil, creamy *alfredo*, and spicy *arrabbiata*. Pairing the pasta with the right sauce is a subject in itself, and one that can provoke fierce debate.

What you can't get in an Italian supermarket is anything that isn't Italian, or at least European. Asian spices for example are virtually non-existent and can generally only be found in the very few Asian groceries that survive here and there. Australian, American and British supermarkets usually have fairly extensive sections selling Indian spices, Japanese sauces, Mexican tortillas and so on. Except in the biggest supermarkets, you'll struggle to find a bottle of soy sauce, let alone anything more exotic.

Italy, you see, is a food monoculture. Foreigners of course flock to the country expecting to eat the local cuisine. But the locals like it too, and don't really have any curiosity or interest in strange foods from the orient or the Americas. Italian cuisine might be a monoculture, but that doesn't make it boring. To return to the apparently simple matter of pasta: not only are there more than fifty types of pasta, and over three hundred different shapes, but the sauces with which they can be combined create an infinite variety of possibilities that have been refined over the centuries. Every region has its own particular combination of pasta and sauce, leading to endless debates about the merits of each.

The hallmark of Italian cooking is simplicity. The Italian journalist and humourist Beppe Severino wrote that when Italians opened cafes and restaurants, they offered the only kind of cooking they knew—the home variety. It was, he says, a stroke of genius, and I am inclined to agree with him. The whole point of Italian cooking is that it is grounded in the dishes mamma makes back at home in the village, and if you try and gentrify it all you do is mess with its very appeal: simple, uncomplicated recipes using fresh ingredients in combinations that have been tested in Italian domestic kitchens over generations.

To give you one very simple example, one of the local supermarket chains was running a poster campaign promoting various combinations of food that was available in their stores—a simple and routine marketing tactic, of course, used all over the world. But as we passed by one of their shopfronts in Rome, the poster that for some reason caught our eye was selling the combination of basil pesto and a pasta called *trofie*, topped with a dob of ricotta cheese. Trofie is a short, thin pasta shape that is given a half-twist when it is made, producing little torpedoes. It originates from Liguria, up in the northwest, so naturally it is traditionally paired with the basil pesto that is associated with that region (and which is often called pesto Genovese).

What we discovered was that this really is a perfect pairing. You can use pesto Genovese with all sorts of other pastas, of course, or with gnocchi, but we have never tasted any combination that is quite so perfect as trofie with basil pesto. And so it goes, all over the peninsula. I don't know, for example, which Bolognese came up with the idea of floating meat-filled tortellini in a thin chicken broth, but whoever he or she was (probably she), they were a genius. The same accolade could be bestowed on the Roman chef (or *nonna*) who decided to make a sauce to go with fettucine made of nothing more than eggs, grated *pecorino* cheese and fried *guanciale* (pig's cheek).

The flip side of this very attractive formula is that Italians have also evolved lots of rules for the preparation and consumption of food, to which they cleave with something that verges on a very un-Italian fanaticism. We had an amusing encounter with this trait at a shop in the Sant'Ambrogio market, in Florence. Robert had bought from one of the other stalls a pasta sauce, with no very definite idea as to how he was going to use it. The next day we returned to the market, and went to a shop that sold every kind of fresh pasta imaginable, intending to complete the simple task of buying an appropriate type of pasta to go with the sauce. That, of course, necessitated explaining to the stallholder just what the sauce actually was, and what kind of pasta we wanted.

Unfortunately, this conversation took place while he was surrounded by Italian ladies waiting their turn. Unable to restrain themselves, they all had to have their say about exactly which pasta (Tortellini? Ravioli? Fettucine?) was the correct choice for this particular type of sauce. Conducted in a mixture of Italian and English, the debate went on for some time, growing ever more vociferous, until eventually I got tired of it all and just made a decision. But the Italians had to have the final say and we left with the words 'this is not approved!' ringing in our ears, though the sentiment was robbed of any serious intent by the laugh and wagging of fingers with which it was accompanied.

Coffee is another example. Australians, as the world knows, are enthusiastic and inventive coffee consumers. Any barista worth his salt in Melbourne can make any one of a dozen combinations of espresso coffee and various kinds of milk on demand. As coffee lovers, we thought we would at least be dealing with something familiar in another country for whom the consumption of the bean is equally sacred. Not a bit of it.

To begin with, Italians do not have our buccaneering approach to when and how coffee is consumed. There are strict rules, and not following them marks you out as (gasp!) a tourist. Eyebrows will be raised if you order a cappuccino after ten in the morning, as doing so is regarded as ruinous to the digestive system, a subject Italians take very seriously. In fact, it is fair to say that Italians are very doubtful about any combination of milk and coffee and approach the subject with a great deal of caution. The standard Italian coffee is an espresso, and if you simply ask for 'un caffe', that is what you will get. It is meant to be consumed quickly, as a pick-me-up, and is always accompanied by a glass of water, which you can have *naturale* or *frizzante* (carbonated). An espresso after lunch is perfectly acceptable but consuming a cappuccino on top of all that food is simply barbaric.

Speaking of milk, we did know that if you order a 'latte' in Italy, you will get a glass of milk, so at least we didn't make that mistake. But a cappuccino or a caffe latte would invariably be served lukewarm, unless you specifically ask for it *'ben caldo'* (good and hot), and even then your request will be fulfilled with a sniff of disdain. Similarly, adding hot water to espresso coffee to make what we call a long black coffee seems to be conceptually confusing to an Italian barista; the closest we could ever get was to order an 'Americano', but even that was a hit and miss exercise. In short, the Italians have their rules for coffee, and they will mess with them only very reluctantly, and only to please the tourists.

The same is true for breakfast, another culinary realm to which Australians have developed a unique approach. Eggs for us are a staple, made to be combined in dozens of imaginative ways with all sorts of other ingredients. But for Italians, breakfast is a coffee and a cornetto, and that is about it. The bitterness of the coffee balances the sweetness of the pastry, and the whole thing is light on the stomach. That approach is entirely rational, and probably many a nutritionist would say it is exactly what one should have for breakfast, but it does mean you are out of luck if you enjoy an occasional big breakfast of eggs and bacon, say, or an omelette. A couple of fried eggs accompanied by slices of cold ham and a bit of salad is the most you'll get from any restaurant that isn't part of a major international hotel chain.

There is one other very simple over-arching rule for consuming food and drink in Italy: do not over-indulge! Take alcohol, for example. Italians simply find it incomprehensible that anyone would want to drink until they are so inebriated that they can barely stand up. Wine is an accompaniment to food, not a path to oblivion, and should be enjoyed for its taste as much as for its intoxicating effect. The brilliant Italian invention of *aperitivo*, when snacks (though that seems an inadequate word to describe what is often a veritable smorgasbord of tasty food treats) are provided free of charge with the purchase of wine or cocktails, reinforces the rule that booze must be accompanied by food. It is also a handy substitute for dinner for poverty-stricken students, who nurse a single glass of wine or spritz for hours so that they can make as many trips as possible to the food counter.

I could go on. The only acceptable dressing for your salad is oil and vinegar, so don't even think of asking for any other kind. Even then, use the condiments sparingly—you are meant to be tasting the food, not the stuff you slather on it. You won't get butter to go with your bread unless you ask for it: bread is for mopping up the sauce left after you've finished your pasta, something you are expected to do to express your appreciation of the meal. Speaking of bread, you'll only get the plain white variety served in a restaurant; the Australian/American concoction of garlic bread would be outlawed in Italy. As would adding parmesan to any fish-based pasta. And if you meet a new Italian friend, don't surprise him by suggesting you share a pizza: it's just not done it Italy.

*

Food, you will have gathered by now, is not a subject to be taken lightly when among Italians. Mealtimes, whether at home or out in a restaurant, are an occasion for socialising, not merely for refuelling, and Italians expect to take their time when gathered around the table. In fact, so central is food to domestic life that the most prominent piece of furniture in many an apartment is the dining suite, which stands in the middle of the living room, relegating the sofa to an ignominious junior place against the back wall.

Traditionally, an Italian menu will comprise four courses: *antipasto*, *primo*, *secondo*, and *dolce*. That might sound like a lot, but usually each course is quite small, at least by Australian standards. The *antipasto* course is generally cheeses or cured meats accompanied by olives or dried tomatoes; *primo* is either soup or a fist-sized serving of pasta, probably half the quantity that Americans or Australians customarily consume; *secondo* is the meat or fish course, again generally small serves and always accompanied with salad or vegetables; and *dolci*, or dessert, is typically a *tiramisu*, a *semifreddo*, or a *pannacotta*, all relatively light options. It is usual to have at least two of these courses, and often all four. But Italians do so in order to prolong the whole experience, enjoy the taste of the food, engage in convivial conversation, and along the way get mildly intoxicated, rather than simply to consume the necessary calories.

Wander around a typical Italian piazza at any time of day and observe. In the fresh coolness of the morning, groups of older people gather under the umbrellas for coffee and pastries and debate for hours the merits of their various football teams and the perfidy of all politicians. Lunchtimes extend over an hour and a half, every minute of which is spent consuming food and drink and talking over the latest in the never-ending saga of office politics. By late afternoon, it is *aperitivo* time, and the students are gathering to nurse their Aperol Spritz and put away a stack of mini-pizzas, slices of cheese and meat, and other little treats. Dinner is a late meal in Italy, though not as absurdly late as it is in Spain, and the long summer evenings are full of the sound of convivial chatter late into the night.

The phrase *la dolce vita* has passed into common English usage, though if put to it few would be able to describe exactly what 'the sweet life' actually means. There is a certain wistfulness to it, particularly when expressed by someone coming from one of the efficiency-obsessed Anglo-Saxon cultures, something we would all like to have but regretfully are unlikely ever to experience. For me, though, and here I am certainly speaking on behalf of Robert as well, the essence of *la dolce vita* finds its best expression in the Italian approach to mealtimes: slowing down, savouring everything, enjoying the company of friends or family, and generally relegating the humdrum concerns of the more serious world to the back corners of the mind for an hour or two.

And though it might be an Italian phrase, it encapsulates a style of life that you can observe in all of the countries that border the northern coast of the Mediterranean, from the Greek Islands to the coast of Andalusia. The teeming squares filled with the sound of laughter and the squeal of children running about between their parents' legs, the coffee taken at a quayside taverna in a little fishing village overlooking a picturesque harbour filled with brightly painted fishing boats, the siesta taken after a long, languorous lunch, all these food rituals seem emblematic of the good life. Somehow, the people of Italy, southern Spain, and the coast of Spain do manage to do all the other things that are important—earning a living, shopping, educating children—but you do get the feeling that they are having more fun than the rest of us. Maybe they know something we don't.

## Chapter 7

# Hunting Caravaggio

I remember seeing at one of those blockbuster art exhibitions popular in Melbourne a quote from the late Robert Hughes that struck a chord which has thrummed away in the background ever since. 'There was painting before Caravaggio,' he wrote, 'and there was painting after him: but they weren't the same.' Hughes, one of Australia's greatest cultural exports and one of the world's most erudite art critics, seemed to hit the proverbial nail right on the head, capturing in a few words the profound influence of on the world of art of a painter whose story has fascinated me ever since. Naturally enough, once we had found our feet and started exploring Rome, one of the first things we did was go looking for the many Caravaggio paintings that hang in the city.

But first, who was Caravaggio? And why was he important? Some readers will know the answer to both those questions, but for those who don't, let's take a little detour into the rather rugged story of his life. The first thing to know is that his name was not in fact Caravaggio. He was born Michelangelo Merisi, the son of a Milanese architect who was employed by the Marchese of Caravaggio, a small town just south of Bergamo. He grew up there, and hence in adulthood became known as Michelangelo Merisi da (from) Caravaggio. The modern town, incidentally, doesn't seem to have much affection for its famous son: the house where he was reputedly born is today a pizza joint, and the only recognition of its importance as the artist's birthplace is a rather faded inscription on the façade of the old building.

In 1584, the thirteen-year-old Michelangelo Merisi moved to Milan, where he was to be apprenticed to a painter named Simone Peterzano, a student of Titian. A few years later, he fled the city, apparently after a quarrel that resulted in the wounding of a police officer: it was the beginning of a pattern of violence that would be a recurring feature of his life. But he arrived in Rome at the perfect time, for the city was undergoing one of its periodic building booms and there was great demand for artists who could fill the new churches and palaces with pictures and frescoes. He was to spend the next decade living and working in the eternal city, years in which he was to make his reputation.

Almost immediately he began to produce images that pointed the way towards his later genius. Initially, they were small-scale genre paintings that demonstrated the painter's ability to capture images in extraordinary detail. *Boy with a Basket of Fruit*, for example, shows a handsome youth (probably Caravaggio's friend Mario Minniti) whose arms nestle a huge basket full of every kind of ripe fruit. Today it hangs in the Galleria Borghese in Rome, and the detail is remarkable, from the folds of the cloth of the boy's shirt to the precise reproduction of each individual piece of fruit.

But it was his next series of paintings that would make the Roman art world sit up and take notice. Their subjects are entirely secular: *The Fortune Teller*, *The Cardsharps*, *The Musicians*, *The Lute Player*, and *Boy Bitten by a Lizard*. Each is an intimate chamber piece depicting people and scenes that the young painter might have encountered all over Rome, but painted with a natural realism, a sense of drama and a cheeky charm that was quite different from the ethereal Mannerist paintings popular in Rome at the time.

They proved to be the key to his first taste of financial success, coming to the attention of his first great patron, Cardinal Francesco Maria del Monte, who took the young artist up and provided him with secure employment. The cardinal's support soon got him commissions to paint on more religious subjects, and what emerged from his brush was a truly remarkable series of pictures in which that sense of the dramatic was married to a powerful spirituality that produced unforgettable images of some of the seminal moments of the Christian story, the martyrdoms of St Peter and St Paul, the stories of St Matthew and John the Baptist, and more obscure tales such as that of Judith and Holofernes.

But the painter who was so brilliantly capable of creating uplifting visions on canvas had a troubled darker side. From the very beginning of his career, he had acquired a taste for the rough life. A contemporary wrote of him that 'after a fortnight's work he will swagger about for a month or two with a sword at his side and a servant following him, from one ball-court to the next, ever ready to engage in a fight or an argument, so that it is most awkward to get along with him'. This temperament constantly got him into trouble. On one occasion he beat up a nobleman, he was jailed several times for brawling, and in 1605 he was forced to flee temporarily to Genoa after another brawl.

His real problems began a year later, when he killed Ranuccio Tommasoni in a duel; this proved to be the last straw for the authorities. Though he was himself an unsavoury character, Tommasoni came from a wealthy family who demanded justice, from whose course even the cardinal couldn't shield Caravaggio this time. Condemned to death and a bounty put on his head, he was forced to flee south to Naples. There, safe from the Roman authorities and under the temporary protection of the Colonna family, he continued to work, producing among other paintings *The Seven Works of Mercy*, a complex and brilliantly imaginative composition that still hangs in the church for which it was made, Pio Monte della Misericordia.

Alas, the restless artist did not settle permanently in Naples, and instead moved on to Malta, where Alof de Wignacourt, Grand Master of the Knights of Saint John, inducted him into the order, thereby affording him some protection from prosecution. De Wignacourt was rewarded with a fine portrait of himself, and the largest canvas that Caravaggio ever painted, of the beheading of Saint John the Baptist, which you can still see in the cathedral in Valletta. No doubt the artist hoped that the Grand Master could secure him a pardon in Rome, but his turbulent nature intervened once again, and he was imprisoned after yet another scandal. Rather miraculously, he managed to escape and fled once more, this time to Sicily, where he stayed for nine months, painting feverishly.

Meanwhile, a new pope had ascended the throne of St Peter, and hoping to secure a pardon, Caravaggio made his way back to Naples, and the ever-supportive Colonna family. An insight into his state of mind might be gathered from two pictures he painted at this time, *Salome with the Head of John the Baptist*, and *David with the Head of Goliath*, in both of which he used his own face as the model for the severed heads. Still, Colonna lobbying in Rome seemed to be promising, and things looked hopeful enough for him to board a ship heading north for Rome.

He was never to arrive. The exact date and causes of his death are not known and have been the subject of a great deal of conjecture. It seems likely that he had a fever, and succumbed in the little town of Porto Ercole, on the Argentario Peninsula in Tuscany, a somewhat odd location, given that the town is well to the north of Ostia, the usual port for Rome. On a visit to this picturesque holiday town, we stood on the very beach where his body was supposedly found.

But theories have also been advanced that he might have died from all sorts of other causes, including syphilis, lead poisoning, or sepsis of a wound earned in yet another brawl in Naples. More sensational is the notion that he might have been killed by the Tommasoni family in an act of *vendetta* for Caravaggio's killing of Ranuccio Tommasoni.

Whatever the actual cause of death, his demise at the age of just thirty-eight robbed the world of a true artistic genius, who really did change the way that artists saw and represented the world. Even in his lifetime he had his followers, some of whom, inevitably, he quarrelled with—most notably Giovanni Baglione, with whom Caravaggio carried on a spirited feud. But after his death Italian painters such as Carlo Saraceni, Bartlomeo Manfredi, Orazio Borgianni imitated and developed his techniques.

The *Caravagisti* movement, as it became known, leapt beyond the borders of Italy. Orazio Gentileschi took the movement to England, where he painted for the court of Charles I, and his daughter, the remarkable Artemisia Gentileschi, was one of the most gifted of the master's successors. In Spain, Caravaggio's style was taken up by Guseppe Ribera, and in the Low Countries by a group of painters known as the Utrecht Caravagisti, and the longer-term influence of his work can be seen, though somewhat attenuated, in the work of the next generation of painters, from Velazquez to Rembrandt and Vermeer. All of these artists, and many more besides, created a body of work that is absolutely distinctive. They are still the pictures that immediately draw the eye when you walk into the room of a gallery, dramatic images that seem to capture real flesh and blood people at crucial moments of introspection, inspiration, agony, and despair.

*

But all that came after the artist's death, and the cockpit of the particular drama of his life was always Italy. So, if you are beguiled by the artist's output, this is the country to conduct your Caravaggio hunt, and the place to start is Rome, where he had his greatest burst of productivity and where he found fame and fortune.

For me, the place to start my Caravaggio hunt is always the church of San Luigi dei Francesi, near Piazza Navona, where you can see three of his finest works, absolutely free. Tourists crowd around the dimly lit niche of the Contarelli Chapel to peer at the scenes from the life of Saint Matthew. They are all extraordinary pictures, but the most striking is his image of Matthew being called by Christ to join his band of disciples.

Matthew was a tax collector, so Caravaggio shows him sitting at a table, around which are gathered various other figures. On his right, a young man sits with bowed head over a few coins that he is reluctantly doling out from his purse, over whose shoulder an older bearded man peers down through his spectacles, making sure that the youth is paying over the right amount. A couple of dandified toughs sit at the other end of the table, one with his back to the viewer, and in between these two groups sits another bearded man, generally taken to be Matthew himself, whose left hand seems to be pointing towards the youth.

And Christ himself? He is barely present, a figure shrouded in gloom, just visible behind the body of the innkeeper who stands to the right of the group of seated figures. Christ's arm is extended and points towards someone at the table, though exactly who he is pointing at is ambiguous (most scholars believe he is pointing at the bearded figure in the middle, but some have suggested that it is the youth who is in fact the future martyr). Everyone except the youth is looking towards Christ, and the entire scene is illuminated by a shaft of light coming from over his shoulder.

Contained in this one picture are all the elements that make Caravaggio's style so arresting. Firstly, he has made the moment dramatic by making it enigmatic. The presumed figure of Matthew's gesture could be saying 'who, me?', or perhaps he is pointing at the young man, asking 'who, him?' We don't know exactly who Christ is calling, and so we don't know how the scene will resolve itself. Then there is the realism. The scene is one that Caravaggio himself might have come across in any tavern in Rome—the tough, bearded tax collector squeezing the last few pennies from a young man, his security guaranteed by the presence of his youthful bodyguard. But this secular transaction has been interrupted by the apparition who has seemingly appeared from nowhere to make his extraordinary demand that the tax-gatherer leave off his petty life and join Christ as an apostle: every figure, the innkeeper included, seems to radiate astonishment, adding to the drama of the moment.

And then there is the final element for which Caravaggio's work was to become famous, the use of *chiaroscuro*, the use of strong contrasts between light and dark. This wasn't a new idea—in fact, its use is central to much of Renaissance art—but few painters have used it to such dramatic effect as Caravaggio. In this picture, that powerful shaft of light not only suggests Christ's divinity, but it also illuminates all the faces turned towards him and deepens the darkness of the rest of the picture.

I've seen reproductions of this painting many times, but seeing it in its original setting is always a remarkable experience—though somewhat marred by the cheapskates of the Catholic church, who refuse to illuminate it properly: the lights all go off after a few minutes, until someone puts a euro coin into the little meter box, a process that causes considerable confusion among the assembled tourists. Even so, you can understand why *The Calling of Matthew* and the other two paintings of scenes from the saint's life made Caravaggio famous as a new and daring artist in a city full of brilliant young painters.

San Luigi is, as I said, just the start. Twenty-five of the painter's eighty-eight known works can still be viewed in various places in the Italian capital. Just up the street from San Luigi, in the basilica of Santa Maria del Popolo, for example, you can see the *Crucifixion of St Peter* and the *Conversion of St Paul*, both powerful and original evocations of the key moments from those two saints' lives. Then a wander into the adjacent gardens will bring you to the splendid Galleria Borghese, where you can overdose on a collection of no less than eight pictures.

The Palazzo Barberini is home to one of his most recognisable images, the gruesome *Judith Beheading Holofernes*, illustrating the biblical tale in which the widow Judith slays Assyrian general Holofernes after a banquet. It is a masterpiece of emotional language: a rather demure Judith is both determined and at the same time repulsed by the act she is committing; her maid Abra is pictured as a somewhat bloodthirsty old crone, grimly fascinated and ready to catch the severed head in her pinny; while the look of horror on Holofernes' face is palpable, having presumably just woken from his drunken slumber as the sword is cutting into his neck.

The rest are scattered in various other museums around the city, prompting a small thrill of recognition as you spot one of the master's works in the Capitoline Museum (an extraordinarily sensuous St John the Baptist), or the Palazzo Doria Pamphilj (a surprising *Penitent Magdalene*).

To find the next largest concentration of his pictures you have to go up to Florence, where there are eight of them in various museums (and we stumbled across a ninth, whose authenticity is disputed, in the Pitti Palace, a picture entitled *The Tooth-Puller* whose most prominent character is an old woman who is a dead ringer for Judith's maid in *Judith Beheading Holofernes*).

But every place in which he spent any time seems to have acquired a picture or two. There are three in Naples, including his last known work, *The Martyrdom of Saint Ursula*, and Milan's Pinacoteca Brera possesses an early work, *Supper at Emmaus*. Cremona has its *Saint Francis*, Genoa's Palazzo Bianco plays host to a brilliant *Ecce Homo*, and down in Sicily, Messina boasts two pictures, *The Raising of Lazarus* and *The Adoration of the Shepherds*. The Sicilian capital, Palermo, used to have one, but—surprise, surprise—it was stolen in 1969 in one of the most sensational art heists in history, and has never been recovered; needless to say, the Palermitani believe the Mafia must have been involved.

We even came across, quite unaware that it was there before we walked in, his painting of *The Burial of Saint Lucy* in the church of Santa Lucia, down in Syracuse. Having a beachside break in Otranto, of all places, we were delighted to discover that the art museum located in that town's forbidding fortress was hosting an exhibition of Caravaggisti, including one by the master himself. And a quick side-trip to Malta gave me the opportunity to see his late masterworks *The Beheading of Saint John the Baptist* and *Saint Jerome Writing*.

Not all of the master's pictures remained in Rome. There are Caravaggios in London, Madrid, Berlin, Paris and New York. Over the years we have seen many, though not all of them. If all this sounds a little obsessive, it is a label I am happy to wear without qualm. There are many geniuses in the great pantheon of artists who have so enriched western culture and given expression to human spirituality, yearning, pathos, and joy, and I get a great deal of pleasure and intellectual stimulation from looking at pictures by Rembrandt, Vermeer, Van Gogh, Turner, and many others. But few of them speak to me quite so directly or as vigorously as the pictures of Michelangelo Merisi da Caravaggio.

# Chapter 8

# Opera and Shakespeare in Verona

There are few cities in Italy with more romantic associations than Verona. Enclosed by a loop of the Adige River, the old town's character seems almost to have been preserved untouched since the Middle Ages, even though the city is crammed with tourists all year round and most of the old building facades now have modern glass and steel shop fronts hosting boutiques and bustling cafes. But those distractions aside, it is remarkably easy to walk around Verona and imagine you are back in its fourteenth century heyday.

The city is of course also indelibly associated with William Shakespeare, who set *Romeo and Juliet* in Verona, along with his early play *The Two Gentlemen of Verona* (though in fact much of the action in the latter play takes place in Milan). The place trades shamelessly on the Romeo and Juliet connection, and a huge number of visitors come purely for that reason, drawn by the timelessly tragic tale of the star-crossed lovers. No doubt that is great for the city's coffers, but there is a good deal more to Verona than that, as we discovered.

On our first visit to Verona, we arrived by train from Venice, having booked a three-week stay in an apartment, and though it was a warm day we opted to walk there from the station, which is located just outside the old town itself. Not, as it turned out, an entirely wise decision; it took us a sweaty forty-five minutes to navigate our way past the massive Venetian-built city gate (now stranded in the middle of a roundabout), along a broad avenue lined with Liberty-era apartment buildings, through Piazza Bra, full of tourists gawping at the immense Roman arena, and up the cobbled and boutique-lined Via Mazzini, to finally arrive in the Piazza dell'Erbe, an irregular oblong with a lively market in the middle and lined with cafes and restaurants.

At the far end of the piazza stands the Palazzo Maffei, behind whose grand baroque facade perched our apartment, a small but very stylish one bedroom flat from whose windows we had a fine view of the piazza below. The owner, when we eventually met him a week or so later, turned out to be a young gay man (several tell-tale signs around the apartment had already tipped us off on this point), a builder by trade, who split his time between Verona and another apartment in Milan, using AirBNB to rent out whichever one he wasn't using.

Having an apartment looking out across a busy and famous piazza at first seemed to us to be exactly the kind of uniquely Italian experience we had imagined when we were back in Australia, but we soon discovered that it had a downside: noise. The Italians are like the Spanish—they eat late and if they plan to drink, they do that even later. Unfortunately for us, one of the most popular bars on the Piazza dell'Erbe was right below us, and since the apartment had no air conditioning, we had to keep the window open to get a little air into the place. So whether we liked or not we had little choice but to keep Italian night hours, either sitting on the windowsill glass in hand to watch the crowd, or else going down to join the party.

The piazza dell'Erbe occupies what was in Roman times the city's forum, the commercial and civic centre of any Roman town, and since then it has always been the commercial heart of Verona, hosting the fruit and vegetable markets (hence the name). Today, beneath the immense white umbrellas that provide shade from the sun and shelter from the occasional summer rainstorm, the market still sells foodstuffs, though that function has been relegated to secondary importance and replaced by lots of stalls selling tourist tat. On its northern side there is a long four-story structure called the Casa Mazzanti, whose upper facade sports fading but still beautiful frescoes that date from the fifteenth century. The ground floor arcades of this building originally contained workshops and shops, but are today occupied by restaurants and cafes, perfect for alfresco dining and people watching. Of these, our favourite was the Caffe Fillipini.

Like its competitors, the Fillipini necessarily caters primarily for tourists, but it is a little more upmarket than the others. The tables are covered in white tablecloths clipped securely to defend against even the most zephyr-like of breezes, the cutlery is polished to a shine that would make a guardsman proud, and even if you are the millionth tourist that has crossed the imaginary threshold between the piazza and the restaurant you are greeted as if you are the first ever to do so by sartorially splendid waiters kitted out in blindingly white shirts, waistcoats and black bowties. It is the kind of restaurant that you know the minute you walk in that they have been doing this for a very long time indeed, and they have not changed their formula in living memory.

But we weren't in Verona to sit about drinking coffee and having lunch, however pleasant such occupations may be. Our original impulse to come to the city was actually the opera festival that is held every year in the Arena di Verona, the former Roman amphitheatre, famous for the scale and grandeur of its performances. Now, I know that opera is not everybody's cup of tea: in fact, I know people who would prefer having an arm gnawed off by a bear rather than sit through an opera performance. But for Robert and I, opera is a sublime art form, with its magical combination of luscious music, sumptuous staging, and virtuosic singing. And occasionally you get some excellent acting thrown in as well.

Of all the composers who have created operas, the great Italians are for us the most endearing. The art form was invented in Italy, when Claudio Monteverdi composed his *Orfeo* for the Gonzaga court at Mantua, and the word itself is Italian (*opera* literally means 'work', in the sense of a work of art). But it was the genius of Verdi and the giants of the *verismo* ('realism') school of opera—Pietro Mascagni, Ruggiero Leoncavallo, Umberto Giordano—who created the body of works that are so beloved of modern audiences. And no-one stands taller in that pantheon than Giacomo Puccini, a composer for whom we had always had a soft spot. Robert in fact cut his operatic teeth on Puccini, when he joined the Victoria State Opera as head of publicity. His very first task was to promote the company's new production of the composer's last opera, *Turandot*; this involved a very steep learning curve, for he was then in his twenties and had never even seen an opera, let alone promoted one. So when we saw that it was on the programme at the Arena di Verona, we just had to book tickets.

The arena itself is spectacular. The external wall that we see today encloses an area of nearly 20,000 square metres; originally, there was another outer wall, some thirty metres tall, made of white limestone and highly decorated; much of it was destroyed in an earthquake in 1117, leaving only a small portion to hint at its past glory. Like the Colosseum in Rome, its seventy-two arches allowed up to thirty thousand spectators to enter or leave with an efficiency that would be impressive even in a modern arena of comparable size.

Not surprisingly, the Roman civic authorities were always nervous about such large concentrations of common citizens, particularly citizens whose blood has been excited by gladiatorial combat and the sight of wild animals tearing each other apart, and so they insisted that the arena should be built outside the city's walls, allowing gates to be shut in the event that the people got a little *too* boisterous. Today, needless to say, the more genteel crowds who are drawn to the opera pose no such threat to public order, and the Piazza Brà, the vast open space outside the arena, is usually filled with happy visitors in search of food or drink from one of the restaurants that line its northern side.

Opera performances have been held in the arena as far back as the Renaissance, and there were a few experimental productions in the 1850's, but it was on $10^{th}$ August 1913 that the modern opera festival got under way with a performance of *Aida*, a work chosen to celebrate the centenary of the birth of Giuseppe Verdi; Puccini and Mascagni were both in the audience. Since that inaugural event a festival has been held every year, except when interrupted by the two world wars, and attracts over half a million visitors to the city. Opera in this town is big business.

So, at considerable expense to our limited budget, we had booked well in advance to see Franco Zeffirelli's fabled production of *Turandot*. Set in ancient Peking (modern Beijing), the opera revolves around an icy-hearted princess, the Turandot of the title, who has vowed she will never marry, citing the fate of a long-dead ancestor as her justification. But Princesses cannot avoid the marital knot, and so to avoid having to be married off for reasons of state, she declares that she will only marry a man who can answer three riddles set by her wise men. One after another her suitors appear, only to fail and be sent to the chopping block, which does seem a rather extreme penalty for failing a quiz.

And then an exiled prince of Tartary appears, accompanied by his blind father and their devoted servant-girl, Liu. You can guess what happens next: Prince Calaf falls for the princess and succeeds in completing the three riddles. Turandot can't bear the implications of that and refuses to complete the bargain; Calaf, in a rather inexplicable act of chivalry, says he will let her off if she can guess his name before dawn breaks the next day. Despite ransacking the town to find someone who might be able to solve this puzzle—the subject of the opera's most famous aria, *Nessun Dorma*: 'none shall sleep in Peking'—and some unpleasant arm-twisting for Calaf's father Timur and the slave-girl Liu. But Turandot's cold heart begins to melt when Liu suicides rather than reveal her master's name (of course, she was secretly in love with Calaf). The prince, meanwhile, take a gamble and reveals his name to Turandot, daring her to do her worst. She finally relents, declaring that Calaf's real name is 'love'; he accepts this rather lame effort and takes her in his arms for the rousing finale.

It is a grand tale, written by a composer at the height of his powers and laced with some of the most gorgeous tunes and arias in the operatic canon. There is also a pathos about it, partly because it was Puccini's unfinished last work (at its premiere the conductor Arturo Toscanini stopped at the point where the composer had laid down his pen, turned to the audience and said '*Qui finisce l'opera, perché a questo punto il maestro è morto*'—'Here the opera ends, because at this point the maestro died.'). But there is also the faint echo of a tragic event from the composer's own life in the character of Liu. He had, it seems, a servant named Doria, who Puccini's high-strung and chilly wife accused of being his mistress. In the small village of Torre del Lago the entirely unfounded gossip became too much for the poor girl who, like Liu, killed herself. Puccini struggled to complete the work, perhaps because it tapped into some deep emotional conflict that he could not resolve, and it was left to a pupil, Franco Alfano, to finish it after the maestro's death.

Having seen *Turandot* performed several times over the years in Australia, we were very excited to have the opportunity to see it in the Verona arena, where Zeffirelli was able to use the vastness of its stage and the unique atmosphere of a performance under the stars to create a much-fabled production. Alas, on the appointed day the weather was less than perfect, raining on and off, and we spent the day fretting about the whole event. By the time we filed into the arena, still digesting dinner from one of the restaurants on Piazza Brà, it was drizzling slightly, and all we could do was hope for the best.

Today, capacity of the arena is about 15,000 patrons (half the number it was reputed to be able to hold in Roman times—we are more safety-conscious than they were), seated in three grades. The most expensive tickets get you a place down on the arena floor where well-dressed opera goers chat and find their way to their comfortable cushioned seats on ground where gladiators once fought wild animals; the next level of expense is the lower tier, which is also equipped with proper seats but no cushions, while those in the upper tiers have to make do with an allocated spot on a stone bench, which they can make more comfortable with a cushion rented from the vendors dotted about the stadium.

One of the things we had learnt from previous experiences of outdoor productions is that the romantic appeal evaporates pretty quickly when your backside begins to go numb on cold stone and your spine starts to wilt in the absence of any support, so we had opted for the middle level, rented some cushions to provide a little comfort for our posteriors and grabbed a couple of plastic ponchos as risk mitigation against the possibility of more rain.

But by now, the rain seemed to have stopped, and the arena was filled with an anticipatory buzz of conversation as we waited for the production to get under way on the enormous confection of a set whose gabled roofs and soaring towers were a remarkably realistic facsimile of the Forbidden City. The last of the sun disappeared, the lights went off, the opera got under way with its short, stirring overture and opening command for the people of Peking to listen to the recitation of Turandot's laws, and we all settled in for a thoroughly enjoyable first act.

Maybe five or ten minutes before the end of the act, the rain started to drizzle down once more. Those who had the foresight to bring umbrellas unfurled them, and the rest of us just put up with it under our plastic ponchos. On stage, the opera wound its way to its spectacular first-act climax, there was a burst of applause and a rustling as people prepared to get up for the interval. But then, to general astonishment, the orchestra struck up again and launched straight into Act Two; we all sat down again, somewhat mystified, and tried to enjoy the performance through the rain, which by now had become quite heavy.

After perhaps another ten minutes the performance was stopped, and an announcement made to the effect that this evening's event was 'suspended indefinitely' in order to 'protect the musicians' instruments'. This is where Italian cunning comes in: buried in the conditions of sale of the tickets was a clause saying that refunds would only be given if the performance was cancelled before the end of the first act. That explained the missing intermission; by skipping it they had taken the performance well beyond that deadline and so, like everyone else, we were unable to claim a refund for that night's performance. All we could do was to book again at full price, for a subsequent night; the second time we were luckier, and though there were a few spots of rain early on, it wasn't enough to stop proceedings, and we ended up having a wonderful evening.

*

I said at the beginning of this chapter that Verona trades shamelessly on its connection with Shakespeare, and though we resisted for a while, eventually we just had to go on the Romeo and Juliet pilgrimage. Probably the biggest shrine to this cult is the so-called Casa Giulietta, where thousands of people turn up every day and go through the little arched gateway from the Via Cappello, and into a short tunnel whose walls have been obliterated by graffiti—love messages scribbled by love-struck acolytes of the cult. Beyond the tunnel, there is a little courtyard, containing a statue of Juliet, whose right boob has been polished to a bright shine by a million kisses and gropes from the faithful (evidently it is supposed to bring you good luck). And above, a fourteenth-century balcony hangs over the scene, from which those girls who are prepared to pay the entrance fee to go into the house itself can be photographed by their boyfriends, mouthing 'Romeo, Romeo, wherefore art thou, Romeo?' Probably the only line from the play that they know.

It is all completely fake, of course. If there ever was a real Juliet/Giulietta, it would be the wildest of coincidences if she actually had lived in this particular house, which some very enterprising city councillors in the 1930's simply picked out from dozens of others, probably because it was on the Via Cappello (Capulet—get it?), and then added a concrete imitation of a balcony from the period. This little investment has paid off in spades, and the House of Juliet is now a major tourist drawcard.

The house itself is actually quite fascinating, though relatively few tourists go inside, preferring to take their selfies in the courtyard and head off to lunch rather than pay the entry fee for the museum. It is a very tall building, five stories high, and is a fine example of thirteenth century domestic architecture. Inside, the museum features period furniture and lots of exhibits from Franco Zeffirelli's film of the play, still in my opinion one of the best film adaptations of them all.

Of course, it wouldn't make sense to have a Casa di Giulietta without also having a Casa di Romeo also, and, again without any evidence, a nearby house has been designated as Romeo's home simply because it was owned by the prominent Montecchi family (i.e., Montague family—you get the idea) in the thirteenth century. It is still a private residence, and you can't go in; the nearest you can get is to have lunch at the Osteria al Duca next door. And not content with creating two fictional residences for these two fictional characters, someone went even further and found a burial place for Juliet, at the church of San Francesco al Corso. In one version of the story, Fra Laurence marries the pair at this convent, which was then just outside the city walls. Naturally, when an open sarcophagus was found down in the crypt of the church it was instantly adopted as Juliet's tomb.

So, is the whole Romeo and Juliet connection with Verona completely fake? Not quite. There have been many versions of the story from which Shakespeare probably drew his plot, including one where the key events took place in Mantua, not Verona. But every version has at its heart the conflict between two feuding families. The cause of the feud is never made explicit, but in the thirteenth century one probable cause could easily have been the long conflict between the Guelfs, who supported the papacy in that institution's long-running dispute with the Holy Roman Emperors, whose supporters were known as Ghibellines.

At the heart of the dispute between the two sides was, as always, a question of power; in this case it was the claim of the popes to be the ultimate overlords of the emperors. For those who have never come across this odd, amorphous political creation, the Holy Roman Empire encompassed most of what is now Germany, whose cities and states elected an 'emperor' to rule over them. Their authority was often notional at best, so the question of whether or not the pope could make or unmake emperors was not a trivial one. The whole Guelf-Ghibelline thing was kicked off in eleventh century Germany (the names that the antagonists took were in fact Italian derivations of the names of prominent German dynasties) but as so often happened in European politics the rivalry shifted its focus to Italy, and the feud motivated various political machinations right up to the fifteenth century.

The Montecchi were in fact a prominent Guelf family in Verona in the early fourteenth century, and the Capuletti were a Ghibelline family from nearby Cremona, while the rulers of Verona, the aggressive della Scala family, were also Ghibellines. The greatest member of that family was Cangrande I, a remarkable condottiere, who embarked on a program of territorial expansion in the early fourteenth century, and was regarded at the emperor's right-hand man in Italy. Like so many Italian grandees, he was a paradox, both military genius and patron of the arts, famous for sheltering the great poet Dante Alighieri after the latter was thrown out of Florence for being on the wrong side of a convoluted political dispute, never to return.

So if you close one eye and squint, it would be possible to reimagine a tale of lovers in fourteenth-century Verona whose amorous ambitions are disrupted by this conflict; in fact, writer David Blixt has done just that, with his *Master of Verona* series of novels. But wonderfully entertaining though his books are, they are, like Verona's own appropriation of the story, entirely speculative and fictional.

Which brings me to an appropriate note on which to end this chapter. Early one morning, while Robert was still sleeping and before the heat of a summer's day was upon us, I went out for a walk that led me across the Ponte San Pietro, a fine bridge across the Adige that dates back to Roman times, and up the hill past the remains of an ancient Roman theatre (still used today for concerts and plays). After a climb that left me puffed out, I arrived at a viewing platform just below the Castel San Pietro, the old palazzo that tops the hill. Sitting there and looking across the red roofs and church towers of the city, the thought came to me that perhaps a young William Shakespeare himself might have sat on this very spot.

To the best of historians' knowledge Shakespeare never left England, so the thought was entirely ahistorical and probably absurd. But it stayed with me, and a year or so later I started writing my first novel, *What News on the Rialto?*, which explored the possibility that young Will might indeed have visited Italy and Verona. The more I dug into the mystery of the missing seven years of his life before he became known as an actor and playwright in London in the early 1590's, the more plausible such an adventure seemed, and so I like to think that perhaps young Will did indeed sit up on that hill, sometime in 1586, and absorb something of the atmosphere of this lovely Italian gem of a city. And maybe, just maybe, a story about two lovers from opposite sides of a feud lodged in his mind, to be resurrected years later when he was a successful playwright looking back nostalgically at his time wandering Italy.

# Chapter 9

# A Quick Tour of the Renaissance

Renaissance is a French word that has been universally adopted as the descriptor for the great flowering of western art, science, literature and music that took place in the fifteenth and sixteenth centuries. But the term was first coined in Italy, when Giorgio Vasari used the word *rinascita* (rebirth) to describe the phenomenon in his book *The Lives of the Most Excellent Painters, Sculptors and Architects*, published in 1550. For it was Italy, not France, that provided the cradle wherein was born what the Italians call the *Rinascimento*.

Rebirth is a very apt term to describe the emergence of Western culture from the centuries-long sleep of the Middle Ages. Though to be fair, painting, sculpture and literature had not been entirely comatose throughout that long period after the final collapse of the Western Roman Empire: in fact, there was a flourishing and well-developed artistic tradition. But it had been focused almost exclusively on religious subjects. Painting and sculpture were trades, whose proper employment could be found only in the glorification of God and the telling of the Christian story. Ancient learning and scholarship had never existed, the Church tried to pretend, and to the extent that their existence was impossible to deny their importance was downplayed. In the great Christian tradition of cherry-picking, only those moral philosophers whose teachings suited the Christian ideal were accepted (even though, it was explained, their souls were damned), and the rest were demonised where they weren't ignored completely.

The engine of the movement we call the Renaissance was humanism, a philosophy that goes back to Socrates and Aristotle. It emphasises the individual and argues that all serious discussion of moral and philosophical enquiry should start with understanding the relationship between people and the world. Needless to say, the Church didn't quite see things in those terms, and that conflict is still not fully resolved to this day. But for the early writers and artists of the Renaissance the slow emergence of humanist ideals enabled a freedom of expression that released them from the stultifying influence of the religious authorities, enabling them to re-examine the ideals of the philosophers of ancient Greece and Rome and to build new theories upon those foundations. In that sense, the Renaissance was indeed a rebirth, new life springing from ancient roots.

Things kicked off in the world of letters, with the writings of Francesco Petrarca (whose name is usually anglicised as Petrarch), Dante Alighieri, and Giovanni Boccaccio. Since they were writing in the fourteenth century, they expressed their ideas within traditional religious frameworks, but with a distinctly human-oriented bent. Even so, they were laying the ground for the great secular writers of the following two centuries, poets like Ludovico Ariosto and Torquato Tasso, and philosophers such as Marcillio Ficino, Giordano Bruno, and Niccolò Machiavelli.

But it is in the world of the visual arts, painting and sculpture, that the influence of the Renaissance finds its most potent expression. And nowhere was more important to the development of art in this period than Florence, the cockpit of artistic development for two hundred years and more. There is no mystery as to why this should have been so: quite simply, Florence was filled with very wealthy people who, having made a fortune in trade and banking, wanted to display that wealth—and their pretensions to aristocracy—by building grand palazzi, which they then decorated with pictures and statues. I'm simplifying a bit, but that is the heart of it.

Foremost among the merchant families of Florence were the Medici. Their family name literally means 'doctor', and their symbol of five balls (or pills?) can still be seen all over the city. But while some ancestor or another might have been a pill-pusher of some kind, the Medici of the fifteenth and sixteenth centuries were about as far as it is possible to be from the kindly craft of medicine. The family elder, Giovanni di Bicchi de' Medici, was a wool trader who turned his commercial talents to banking, and then proceeded to build the world's first great international bank. Florence was at that time notionally a republic, but Giovanni's son and successor Cosimo used the family wealth to create a political system that entrenched his family's dominance of public life for the next three hundred years (with a couple of interregnums).

Cosimo is recorded as saying that 'for fifty years, I have done nothing else but earn money and spend money; and it became clear that spending money gives me greater pleasure than earning it.' How he spent it was on creating the Palazzo Medici, his austere but beautiful family home in the centre of Florence, just by the family church of San Lorenzo, and decorating it with the work of Donatello, Fra Angelico, and Filippo Lippi, the early geniuses of the Renaissance. His grandson Lorenzo was to be even more extravagant, earning the sobriquet 'il Magnifico' for his grandiose spending and patronage of artists such as Andrea del Verrocchio, Sandro Botticelli, and those twin giants of the Renaissance, Michelangelo Buonarroti and Leonardo da Vinci. In the process, he brought the Medici bank close to ruin, leaving a financial legacy that would contribute in no small way to the end of Medici political mastery of Florence for some fifteen years.

It is therefore no surprise that modern Florence is a veritable treasure-house of art from the century that the Italians call the 'Cinquecento' (in a typical piece of Italian verbal economy, rather than saying 'the fifteen-hundreds' or using the confusing '16th Century', they simply ignore the first thousand years of the Christian era and label each century accordingly: by this reduction the 1500's become simply '500', or *cinquecento*, the 1600's become '600', or *seicento*, and so on). You encounter the painters, sculptors and architects of that brilliant era all over the place, from the statues that line the courtyard of the Uffizi to the life size sculpture of Filippo Brunelleschi, staring for all eternity at his miraculous dome on the cathedral of Santa Maria de' Fiori. You can escape the heat of the day in the otherwise nondescript church of Santa Trinità and find yourself contemplating Domenico Ghirlandao's masterwork, a gorgeous set of frescoes decorating the Sassetti Chapel that portray scenes from the life of St Francis. Or you can wander among the sculptures in the Loggia dei Lanzi and admire the sinuous bronze brilliance of Benvenuto Cellini's statue of Perseus holding a rather grisly severed head of Medusa.

The city also has an abundance of churches and chapels where for a small fee you can gaze on some of the most profound exercises in artistic expression. The vast cavern of Santa Croce is one big art gallery, with paintings and sculptures from almost every big Renaissance name ; you can see a newly-restored painting by Pontormo in the little church of Santa Felicità just by the Ponte Vecchio, then wander round the corner to Santo Spirito to have a look at a crucifix made by the young Michelangelo, before walking over to another church, Santissima Annunziata, and visit the Capella dei Pittori (the painters' chapel) where many Florentine artists are buried and which is, fittingly, decorated with many fine sculptures and paintings.

Then there are the museums, the Uffizi, the sprawling Palazzo Pitti, and the more compact Palazzo Strozzi, as well as several less well-known venues. The Uffizi alone has over a hundred rooms occupying thirteen thousand square metres of space, which host over two million visitors every year: you can literally lose yourself for days looking at its collection. The Strozzi, former home of a family that was able for a time to rival the Medici in power and influence, is the venue for blockbuster exhibitions of both old and new art, and the frequently underrated Pitti is the place where most of the Medici family's private art collection ended up, with over five hundred Renaissance paintings on display.

Being exposed to all this was a little overwhelming at first, as we staggered from palazzo to church to museum drinking it all in with the frenzied enthusiasm of a parched man newly emerged from the desert. Though we both knew something of the art of the Renaissance, ours was an amateur knowledge, gleaned over many years in the haphazard way in which most of us who are not professional acquire some degree of expertise. While we knew what we were looking at, what we lacked was context, the background understanding of time and place and technique that could make sense of the images in front of us.

Cue the arrival in our lives of Dr Alan Pascuzzi. Introduced to us by a mutual acquaintance, Alan is a brilliant art academic (he has in fact published a book on Michelangelo's drawings), and he agreed to show us around some of the great art works in Florence. We started with the Museo dell'Opera del Duomo, the museum not far from the cathedral where the art and artifacts that had previously adorned the interior of the church are now stored, conserved, and displayed. This is a museum that is easily overlooked by casual tourists, but it is a brilliant place, containing over 750 works, mostly statuary and votive pieces. One of the most famous—and certainly most affecting—is Donatello's stunningly original Penitent Magdalene, an intricately carved wooden statue of the saint whose rags seem so real that you expect them to shimmer in the breeze. The Museo is also the home to the original of Ghiberti's bronze doors made for the Baptistry (the doors that tourists crowd around to admire out in the piazza are in fact nineteenth century copies), the so-called 'Gates to Paradise'; the copies are superb, but seeing the originals, and having them explained in detail by Alan, was a much more edifying experience.

Apart from taking us on several tours of the Uffizi, each time focusing on a different part of that vast collection, he also arranged visits to places that can be difficult to access, such as the sculptures that are hidden away upstairs in Orsanmichele, the former granary that was converted to a church. But one of the most memorable tours that I remember was to a place that is often thought of as the very birthplace of Renaissance painting: the Brancacci Chapel.

This chapel, attached to the church of Santa Maria del Carmine, was decorated over a two-year period by a number of artists. Felice Brancacci originally commissioned Masolino da Panicale to decorate it, but Masolino was recalled to Hungary, where he was court painter to the Hungarian king, and his 21-year-old assistant Masaccio took over. Masaccio in turn was called to Rome, where he died at the young age of twenty-seven; the frescoes were finally completed by Filippino Lippi. So the images we see today are the work of several great artists' hands.

But what they created was a masterpiece, and a deeply influential work of art. For its time it was revolutionary in its use of perspective, lighting effects, and above all its focus on presenting human figures in a realistic and naturalistic way, as opposed to the more idealised representations of medieval art.

These characteristics, Alan explained, lie at the heart of Renaissance painting, along with its perpetual quest for balance and harmony in the composition of images.

He also told us an amusing story: among the many artists who learned their trade by copying Masaccio's masterpieces was a young Michelangelo Buonarotti. One day he was working away, standing where we had stood, drawing a section of the frescoes alongside another young sculptor, Pietro Torrigiano. Glancing across at the other man's easel, Michelangelo offered an unflattering critical appraisal of what he saw. Torrigiano wasn't open to criticism, however, and landed a punch on Michelangelo's nose so powerful that, in the words of Benvenuto Cellini, 'it was crushed like a biscuit'. Thereafter the powerfully built Michelangelo's visage resembled that of a boxer more than an artist.

Alan also introduced us to several other places in Florence that we would never have known existed were it not for his encyclopaedic knowledge of the city and its art works. One such was the Oratorio dei Buonomini, a tiny chapel on a small, nondescript piazza that you could easily walk past and never notice. The oratory was built by a Florentine confraternity formed to provide financial help to the *poveri vergognosi*, or the 'shamed poor'. These were not your ordinary poor people: for the most part, they were respectable merchants who had fallen on hard times, and the fraternity was at least partly funded by Cosimo de' Medici.

But fascinating as this early example of middle-class welfare is, it is the interior decoration of the little chapel that is of most interest. When you walk in, your eyes are immediately drawn upwards to a dazzling set of nine frescoes that depict the brothers of the confraternity doing their good works—giving food and drink to the thirsty, clothing the naked, visiting the sick, giving shelter to pilgrims, releasing a debtor from gaol, making a visit to a family in need, and so on. Who painted the frescoes is not known, but they are attributed to the workshop of Domenico Ghirlandaio, the master of fifteenth-century fresco technique.

An artist friend of ours once told me that, according to some study or another, the average amount of time that viewers spend looking at a painting is twenty-seven seconds. I'm not sure whether I am more staggered by the actual finding, or the fact that anyone invested the time and energy in trying to work it out—but if true it is a little dispiriting when you consider just how much effort goes into creating art works. Alan, it turned out, is also a working artist specialising in religious sculptures, and he gave Robert a real taste for those realities by giving him a series of private lessons on some of the techniques commonly used in the Renaissance: tempera painting, fresco, and the application of gold leaf.

That the great painters of the Renaissance were artistic geniuses goes without saying. But, as Robert learned, they were also highly skilled technical craftsmen. Take tempera, for example, which involves mixing egg yolks with various pigments to create the desired colour. Sounds simple, doesn't it? Not a bit of it: first, the egg yolk must be very carefully extracted from its membrane by piercing it and allowing the inner yolk to drain. Then water or a small amount of vinegar is added to stop the yolk from drying out too quickly. Meanwhile, pigment must be ground to a fine powder that can be added to the yolk mixture. But the egg yolk thickens on contact with the air, and so more water must be added to make sure that the right consistency is maintained. And tempera is a fussy medium: once prepared, the paint cannot be stored, so it must be used immediately. It is water resistant but not waterproof, so it needs to be painted onto a stiff surface of wooden board (since it will flake if applied to canvas), and as it dries rapidly it must be applied to the surface very quickly.

Fresco painting, in which the artist applies pigments directly onto wet plaster, is similarly complicated. The pigments chemically combine with the plaster as it dries, creating a durable image that will last for as long as the plaster itself survives. The challenge with this technique for the Renaissance artist was that he had to work very quickly to fix the paint in place before the plaster dries. That meant he had to do everything in small sections, which in turn led to a great deal of preparation and planning. For example, it was usually necessary to draw the overall image on the wall first, so that the artists and his assistants knew what they were working towards. Moreover, the final image had to appear completely seamless, so that the viewer could not see without looking very closely the borders between each of the sections.

The application of gold leaf is a similarly exacting process, requiring a steady hand and a sharp eye, and it goes without saying that it is also a very expensive way of producing images. But that is true too for the other techniques: the cost of pigments could be extraordinary. Take that lovely ultramarine blue that you see in so many Renaissance paintings (a small Alan Pascuzzi gem: in religious art, the Madonna is always painted in a blue dress). It is made with lapis lazuli, a type of deep blue crystal to this day only found in a remote corner of Afghanistan; by the time it made its way across Asia to Europe it had acquired a value that was almost the same as that of gold.

Though Alan's tutelage helped Robert produce several quite creditable copies of some small pictures, it is fair to say he will never be an artist himself. But the experience taught him, and vicariously taught me, to appreciate the fact that those extraordinary pictures that we wandered past and stopped to examine for our allotted thirty or so seconds had taken many weeks, months and in some cases years to produce. Unless you are going to devote your entire life to the task, it is of course not possible to give every picture the attention that it deserves, but I like to think that perhaps we might gaze with a little more reverence and a little more humility upon the art works we encounter, whether ancient or modern, and whether or not we are moved by them to at least recognise the sheer effort and skill that has gone into their making.

Florence might have been the cradle of the Italian Renaissance, but once born it did not remain a toddler for long. Artists living in Padua, Mantua, Milan and Venice were soon inspired to imitate and evolve the techniques and themes that the Florentines had developed. Michelangelo, Leonardo, Titian, Raphael, del Sarto and many others contributed to what we call the High Renaissance, in which the hallmark style of Renaissance art, with its emphasis on order, balance and harmony, was extended by all sorts of innovations of technique. Artists experimented with tonal contrasts such as *sfumato* (softening the transition between colours) and *chiaroscuro* (contrast between light and dark), explored the mathematical properties of linear perspective, and depicted both physical and psychological features with a new realism. Over the course of the Cinquecento this vast and innovative outpouring of creative talent turned Italy into the western world's greatest centre for art and left as its legacy the immense collections that still turn our heads today.

Though the ideals of Renaissance art soon migrated across the Alps to be picked up by artists in the Netherlands, France and Germany, like everything, art is subject to the fashions and tastes of the society in which it exists, and by the end of the century Italians had moved on, embracing the riotous excess of the Baroque and a new generation of painters. The Carracci brothers in Bologna and the towering genius of Caravaggio in Rome kicked off a new style that emphasised compositional drama, in scenes painted in rich, deep colours, intense light, and dark shadows, innovations that were made possible by the emergence of oil painting as a technique to replace the old tempera methodology.

Yet the influence of the Renaissance is inescapable, and its ideals of equilibrium and harmony are as appealing today as they were five hundred years ago—and for the same reason: in a world that seems always to be in turmoil, we take comfort from images that express our yearning for balance and stability and express the eternal rather than the ephemeral. That such perfection should have emerged in the turbulent, chaotic world of sixteenth-century Italy is a mystery for the ages, but the fact that it did means that Italy possesses an unparalleled artistic legacy that makes travelling through the country such a joy for any lover of art.

# Chapter 10

# Portrait of a Piazza

In Italy, it's called a *piazza*. In Spain, a *plaza*, in France, a *place*. No matter where you go in Mediterranean Europe, the town square is the focus of local life and organisation. In Italian towns and villages, the piazza is the setting for countless conversations over coffee or *aperitivo* about everything from politics to the price of olive oil, the place where the local market is held, where you go to buy a newspaper or cigarettes, or, if you are young, just hang out with your friends and flirt with the opposite sex. And the Italian phrase 'scendere in piazza', literally 'going down on the square', means the coming together of people to protest, highlighting another role of the town square in always-volatile Italian politics.

The piazza also provides a stage upon which the performances of Italian civic life can be acted out. Take the *passeggiata*, for example, the daily evening ritual in which couples and groups of friends stroll up and down the main street, taking in the evening air, chatting and gossiping at the end of a hot summer's day, being seen and showing off your new clothes or, if you are a young male, your new white sneakers. The whole exercise usually starts with a turn around the piazza and ends in the cafes and restaurants.

Similarly, the formalities of Italian weddings might take place inside the church, but the really fun bit happens back out in the piazza, where the newlyweds are showered with rice by wedding guests and passers-by stop to admire them and their families. And at Easter and Christmas the piazza is the amphitheatre for that ultimate piece of Italian showing-off, those gorgeous religious processions which can be uplifting to the spirit of even the most hardened atheist.

Naturally enough, as towns and cities evolved and grew, the piazza as an urban form grew with them, essentially replicating its rural function by becoming the focus for the neighbourhood. Many became larger, grander, dominated by ever bigger churches and town halls, and in the process lost their intimate character. But in most Italian cities there are still many piazzas that function much as they always have, like Piazza Santo Spirito, our local square in Florence for three months when we rented an apartment on nearby Via Maggio, in Florence's Oltrarno—'the other side of the Arno'—district. Indulge me while I give you an extended description of it, as an exemplar of the kind of piazza that we came to know and love during our Italian travels.

The piazza itself is a kind of irregular quadrilateral, widening slightly towards its southern end, lined on each side with what were originally town houses, and are now mostly apartments. They are uniformly four stories high on the eastern side, and five stories on the western, giving the square a slightly lopsided appearance. The western side is also the side where the bulk of the restaurants are, six of them, each with outdoor seating under massive umbrellas. Two rows of trees—a rarity in central Florence—flank the long centre of the piazza, providing welcome shade in the summer. In the very centre there is a fountain, which serves as a perfect rendezvous point.

Most public places all over the world host a statue to someone or other whose contribution to society has long been forgotten by all except the most enthusiastic local historians. Santo Spirito is no exception: located at the southern end of the piazza, almost tripping up the traffic on Via Sant' Agostino, stands the kindly image a gentleman named Cosimo Ridolfi. An agronomist and politician, he came from an ancient Florentine family. In between serving in various governments of the Grand Duchy of Tuscany, he found the time to establish a bank which was dedicated to encouraging investment in farming. Operating from the family palazzo round the corner in Via Maggio, it eventually became the Cassa di Risparmio, still an important financial institution today. So I guess a statue is probably justified.

Also at this end of the piazza is its second-most important building, the Palazzo Guadagni. Built in 1502 for a merchant who decided to consolidate several households into one palazzo, it follows the standard Renaissance design for grand houses—fortress-like rusticated stonework at the ground level framing an imposing gate, two further elegant stories above, and topped by a wide loggia to catch the breeze (and probably also to keep an eye on the people in the square below!).

Balancing Palazzo Guadagni and Signor Ridolfi at the opposite end of the piazza is the off-white face of Santo Spirito church. It was designed by Filippo Brunelleschi—the guy who put the dome on the main cathedral of Florence—but it was not completed before his death in 1446. The architect did in fact plan a facade for the church, but it was never built due to financial disputes, and so the church still presents a rather blank face to the world (a common fate for Florentine churches, where the desire to glorify God often competed with the natural parsimony of the Florentine merchants who were paying the bills). An unfinished exterior does not however mean a drab interior—quite the reverse; inside, Santo Spirito's nave and dome are glorious, and the various chapels host a dazzling array of art works.

In the cloisters of the monastery next door, you can see a stunning and newly restored wooden crucifix that was made by none other than Michelangelo. The great artist was afforded board and lodging by the monks who also turned a blind eye to his rather grisly (and at the time highly illegal) study of human anatomy, carried out by dissecting corpses supplied by the monastery's hospital.

Of course, any modern piazza worthy of the name must have at least one restaurant; Santo Spirito has nine. Let's do a quick tour. Starting from the north-eastern corner, the first cafe you come to is called *Gustapanino*—which roughly translates to 'tasty sandwiches', actually a pretty accurate description of their specialisation: *panini, foccacie,* and *crostini*. Needless to say, this place is very popular with younger people. Next to that is another little cafe, Volume, which is a kind of trendy hipster hangout. The first proper restaurant is *Borgo Antico* ('The Old Village'), another accurate description for a place with a simple menu, cheerful staff, and communal tables where complete strangers readily find themselves engaged in conversation. Next door is *Caffe Ricci*, similar in style but with a more extensive menu of Tuscan specialties. Finally, at the end of the run is *Tamero*, best known for the fact that they make all of their own pasta on site, which they also sell separately if you want to cook it at home (though you have to be quick, since they usually sell out of fresh pasta by lunchtime).

On the other side of the square there is the Pop café, which we really liked because unlike most Italian cafes they serve their coffee hot without being asked—Italians prefer their coffee lukewarm so they can drink and go. A little further up is *Pitta M'Ingoli*, and on the corner is *Osteria Santo Spirito*, which is very popular and probably has the best food on the piazza.

So those are the restaurants—plenty to choose from. But the piazza also has a couple of other important shops that are very typical. One of these is the local *tabacchi*, whose principal function, as the name suggests, is the sale of cigarettes and tobacco products, though over time they have also become the main outlet for all sorts of other small but important services.

For example, you can generally get your phone plan topped up, buy bus passes and lotto tickets, sift through an array of tourist related items such as maps and guides, and get cash from their ATM. After hours, if you want cigarettes you have to buy them from a dispenser located outside the *tabacchi's* shuttered shopfront—but there's a catch: to use the machine you must insert a valid Italian identity card. Needless to say, this has perplexed many a hapless tourist in need of a nicotine fix. But in Italy bureaucracy just stimulates innovation, in this case encouraging an enterprising local who hangs about the machine offering the use of his ID card for €1 to anyone who needs it!

If you want to buy a newspaper or magazine in Italy, you usually do so by going to an old-fashioned news kiosk, like the one on the corner of the square next to Osteria Santo Spirito. It is little more than a kind of metal box with doors that fold outwards, on which are displayed an array of newspapers and magazines; the proprietor lurks in the back, a barely visible grey-haired guy who gives you a grumpy look if you don't produce the exact change—in my case €3.20 for my copy of the *New York Times*, the only English language newspaper that he sells. At around 1:00pm, the whole thing is shuttered up while the proprietor, no doubt exhausted from his morning's labours, goes off for a couple of hours lunch, before reopening from 3:00pm until the early evening.

For food shopping, the needs of the local residents are served by the various shops in and around the piazza. There is the local *pasticceria*, a source of fresh bread as well as pastries of every kind, the *macelleria*, or butcher's shop, run by the cheerful, white-smocked duo Leonardo and Massimo, as well as a *polleria* (poultry shop) and several good *alimentari* (small grocery stores, where you can buy fruit and vegetables as well as basic grocery staples). Venture into any of these shops, and you'll find locals buying their daily provisions, zeroing in on whatever is fresh that day.

As well as all these permanent shops, there is also a daily market which sets up at the southern end of the piazza. There is a fruit and vegetable vendor who sets up every day, and other goods turn up depending on the day of the week; one day it's men's clothing and shoes, the next day women's clothes, and then later in the week all sorts of hardware and household items appear. Once a month, things culminate in a mega-market, when the whole piazza is filled with stalls selling leatherwork, second-hand goods, art works, cheeses, meats and pastries.

The opening of the market starts the daily routine—first thing in the morning the vendors are busy carefully and painstakingly setting up their stalls, while the street sweepers are still at work giving the square a brush-up. By about 9:30 or 10:00 students and other locals who are at leisure have begun to appear and are settling into the cafes on the sunnier western side of the square. The market generally packs up at around 1:00pm, which is also when the lunchtime trade starts to fill the bigger restaurants on the eastern side, and by 3:00pm the place is filled with the sound of people enjoying lunch. About this time, too, the paved area in front of Santo Spirito church fills with people, mostly students, eating their *panini* and soaking up the afternoon sun.

There's a bit of a hiatus until around 5:00pm, when the excellent Italian tradition of *aperitivo* kicks off as a prelude to the dinner hour. During the week, this is the time when Italians get together with friends after work, enjoying a Campari or an Aperol spritz, and feasting on the array of finger food that is provided by most bars either free or for a small cover charge. *Aperitivo* leads into dinner and the restaurants on the square pump until midnight or later, when peace and quiet finally descend and the piazza goes to sleep until the whole routine starts again the next day.

Piazza Santo Spirito also has a special vibe owing to the fact that the Oltrarno is filled with thousands of students who study at the offshoots of American (and Australian) campuses that are based there, most studying fine arts or art history. That makes it a lively spot at the weekends, when students gather in large numbers on the broad platform in front of the church to drink, eat their gelati, and chat in the sunshine, and the cafes and bars are noisily active until late. No doubt many of them are also customers for the occasional drug dealer hanging about by the big fountain in the middle of the square, where they ply their trade mostly unmolested either by the local police or *carabinieri*.

Santo Spirito is not, of course, the only piazza in Florence; in fact, the city is chock-full of them. The most famous is the Piazza della Signoria, dominated by the castellated splendour of the Palazzo Vecchio and the porticoed Loggia della Lanza. This has always been the civic heart of Florence and is still the place where you are most likely to see a ceremonial parade by one of the city's old guilds or witness a political rally. Then there is the imposing expanse of the Piazza della Repubblica, which stands on the site of the original markets that were cleared away in order to build a space that would be a worthy glorification of the new Italian Republic in the 1880's, complete with an imposing triumphal arch that today looks benignly down on the hustle and bustle of the city's most elegant cafes and restaurants.

Other piazzas in Florence are less showy. Piazza Massimo d'Azeglio, named after one of the pivotal figures of Italian unification, is a lovely, peaceful square surrounded by elegant houses that once served as embassies and consulates when Florence had its brief moment as capital of the republic, from 1865 to 1871. Then there is Piazza Santissima d'Annunziata, another local haunt during one of our stays in Florence; named for the church on its northern side, the renaissance porticoes on the eastern and western sides combine with the Liberty-era palazzi on the south to give the square an architectural unity that is a delight to the eye.

One of the original functions of the piazza was to provide an open space where religious processions could arrive or depart from the principal church of the town or village. That function can be seen in the design of Piazzas Santa Croce and Santa Maria Novella, both of which are dominated by their respective church facades (though both have been put to more secular uses over their history, the former as the site for games of *calcio*, the rather brutal Florentine form of football, and the latter as a place for carriage races, which must have been quite an alarming spectacle). And of course, there is the granddaddy of them all, the Piazza del Duomo, the space in front of the gorgeous facade of the massive cathedral of Santa Maria del Fiore, though that building is so vast that it makes even this expansive open space seem cramped.

Mind you, not every piazza in Florence (or elsewhere in Italy for that matter) has been able to retain its pleasant, pedestrian character. Piazza San Marco, for instance, is the main hub for many of the city's bus routes, so it has been rather overwhelmed by the queues of people waiting for an endless stream of loud and smelly buses. And the historic triumphal arch and town gate in Piazza della Liberta are stranded in the middle of a square that has been converted into a big traffic roundabout. But egregious as they are, these are exceptions in a city where, for the most part, the pedestrian rules.

Nor does a piazza have to be grand to be charming; not far from one of the places we stayed in Florence there is a little, irregular open space called the Piazza di San Pier Maggiore. Every day there is a fruit and vegetable stall that sets up just outside the *pasticceria*, where locals can buy their tomatoes and capsicums after a visit to the nearby butcher, before settling down for a coffee and a read of the papers or a gossip with friends at one of the two cafes. Small it might be, but this piazza performs the same civic function as its larger cousins; nor is it unique, for similar spaces can be found all over Florence.

Though I've focused this chapter on Florence we felt the attraction of the piazza all over Italy, in towns big and small. As we sat having coffee in the Piazza del Popolo in Ravenna, drinking a glass of wine in Urbino's diminutive Piazza della Repubblica, or having dinner in the crumbling Piazza Plebiscito in Martina Franca, the same question occurred to us over and over again: what is it that makes the Italian piazza so special?

No doubt a swarm of urban planning experts could provide answers to that question, but here are our thoughts. First and foremost is the nature of the urban fabric within which most piazzas nestle, for the most part made up of medium density apartment buildings and narrow streets in which car traffic is deliberately limited in favour of pedestrian movement. Italians are not shy about pedestrianising their streets, even in more modern car-oriented sections of their cities, and they walk everywhere, creating a street-level ecosystem that is quite different from the traffic-choked roads that are characteristic of cities in Australia and America.

Secondly, most piazzas (other than those designed purely as ceremonial spaces, like St Peter's in Rome) have an appealingly human scale, big enough to provide a sense of openness as you decamp from the cramped and narrow streets of the *centro storico*, but small enough to feel intimate and inviting. That balance is an essential ingredient in making the piazza a place that is above all designed around people.

Lastly, the fact that most piazzas are surrounded by residences adds to the sense of theatre, as ancient *nonnas* sit on their balconies or lean on their windowsills keeping an eye on the goings-on below. Even as a tourist, you know they are judging you, as they and their forebears have judged visitors for hundreds of years, while returning their stare seems like impudence. Think of the piazza is a public stage, where your performance is always being judged, where social norms are reinforced, and from which a disgraceful exit would be, at the very least, embarrassing.

That thought leads naturally to another observation: the Italian piazza is very much a multi-generational space. Little children roam freely about, under the benign and watchful eyes of every grown-up in the square, and young adults are as ubiquitous as grey-haired seniors. This seems to create an atmosphere of easy-going tolerance (though perhaps that is just part of the Italian psyche) combined with an attitude of respect between generations that often seems a million light-years away from the self-obsessed isolationist attitudes of many, both young and old, in other western societies.

All of these factors combine to make it impossible to feel lonely in an Italian piazza, even if you are an introvert sitting by yourself reading the newspaper over a coffee. You might not have any real connection with the matrons out doing their daily shopping, the young people gathering to chat about the latest fashions, or the older men commiserating with each other over the latest outrages in Italian politics, but you can't help feeling a sense of kinship with the social life that is going on around you.

Perhaps the piazza is successful because of the unique characteristics of the Italians, and therefore difficult to replicate elsewhere. But maybe there are also intrinsic social benefits from which other countries could learn and even seek to emulate. It would be nice to think so.

## Chapter 11

# The David(s) of Florence

'How many statues of David do you think there are in Florence?'

Robert posed this question as we stood outside one of the many shops in the city that sell tourist bits and pieces. This particular shop window was dominated by the serried ranks of dozens of plastic replicas of Michelangelo's famous statue, reproduced not in any facsimile of the original's white marble, but rather in garish blue or yellow. The whole thing seemed to us to be a somewhat amusing exercise in tackiness.

'Must be thousands of them,' was my rather sniffy response. But the question did get us thinking, and we realised that, tourist fakes aside, there was definitely more than one image of the biblical hero, and so we set out to count them.

In fact, there are five separate and original representations of the biblical hero made by the greatest sculptors of the Renaissance, which might seem a bit excessive. But then again, Florentines have always identified with the biblical hero's struggle against the giant Goliath, which they saw as a metaphor for their own position as a small and relatively weak state often beset by the giants that surrounded them.

Let's start with the big fella, Michelangelo Buonarotti's extraordinarily evocative work that stands in the Accademia

Gallery. This is obviously the most famous image of David in Florence, and probably the world, and despite its ubiquity it is still an incredibly popular attraction. Like the Mona Lisa, you can't see it without being in a crowd of awe-struck and picture-popping tourists, and every day of the week, all year round, there is a queue waiting patiently down the street outside the Accademia.

The story of the statue is well known. Originally it was a huge block of Carrara marble that was brought to Florence to make one of twelve large statues of Old Testament figures that were to stand on the buttresses of Santa Maria del Fiore. The project was abandoned, and the marble stood unwanted in the cathedral workshop for twenty-six years. Eventually in 1501 the young Michelangelo was contracted to start work on carving an image of David, a task that took him another two years to complete.

The finished article weighed more than six tons; the committee that was convened to decide where it should be put soon realised that hauling it up on the roof would be an impossibility, and so they had to choose an alternative. Sandro Botticelli and Leonardo da Vinci were both members of this committee, and the debate became quite passionate. Eventually it was decided that the statue would be placed in front of the Palazzo della Signoria (today called the Palazzo Vecchio), replacing Donatello's sculpture of Judith and Holofernes. There was a nice piece of political symbolism in this: so placed, David's baleful and determined gaze would be directed towards Rome, at that time one of several Goliaths that Florence was trying to fend off, and sending a clear message: don't mess with us! The statue stayed there, slowly deteriorating, until it was shifted in 1873 to its present position in a purpose-built podium in the Accademia dell'Arte, where it could be protected from the elements. Donatello's sculpture, meanwhile, found its way to more sheltered surroundings inside the palazzo.

So, what is it about this work that gets Italians and tourists alike out of bed, even on a cold and wet Sunday morning, as it was on the day that we went to see it? Of course, long before you get there you know what it is going to look like. Yet, even seen over the heads of the crowd as you approach, there is something different about it that none of the photographs ever quite capture: it is luminous—the statue seems almost to glow with a purity that is not just a trick of the light.

When it was first unveiled, the Florentines called it *Il Gigante*, and you can certainly understand why, for close up it really is an enormous statue. Interestingly, the famously odd proportions (the disproportionately large head and hands) really do work when viewed from below, and it ends up looking just right from every angle, including the back. It is a genuinely beautiful work of art.

This is a particularly virile representation of David. He is shown as a strong, perfectly muscled young man (many a gym bunny would die for these pecs and abs), mature and confident. The expression on his face is one of intense concentration, although it is not exactly clear whether the artist intended to represent David in the moments before or after his triumph over Goliath, since Michelangelo didn't include the traditional head of the vanquished giant under the hero's feet. But all in all, the statue is undeniably one of the world's most iconic images of male physical prowess.

There are a couple of copies of this masterwork elsewhere in Florence; most famous is the one that stands in front of the Palazzo Vecchio, the ancient seat of Florentine government, placed there after the original was removed to its present home. Grey and weather-stained, it doesn't really come close to the original, even though it is a reasonably faithful copy, good enough that many an innocent tourist has taken their obligatory photo and departed, convinced that they saw the real thing. And then there is an inferior bronze copy high up on the Piazzale Michelangelo, the viewing platform that overlooks the city—up here, the famous calm face seems to have an expression of distaste as it looks down on the legions of tacky souvenir sellers flogging plastic copies of himself by the hundred, and the busloads of cruise ship tourists leering at what they mistakenly believe to be the original.

Back across town, the other three Davids all live in the Bargello Museum. This is a fascinating building in itself. It was Florence's first town hall, then it became the seat of justice, where the Podesta, or chief magistrate, meted out judgements. Eventually as the republic grew and civic functions were transferred elsewhere, it became one of the most feared prisons in the city. Its square, castle-like shape and high stone tower were the model for the nearby Palazzo Vecchio, which echoes the design of this comparatively modest building on a grander scale. Today the Bargello houses what I think is one of the most enchanting and accessible museums in Florence, devoted almost entirely to Renaissance sculpture.

So, let's have a look at the next most important (in my opinion anyway) statue of David in Florence. This is the one by Donato di Niccolo di Betto Bardi—better known as Donatello. To my mind, this statue is almost the complete antithesis of Michelangelo's muscular stud. Where Michelangelo gives us a mature man, Donatello's David is clearly and obviously a youth, perhaps fifteen or sixteen, well-muscled but unformed, coltish, gangling. He wears an elaborate dandified hat of the type that a peasant might have worn in Donatello's own time from beneath which long locks of hair spring and drape over his shoulders. Posed with a hand on his hip and one leg propped on the dead Goliath's head, the statue has a distinctly androgynous feel about it. Donatello gives us David in his moment of triumph, his booted foot on the slain giant's head. Yet the look on his face is rather sly, that of an impudent youth who has just pulled off an unexpected trick.

Giorgio Vasari, the great chronicler of the lives of the Italian Renaissance artists, thought that the statue was so naturalistic that it must have been modelled from life, and given Donatello's known homosexuality it is tempting to think that the model might have been a lover (for a brilliant fictional exploration of that idea, see *The Medici Boy*, by David L'Heureux). Homosexuality, or more accurately the practice of sodomy, was seriously illegal in Renaissance Florence, even if prosecution was a haphazard affair for an offence that in practice was widely tolerated—not least because many of the offenders belonged to the city's ruling classes. Even so, expressing his own preferences in his statue might have been rather dangerous for Donatello, and since he left no other record or explanation, we must consign such thoughts to the realm of speculation.

The statue is important not just for its subject matter, but also for its technical and historical achievement, for this was the first life size male nude to have been cast in bronze since antiquity. It was commissioned by Cosimo de' Medici in 1430, and when completed it stood in the courtyard of the Palazzo Medici, itself designed by another of Cosimo's favourite artists, Donatello's business partner Michelozzo Michelozzi. Like Michelangelo's statue, this David was also a bit peripatetic. When the Medici were expelled in 1494, the statue was seized by the state in restitution for debts which the new republic claimed that Piero de' Medici owed to the government and moved it into the courtyard of the Palazzo della Signoria. After that it was moved to the Palazzo Pitti in the 17th century, the Uffizi in the 18th, and finally in 1865 to its present home in the Bargello.

This wasn't Donatello's first attempt at a portrayal of the biblical hero. Back in his early twenties, he had been commissioned to carve a statue to be placed, like Michelangelo's giant, on one of the buttresses of the cathedral. For various reasons it was never put there, languishing in storage for a while before finally being moved to the Palazzo Vecchio in 1416, where the political symbolism of David was underlined by an inscription placed around the statue's pedestal that read, in Latin, 'To those who fight bravely for the fatherland the gods lend aid even against the most terrible foes'.

This version of David is fully dressed and draped in a cloak, one foot propped on Goliath's head, though the curiously blank face stares vaguely up into space, as if unaware of the grisly trophy beneath his sandals. It is beautiful in its own way, and it shows the promise of the future great sculptor, but its form adheres to the stiffly formal conventions of the Gothic style rather than to the more naturalistic representation of later Renaissance art. It is fair to say that it is a rather bland sculpture, interesting mostly as a counterpoint to Donatello's later effort.

Another great Florentine, Andrea del Verrochio, had a go at the subject of David in the 1470's, some forty years after Donatello's second and more celebrated version. Like Donatello, Verrochio represents the hero as a rather skinny youth (it has been suggested that the model might have been the young Leonardo Da Vinci, who spent some time in Verrochio's *bottega*, or workshop). This is unquestionably David triumphant, his foot firmly planted on a Goliath's head that wears an expression of surprise, as if astonished at the youth of his slayer. It is undoubtedly a remarkable and beautiful statue, though it lacks somewhat the allure of its predecessor. It too found its way into the Palazzo della Signoria, which by the end of the fifteenth century must have resembled a rather crowded sculpture park with all the statuary that had been moved there.

So that's four Davids. The last is not quite as well known, and takes us back where we started, with Michelangelo. Actually, it's a bit of a cheat to include this statue, since it is unfinished, and it is not at all certain that the figure it represents is David at all—the work is equally commonly referred to as being Apollo. The confusion arises because Giorgio Vasari said it represented Apollo taking an arrow from his quiver, whereas whoever catalogued the inventory of the art works of Grand Duke Cosimo I identified it as 'David'. Today art critics hedge their bets and call it the 'Apollo-David'.

The blocky, twisting figure looks downward over his shoulder with a rather melancholy expression, almost as if he is ruminating on the consequences of his victory. It was created in the aftermath of the bloody 1527 siege of Florence which ended the Medicis third exile and reinstated them as hereditary rulers of Tuscany, and it may be that the melancholy stems from the 55-year-old sculptor's feelings about that event, a kind of mute protest perhaps. We will never know, but it is most certainly a very different representation of the biblical hero from his earlier work, created in the optimistic first flush of his own youth.

So there you are, five different representations of David in the one city, whose fascination with this particular biblical figure seems to have stemmed from its self-image as a small and weak republic facing the giants that surrounded it—Venice, Milan, the Kingdom of Naples, and the ever-present threat from France and Spain, both keen to control the fractious Italian peninsula. And the subject continues to resonate among modern Italian artists: on a visit to the hillside village of Fiesole, just outside Florence, we were startled to encounter in the town square a modern statue of David and Jonathan—explicitly homoerotic in character—part of a temporary exhibition by modern Italian artist Filippo Dobrilla.

Today, the figure of Michelangelo's David is ever present in Florence. Every tourist shop and souvenir seller has any number of versions of Michelangelo's original in plastic and metal in every colour and size imaginable: there are cooking aprons featuring the statue's not-very-impressive genitalia, and that stern, determined face adorns countless mugs and jugs. You can't escape him. But it is nice to know that you can always drop into the Bargello and have a look in peace at some of his competitors.

# Chapter 12

# Country life: A Farmhouse in Volterra

A farmhouse in Tuscany. It is the great cliché, really, isn't it? The stuff of countless books and films with more or less the same plot: jaded city dweller (usually American) buys a run-down farmhouse in the countryside discovers the true bliss of *la dolce vita* after any number of stupid cock-ups, and in the process gets their angst out of the system. Oh, and of course they turn their back on nasty modern New York or London or wherever and live happily ever after.

The thought of doing anything of that kind had never entered our heads, and in fact all of our planning had been focused on visiting cities, not the country. But when our Sydney friends Peter and Jaycen offered the use of just such a house for a month late in 2017, we jumped at the chance.

The house is called *La Colombaia Vecchia*, which means 'The Old Dovecote', and it was first purchased by Sydneysiders John and Judith Wregg many years ago as a summer home for them and their growing family. Judging from the photos in the album that they showed us charting its progress, it was more or less a shell when they bought it. Over the years they steadily renovated it into a comfortable home; then, once their kids had grown up, they sold a part-ownership to Peter and Jaycen, who ever since have been travelling from Australia to spend a month or two over Christmas (the Wreggs use the house mostly in the summer).

We met John and Judith for the first time on a reconnaissance visit in October, as they were packing up to go back to Australia; they kindly showed us the ropes, handed over a set of keys, and threw in an excellent lunch to boot. Though we didn't know it then, they had given us the keys not just to their house, but to one of the most enchanting months we spent on our whole three-year odyssey.

The house seems to grow organically out of the hillside on which it stands, and it is a typical tall Tuscan farmhouse, three stories of brown stone pierced by small windows flanked with shutters, in one corner a small loggia frames a perfect view of the valley below. Inside, the house is deceptively large; there are six bedrooms, a cozy living room, a rather grand dining room with seating for twelve which was once home to the farm's livestock, and a big kitchen, equipped with every pot, pan and utensil known to man, plus, extravagance of extravagances, no less than *two* coffee machines (one belonged to Peter and Jaycen and the other to John and Judith). This is the real heart of the house, the focal point around which everything else is arranged. Outside behind the main building is a broad platform, home to a fishpond and no doubt the site of many a summer lunchtime gathering under the trees that provide shelter from sun and wind, though it was a little less inviting in late autumn.

From the loggia, the view is spectacular. Immediately in front of the house, a country road loops lazily down the hill through newly ploughed pastures that disappear into a copse of trees at the bottom of the valley. Beyond, rising to a peak in the distance, is the Berignone state forest, a carpet of green shot through with the orange and russet shades of autumn.

The forest is a popular haunt for the local hunters, and from sunup until mid-morning, the pop of rifle shots can be heard as they hunt birds, other small game and probably the occasional wild boar. Further away to the southwest, plumes of steam are visible from the complex of geothermal power stations that tap the energy of underground hot springs.

Apart from the ploughed fields and fences, the only other signs of habitation are a few farmhouses dotting the landscape, and, perching above us, the tiny hamlet of Mazzolla. This is a typical Italian *borgo*, a small village built on a hilltop for defence, from the safety of whose walls the farmers issued forth each day to work the fields and olive groves. Today Mazzolla consists of just a cluster of houses, a church, a couple of B&B's, and a small palazzo that is mostly used as a wedding venue. The only restaurant, Trattoria Albana, is owned and run by Giuseppe and his wife Mary, and serves a fine menu of local Tuscan dishes, beautifully rendered, in an old-fashioned atmosphere enlivened by the presence of an open fire, which was very welcoming in the November chill. It even had a few moments of fame when it scored a brief scene in the off-beat British film *The Trip to Italy*, in which comic actors Steve Coogan and Rob Bryden undertake a culinary tour of Italy, playing (mostly) themselves.

Staying in a country house was a completely new experience for us; we are city boys at heart, and we found the deep silence of the country both beguiling and occasionally unnerving. Not being able to hear any traffic or the noise of passing people chatting in the street felt odd until we got used to it, and began to enjoy the quiet, broken only by the distant twittering of a few birds and the occasional pop of a hunter's rifle. At night, the darkness was almost complete, as there are no streetlights on the road, and in the absence of moonlight the landscape just disappears into inky blackness, pierced here and there by the light from farmhouse windows.

But then we would look up at the staggering visual feast of the hundred thousand million stars of the Milky Way (I didn't make that number up, by the way, it came from National Geographic, and is in fact at the lower end of estimates of the size of our galaxy). Those of our friends who live in the country will no doubt smile if they read this, but for someone who has spent almost all of their life in cities, seeing all those stars in a clear night sky evokes a sense of awe that nothing man-made can approach. Mind you, in November it is a little too cold to spend more than a few minutes out on a Tuscan hillside, so our enjoyment of the spectacle tended to be brief.

Not that our solitude was absolute. Every week, the two cleaners, Roberta and Piera, turned up to clean the whole house and change the bed linen and towels, all of which was taken away to be laundered by the other member of the team, an odd-job man named Luca. Though all three were perfectly charming, none of them spoke more than a few words of English, so there were the usual comic moments as we tried to talk to them. During our pre-arrival briefing, John had jokingly reassured us that communicating with Luca would not be a problem, because he repeated everything three times, even with fluent Italian speakers like himself. That turned out to be exactly the case, and in the end we got on famously with Luca.

Apart from doing odd jobs for the owners of *La Colombaia Vecchia*, and probably for other houses in the area for all we knew, Luca is also a hunter. One morning as we were about to get into the car to drive off into town, he appeared at the top of the road, gun slung over his shoulder, accompanied by a pair of excitable hunting dogs. Naturally, we stopped and had a bit of a chat, as best we could with our limited Italian, and we asked him whether he was off down the hill to go shooting. No, he said, not at all, he had already got his bag for the day; reaching into one pocket he produced, with an air of triumph, a very small, very dead bird. Robert nearly jumped three feet backwards and was even less impressed when Luca reached into another pocket and hauled out an equally dead wood pigeon of some kind. Presumably this was going to be his supper.

Hunting, whether for small birds, for the big wild pigs that roam the forests, or for the deer that we occasionally saw bounding across the fields, is seen as a genuine agricultural activity in Italy. The country has more than 800,000 licensed hunters, and hunting is particularly popular in Tuscany, Umbria and Sardinia, where game is shot both for the domestic table and for restaurant consumption. *Cinghiale*, or wild boar, is a meat staple in central Italy, finding its way into delicious stews or as a ragu to be served with pasta.

Sheep farming is the other major agricultural activity that dominates this part of Tuscany. Unlike Australia, the sheep here are bred primarily for their milk, which is used in the literally hundreds of varieties of *pecorino* cheese that dominate the cheese section of the supermarkets. To ensure that they produce the best possible milk, the sheep are positively coddled by comparison with their more robust Australian cousins, sheltered from the cold of winter in big sheds, and guarded in the summer by immense, shaggy Maremma sheepdogs, who grow up with the sheep and often behave as if they were sheep themselves.

When summer comes, the flocks are released from their confinement and guided by the shepherds across the fields to their newly grown grazing spots. Sheep dogs in Australia are small, hard-working and intelligent creatures who use training and instinct to worry their rather more dim-witted charges into moving in the required direction; in Italy, where the sheep follow a pattern of movements so ancestral it is probably bred into their bones, the same thing is achieved by the shepherd alone with the use of whistles and calls and the occasional wave of his stick.

Once settled under the shade of a patch of trees, the shepherd will go off to lunch and leave the flock in the care of the Maremma, who will make the occasional patrol, issue a few barks, and then settle down for a snooze himself. By the middle of the afternoon, the only sounds that can be heard are the buzzing of insects and the occasional clank of a bell as one of the sheep shakes off the unwanted attentions of a fly. At some point in the late afternoon or early evening, the distinctive sound of those bells builds into a kind of agricultural crescendo when the shepherd returns to move the flock to another pasture for the night. There can be no more bucolic sound in Italy.

*

Volterra, our nearest serious urban centre, is one of the most fascinating towns in Tuscany. About ten minutes away by car, the town hugs the top of a long ridge, some 530 metres above sea level, and has the distinction of being one of the oldest continuously occupied sites in Italy, there having been a settlement here as far back as the 8th century BC. It was an important Etruscan centre, and thereafter a Roman town; vestiges of both civilisations can be seen in the old Etruscan acropolis, and the ruins of the Roman Theatre and baths. In the centuries after the end of the Roman Empire it was the seat of an important bishopric, and an independent commune until it fell under the ever-expanding sway of Florence, in the 14th century.

Volterra's submission to Florence was not easily won, and in 1472 the city rose in rebellion against the Medici government of Lorenzo the Magnificent, after a dispute over who should control an important local alum mine (alum was at that time a highly prized mineral, used for medical purposes and for fixing colours in the dyeing process). Lorenzo's response was savage: he sent 7,000 troops to besiege and sack the town. Once subdued, Florentine dominance was cemented by the construction of the Fortezza Medici, the imposing fortress that stands on the highest point of the hill overlooking the town, and is now used as a prison. The Volterrans never forgave the Florentines, and even today there is a kind of subterranean grudge between the two cities.

Despite the vicissitudes of its history, Volterra survives today as an almost perfect medieval walled town whose cobbled streets and piazza have barely changed since the 16th century. That makes it attractive to tourists, but it is also an irresistible backdrop for filmmakers, as we discovered on our first foray into town. Far from having buttoned itself up for winter as we had expected, the place was buzzing with activity. Emerging from the car park, the first sign that something was going on was the presence of a number of huge trailers of the type used by film companies; sure enough, in a marvellous twist of irony given their ancient grudge, Volterra had become 16th century Florence for the filming of the second season of the TV series *The Medici: Masters of Florence*.

The normally pristine main square, the Piazza Dei Priori, had been given the untidy look that it would have had in the 15th century, complete with wooden market stalls (including fake sides of meat—made of wood!—hanging from their frames), a kind of stage on which simple theatrical performances might have entertained the Florentine masses, lots of straw everywhere on the cobbles, very realistic-looking carts and carriages, and a dozen or so horses, who made their own distinctive contribution to the atmosphere in the form of horse-piss and poo.

No doubt one of the reasons the producers had chosen to make the series here was the similarity between the Palazzo dei Priori, the town hall of Volterra, and the Palazzo Vecchio in Florence. Though considerably smaller in scale, the Volterran building also sports a clock tower and is similarly crenelated; with the addition of fake wooden galleries along the front (entirely unhistorical but visually effective) it was a reasonably good stand-in for its more famous Florentine architectural cousin.

In amongst all this, the actors and extras, dressed of course in Renaissance costume, stood around smoking and talking on mobile phones while they waited for the next take. We joined the locals, many of whom no doubt had relatives filling in as soldiers, servants and what-not, standing around in the cold until they started shooting a couple of scenes. But filming is a long, tedious and repetitious business, and before long we wandered off and left them to it, retreating to the comfort and warmth of a cafe for a cappuccino and a cornetto (the Italian equivalent of the French croissant). This went on for pretty well the whole month we were there, and eventually became vaguely annoying. And it was all in the service of a pretty awful interpretation of Florentine history, as it turned out.

Notwithstanding the make-believe going on in the Piazza dei Priori, Volterra is a real town where real people live, a fact that is more apparent when the tide of tourists has departed. Many restaurants had closed and wouldn't reopen until spring, but those that were open were frequented by locals, who arrived en-masse from their various jobs around the town at between 1.00 pm and 1.30 pm, spending an hour or so enjoying lunch, and then gradually dispersing after about 2:30 pm to go back to work. Though there are two good supermarkets just outside the walls, deep in the old town the *alimentari* (fruit and vegetable shop) and the *macelleria* (butcher) are still the shopping mainstay for residents of the city. And if you need a haircut (as we did) there is an excellent barber whose shop seems to be something of a drop-in centre for the older men of the city, who turn up, have a flick through the newspaper, chat with the barber, and then wander off, none of which disturbs his concentration in the least.

Wandering the narrow streets and lanes of the town is a joy in itself, but Volterra's elevation provides another treat: some of the most spectacular views in Tuscany. Late in the afternoon, Volterrans can be seen all along the Viale dei Ponte, either strolling or sitting on a bench to enjoy the vista across the valley towards Cecina. In November, the skies were frequently cloudy, but occasionally they would part, and we were treated to the sight of the sun glinting on the distant Ligurian Sea, just visible between the peaks of the hills to our west.

Like any Tuscan tourist town, Volterra has many excellent cafes; one of the most popular was *l'Incontro*, whose name means, appropriately enough, 'the meeting place' in Italian. A long and narrow table-filled space with a high wooden counter along one side that displays a dazzling array of pastries, cakes, and paninis, *l'Incontro's* staff are chatty and briskly friendly. On market days the place buzzes with the English voices of expatriates, who have made this particular cafe their haven, ordering their coffees before or after they load themselves up with the week's shopping.

Speaking of expatriates, it is easy to see why Tuscany has such an appeal for the British. It has a romantically beautiful landscape, an equable climate, generally good health services that can be accessed easily and cheaply (or at least they could before Brexit), good food and friendly, tolerant people. And there are so many expatriates in Tuscany that forming a circle of friends is not at all difficult; even in our short stay, we met half a dozen people. It is not even necessary to speak Italian, and many don't, leading them into an odd kind of relationship with the Italians, of whom they speak of with the amused exasperation with all 'foreigners' that the British have affected for centuries, even as they rely on them to solve all the practical problems of their day-to-day existence.

Among the expatriates, our closest friends came to be Siobhan and David, who kind of came with the house, since they generally keep an eye on it whenever it is unoccupied. Irish Siobhan is an artist, who has developed and perfected a very fine style of printmaking; David works selling wine for a local winemaker, and has enjoyed a travelled life, including a stint in Australia. They live in a house that perches on a hillside just outside Montecatini Val di Cecina, a small town on the opposite side of the valley from Volterra, with an enormous dog called Suleiman who, though he stands a good metre or more tall, still thinks he is a puppy. They were our hosts for several lazy lunches and splendid dinners, and our guides for expeditions to nearby towns like San Gimignano, and the coastal town of Cecina, where we had some fun negotiating (not altogether successfully) the vagaries of the big local market that is held there every weekend.

For the first couple of weeks, we had enjoyed our solitude. I was busy writing, having taken over one of the upstairs bedrooms as a makeshift study, and Robert had great fun rattling around in John's kitchen, cooking up brilliant meals (it is something of a miracle that neither of us gained any noticeable weight while we were there). Then, in our third week, we had some visitors, old friends of Peter and Jaycen who came from Australia to spend a week and a bit with us. Deb, her son Alex, and her cousin Esther arrived in the dead of night, having had a bit of misfortune involving a hire car and a tyre on their way from Pisa airport. By now of course we were 'experts' in all matters Volterran, and we had fun showing them round the district, taking them off to nearby San Gimignano, and enjoying dinner at a couple of local restaurants. It was nice to have visitors, but we found we had rather come to enjoy the peace and quiet, and it was also nice to have it back when they left.

By the end of the month, we had so comfortably settled into our country existence that it was quite a wrench to say goodbye when the time came for us to move on. If this were a novel, or a memoir of the more conventional kind, it is at this point that we should have made a life-changing decision to stay in Tuscany forever, buy a dilapidated old house of our own, and have a whole new adventure. Alas for the dramatic literary possibilities, that wasn't to be, either because the stars weren't aligned or, more prosaically, just because neither of us is quite that spontaneous. But who knows, maybe one day!

## Chapter 13

# Napoleon's Island

At eight pm on May 3rd, 1814, Napoleon Bonaparte, the former Emperor of the French, arrived in the pretty harbour of Portoferraio on the island of Elba, aboard the British frigate *Undaunted*; he disembarked the next day at two in the afternoon, to be met by the sub-prefect, local clergy, and other officials. With him were his faithful generals Bertrand, Druot and the former commander of the Imperial Guard, Pierre Cambronne, along with six hundred Guardsmen. Ten months later, on the night of Sunday February 26th, 1815, he departed under cover of darkness aboard the brig *L'Inconstant*, the tiny flagship of his equally tiny navy, and embarked on the inveterate gambler's last throw of the dice—the so-called Hundred Days in which he recovered France and almost defeated the British and Prussians at Waterloo.

Napoleon's exile on the island of Elba is one of those footnotes of history that are always rather intriguing. What must it have been like for this towering military and political genius to be reduced to sovereignty over a mere two hundred square kilometres and 11,400 inhabitants, a speck of rock in plain sight of the coast of Italy, just ten kilometres away? At times, it must have seemed like a sick joke—Napoleon himself disparagingly referred to Elba as 'an operetta kingdom'—yet at other times it seemed as if he had resigned himself to his fate and was content to live out his life there in a kind of retirement.

Mind you, Napoleon's version of retirement would exhaust most people. During his 300 days on the island, he reorganised his new kingdom's defences, gave money to the poor, reformed the customs and excise system, repaired the barracks, built a hospital, paved parts of Portoferraio for the first time, organised regular rubbish collections, set up a court of appeal, and established an inspectorate to widen roads and build bridges. In between times, he read voraciously (and left a library of over a thousand volumes to the city of Portoferraio), grew avenues of mulberry trees, and planted vineyards. I rather suspect that any modern government that was this active would be politically unassailable!

Imagine, too, the effect on the people of the island when this semi-mythical man, demonised and lionised in about equal proportions across Europe, was deposited among them. What must they have thought? They themselves had had little say in the matter. In fact, the decision to send the defeated emperor to Elba was one shrouded in mystery: another emperor, Alexander II of Russia, had simply announced it, leaving his other allies with no choice but to accede. Quite what Alexander's motive was is hard to discern. Most likely it was practicality, placing Napoleon somewhere he could be easily monitored, and perhaps combined with a desire to humble the great ogre by putting him on the smallest, most insignificant piece of territory he could find, albeit one where his personal safety could reasonably be assured.

In any event, history records that the night before his disembarkation from the British ship of the line *Undaunted*, most of the three thousand inhabitants of Portoferraio placed candles in their windows as a sign of welcome. Proclamations telling the Elbans that Napoleon had 'chosen' their island for his 'sojourn' because of the kindness of its people and the mildness of its climate were posted up all over the capital, and thus flattered, the islanders worked through the early morning to build a stage upon which Mayor Traditi could welcome their new sovereign and hand him the keys to the town. The crossing from ship to shore took a full hour, so crowded was the harbour with sightseers in their rowboats, and there was a big crowd on the quay, among them a sergeant who Napoleon had decorated years earlier; on being recognised, the man wept, and the wily emperor had conquered yet another crowd.

Today, Elba is a very popular holiday destination for Tuscans; a mere three hours from Florence by road and ferry, it is accessible and yet it also feels remote. Leaving Piombino, the sheer volume of ferry traffic is a testament to its popularity: in the summer months there are three ferry companies that service the island, providing a virtually continuous service every half hour or so. Forty minutes after leaving Piombino's rather unlovely industrial port behind us, our Toremar ferry was sliding into the sheltered harbour of Portoferraio, which looks much as it must have when Napoleon arrived two centuries ago, a semicircle of water lined with shops and warehouses (and restaurants, which probably weren't there in Napoleon's day).

Beyond the waterfront, the arch of the so-called water gate took us into the town centre and the Piazza della Repubblica, which in Napoleon's time would have been called the Piazza d'Armi. What might once have been a fine open space is now pretty much a car park, ringed with shops and restaurants, the town's fine Duomo at one end facing off against the town hall at the other. As piazzas go, fairly unremarkable.

Portoferraio gets its name from the iron ore that used to be the island's principal export, a trade that was important enough to justify the investment in substantial fortifications to protect it when the Medici took over the place in 1546. Forts Falcone and Stella dominate town and harbour from their rocky perches at the eastern and western extremities of the little peninsula, and the Linguella tower protects the harbour entrance. Thus fortified, early nineteenth century Porto-ferraio would have been as secure a capital as any former emperor might desire.

A steep walk through narrow back streets and up long flights of stairs brings the visitor to the retired emperor's city pad, the Villa Mulini. The building's official title is actually the 'Palazzina dei Mulini', which seems appropriate for a place that is rather larger than your average villa, but nowhere near grand enough to really wear the title of a proper palace. Still, it's a pretty nice retirement option, sited high on the cliffs where there is a breeze even on the hottest days. In fact, there were once two windmills on the site, long demolished, from which the place gets its name, *mulini* being Italian for 'windmills'.

Originally two rather squat buildings that had once been used as a cottage by the island's governor, its position atop a sheer sea cliff and overlooked by the guns of forts Stella and Falcone made it an attractive option from a security point of view, and it was conveniently distant from the hubbub of the town. So the emperor bought it and set about refurbishing the place by adding another storey where he intended to accommodate his wife Marie-Louise and their young son when they were reunited, an event he longed for and that had been promised under the terms of his abdication; he was not to know that this was never going to happen, since Marie-Louise's father, Emperor Francis of Austria, was determined to prevent her from doing so, in direct violation of the terms of the peace treaty.

Inside, the bedrooms and more intimate living rooms are all on the ground floor, and today are furnished with items from the imperial period, either originals or reproductions. A book-lined study contains Napoleon's desk and would once have housed the very impressive library that he had compiled from all over Europe. In another room his campaign bed is displayed, an affair of iron and canvas, a reminder of one of this man's many contradictions: though he had at his disposal such sumptuous palaces as Versailles, the Tuileries, and Fontainebleau, he was also at heart a soldier for whom this simple contraption was as comfortable as a four poster.

The upper floor is dominated by a large and airy reception room whose floor to ceiling windows open to views of the garden, giving it a wonderfully airy feel. It is easy to imagine the diminutive emperor holding court here, charming his rusticated and provincial subjects with his quick smile, boundless energy and formidable memory for faces and names. A man who understood the importance of maintaining appearances, he made sure that a proper court protocol was devised and strictly enforced, both in the palace and as he travelled around the island. Yet, far from looking down on his Elban subjects, Napoleon seems to have treated them with courtesy and affection, surreal though his situation must have seemed compared to his glittering recent past.

Apart from the accommodation for the emperor, the house eventually became a home to his mother Letizia, the fierce old matriarch who was probably the only woman other than Josephine of whom Napoleon was genuinely afraid. The only other member of his rather grasping brood of siblings who came to Elba was his sister Pauline, who faithfully joined him in his exile. She sounds like she would have been rather fun to know. Possessing the same furiously energetic disposition as her brother, she was fond of sailors and loved a party; she was also a natural conspirator and no doubt served as a clandestine carrier of messages back and forth to the mainland as Napoleon's eventual escape was planned.

Villa Mulini wasn't Napoleon's only residence on the island; he paid 180,000 francs to buy a farmhouse in San Martino, virtually in the middle of the island, which he proceeded to have decorated as a summer residence, in a lavish style that nostalgically recalled his victorious time in the Egyptian campaign. Having got it started with his usual energy and enthusiasm, he seems to have got bored by it, and in the end only ever spent a few nights there.

'What a pity the man wasn't lazy', the slippery but witty French statesman Talleyrand once quipped about Napoleon. His energy was legendary, and even on Elba, his supposed 'isle of rest', he seemed to be forever in motion, riding all over the island accompanied by his faithful general Bertrand, or the supervisor of the island's mines, Andre Pons, or occasionally the British commissioner to the island, Neil Campbell. Bertrand at least had become inured to his master's ways over many years, but the other two both complained of their exhaustion after a day spent with the emperor. Inspecting mines, ordering the building of roads, planning upgrades to the port and to fortifications, reforming the taxation systems, issuing a new constitution and overhauling the laws, designing a new flag, drilling his little army, obsessively supervising the renovation of the Mulini, all this and more kept him occupied and consumed all the energies of his aides.

But it wasn't enough. A few days after his forty-fifth birthday, the villagers at Marciano Marina, on the northern coast of the island, reported seeing two women and a child landed on the beach there. The immediate assumption was that empress Maria-Louise had arrived at last, albeit in clandestine fashion. In fact, the visitors were Napoleon's sometime mistress, the Polish countess Marie Walewska, her sister, and Alexandre, Marie's young son by Napoleon. The little party was taken up into the hills behind the town to a little house attached to a shrine which had been commandeered for the occasion by the emperor, where they spent two days with him before sailing off again, just as mysteriously.

Was the visit purely a matter of pleasure? Or did Walewska bring Napoleon news or letters from the outside world? She later hinted as much, suggesting that Napoleon considered his exile temporary and that she had brought information he needed to help him decide when would be the most propitious moment to end it. The briefness of the stay, and the presence of her sister and her child in a small and cramped hermitage, which would no doubt have dampened any amorous intentions, suggest that the visit was a matter more of business than pleasure. This was still some six months before his final escape, and it may be that at this stage he was simply weighing up his options and keeping an eye on events.

For the modern visitor walking in his garden on a bright summer's day it is hard to resist posing the question of why, given such idyllic surrounds, Napoleon would have ever wanted to leave. The emperor himself frequently said that he was content to see out his days here, and that his days of world domination were done. But perhaps he was just gulling his 'gaolers', the commissioners who were appointed to make sure he behaved himself. Of course, such a tiny dominion would probably never have been enough for such a titanic force of nature, and his erstwhile enemies, in their foolishness, also did their level best to offer him sufficient provocation to take his final gamble. They withheld the payments that had been promised for his upkeep, and they denied him access to his wife and son. But most of all, the Bourbons, having returned to power without learning or forgetting anything, soon reduced France to such a state of discontent that Napoleon was pretty sure he would get a good reception if he came back. And so, on that dark and moonless February night, he slipped aboard *L'Inconstant* and sailed off to his destiny at Waterloo.

For most modern visitors to Elba, Napoleon's exile is a matter of, at best, mild interest, since most come to soak up the sun and enjoy the island's pleasant beaches and resorts. But the story of how one of history's giants came to live in a lilliputian kingdom for a while, before going off to face a tragic destiny that ended in yet another island exile on a much more inhospitable rock in the middle of the Atlantic is a fascinating one, full of odd little mysteries and speculation. Ideal territory in many ways for a novel; to the best of my knowledge the only book that has been written along these lines is A.P. Herbert's *Why Waterloo?*, which I read many, many years ago. Perhaps one day I will have a go at writing the story myself.

Chapter 14

# Milan and Leonardo: Art and Power

As a city, Milan is, and believes itself to be, quite different from any other on the peninsula. For one thing, it is the only city in Italy to boast something resembling a 20th century skyline of tall buildings. For another, it sees itself being at the heart of the modern, busy and industrious north of the country. It is of course the design and fashion capital of Italy, and in those fields preeminent in the world. Its urban area is home to 5.3 million inhabitants, making it the second most populous city in Italy, after Rome. It is a city of expositions and trade fairs, and is the home of the Italian stock exchange. In short, if Rome is the political capital of Italy, then Milan is its commercial centre.

Not that politics has passed Milan by. The city witnessed the birth of fascism when Mussolini rallied his blackshirts in the piazza San Sepulcro, and it was from here that he launched his March on Rome in October 1922, the event which precipitated the political crisis that put him into power. And today Milan is the modern heartland of the politically right-wing *Liga* movement of Matteo Salvini. None of that is to suggest that the Milanese are irredeemably right-wing, but it is probably fair to say that Milan marches to a different drum than the fairly consistently left-ish tone of the rest of the country's politics.

Physically, the centre of the city is as handsome a place as anywhere in Europe. The soaring cathedral with its wedding-cake facade is the city's symbol and its heart. Appropriately, just across the piazza from the cathedral is a different temple, this one dedicated to shopping: the Galleria Vittorio Emanuele II, an elegant cruciform space filled with boutiques and cafes opened in 1877; nicknamed *il salotto Milanese* (the Milanese drawing-room), it is a popular meeting place as well as a tourist drawcard. In the middle, where the four arms of the arcade meet, there is a mosaic showing the coats of arms of Milan and the three capitals of united Italy (Turin, Florence, and Rome), and in a typically Italian piece of superstition, it is said that if you spin three times with your heel on the testicles of the Torinese bull, you will have good luck. Needless to say, Italian visitors can be seen hilariously enacting this ritual at any time of day.

Keep walking through the Galleria, and you come out into the pretty little piazza that fronts the opera house, La Scala, where dreams of Italian independence from the Austrian occupiers were symbolically played out in the operas of Giuseppe Verdi, whose very name was co-opted as a slogan: *Viva Vittorio Emanuele, Rei d'Italia* ('Long live Victor Emanuel, king of Italy'). The composer himself was rather more ambivalent about the *risorgimento*, even as a chorus from his opera *Nabucco*, the rather melancholic *Va Pensiero*, became a virtual national anthem. Even so, he was elected to the first Italian parliament in 1861, and he remains the ultimate Italian nationalist composer.

Though Verdi was born near Busseto, in the Po valley between Parma and Piacenza, he moved to Milan in 1839, and spent a dozen years there, writing operas and getting rich, something of which the Milanese no doubt thoroughly approved. Like Shakespeare, his genius wasn't purely artistic: he made sure he was paid handsomely for his work and invested the proceeds in properties in Milan and out in the country, including the Villa Verdi, in Busseto, where he lived from 1851 until the end of his life. This preoccupation with matters material didn't always chime with the artistic side of him, and his biographer John Rosselli wrote that 'I do not very much like the man Verdi, in particular the autocratic rentier-cum-estate owner, part-time composer, and seemingly full-time grumbler and reactionary critic of the later years.' Still, whatever his personal quirks, he remains the most beloved of all Italian composers, and will forever be associated with Milan.

Further north from La Scala is the Brera district, at whose heart lies the city's greatest artistic repository, the Pinacoteca Brera. The collection is immense, with almost every great Italian painter from the Renaissance to the Baroque well represented. Caravaggio's brilliant *Supper at Emmaus* is here, its enigmatic Christ caught mid-parable talking to an audience whose attitudes convey scepticism and fascination in equal measure, and there are any number of Carracis, Corregios and Guercinos. Of all the paintings we saw, the one that really seized my imagination was Andrea Mantegna's superb painting of the *Lamentation of Christ*. This picture is a truly extraordinary exercise in perspective painting. The viewer is sat at the feet of the dead Christ, whose body is laid out on a catafalque, his mother Mary dabbing tears from her eyes at one side; quite apart from the sheer technical genius of the picture, Mantegna succeeds in creating a harrowing vision of death that is immediate, dramatic, and deeply moving.

If, having gorged yourself on art, you leave the Brera and walk westward you very soon come to the Castello Sforzesco, the vast fortress-palace that has brooded over Milan since it was constructed in the fourteenth century for Galeazzo II Visconti. Approached from the centre of the city along the wide boulevard of the Via Dante, the Castello is still an imposing sight, the archetypical Renaissance fortress with its forbidding walls, imposing central gate, and huge drum-towers at each corner. This martial exterior encloses a pleasant open courtyard that would once have been buzzing with military activity, and beyond that, a magnificent palace where the dukes lived.

Had we been wandering through the palace complex five centuries ago, we might have stumbled into a disused ballroom, where we would have been confronted with a thirty-foot high statue of one of the Sforza dukes, mounted on his horse and looking bravely into the distance at some unseen battlefield. The statue, we might have been told, is made of clay, and is actually only a model for a huge bronze that the artist has been commissioned to make, the biggest ever made in Italy, bigger even than Verrochio's statue of Bartolomeo Colleoni in Venice. And the artist? That tall, craggily handsome fellow over there, standing looking at his creation deep in thought—Leonardo, his name is, from the village of Vinci.

In the movie *The Third Man*, Orson Welles' character Harry Lime says 'in Italy for thirty years under the Borgias they had warfare, terror, murder, bloodshed, but they produced Michelangelo, Leonardo da Vinci, and the Renaissance. In Switzerland they had brotherly love, five hundred years of democracy and peace, and what did that produce? The cuckoo clock.' There is probably no more pithy expression of one of the central paradoxes of the Renaissance: how could such a turbulent, uncertain time have produced such an extraordinary outpouring of artistic endeavour? And there is no more perfect example of the intersection between art and power than the life of Leonardo da Vinci.

\*

In 1482, the thirty-year-old Leonardo arrived in Milan, having been dispatched there as by his friend and patron, Lorenzo de' Medici, better known to history as Lorenzo the Magnificent. Though Lorenzo had supported the artist's early career, by this stage his enthusiasm for the young provincial had cooled somewhat, perhaps because he had shown an increasing tendency to abandon commissions when they were half-finished, much to the irritation of his patrons. So perhaps Lorenzo saw an opportunity to get him out of Florence, by sending him to deliver the gift of a silver lyre to the ruler of Milan, duke Ludovico Sforza.

Sforza, known as *Il Moro* (The Moor) on account of his dark complexion, had seized power in Milan the year before, ruling as regent for his twelve-year-old nephew, and then eventually as duke of Milan in his own right. One of the more complex figures in the grand cast of Italian Renaissance rulers, Sforza was at once tyrannical, crafty, indecisive, cultured, and extravagant. Utterly ruthless in the pursuit of his political objectives, he was nevertheless a great patron of artists, which must have appealed to Leonardo, since, having arrived in Milan and delivered Lorenzo's gift, he promptly offered his services to the duke, who gave him an apartment in the Castello Sforzesco. He would live and work there for the next seventeen years.

At first, he was employed producing pageants and other court entertainments; though a seemingly frivolous occupation, Leonardo might well have enjoyed the opportunity to combine his interests in painting and engineering. He had also recommended himself to the duke as a military engineer; whether he in fact undertook any commissions in this character is uncertain, but certainly his notebooks from this time are filled with drawings of military projects and machines.

But it was as a painter that he had made his reputation in Florence, and it was as a painter that his new patron wanted to employ him, and on a spectacular project at that. Not far from the Castello is the Dominican monastery of Santa Maria della Grazie, whose church the duke had decided to rebuild as the Sforza family mausoleum. Under pressure from the restless autocrat, the work had proceeded rapidly, and it was now time to decorate the walls of the church. Leonardo, Ludovico decided, would paint a picture of the Last Supper.

Wall paintings are usually completed using the fresco technique, in which the pigment is applied to fresh (*fresco*, in Italian) wet plaster and allowed to dry, fixing the colour in the process. That sounds simple enough, but in practice the artist has to work quickly and accurately, with no opportunity to change the end result once the plaster has dried. That didn't suit Leonardo, whose natural medium was oil painting, a technique that allowed the painter to work slowly, and make changes as he was going along. Instead of using the traditional fresco methods, he decided to paint in oil and tempera on a wall that had been sealed with a double layer of gesso, pitch, and mastic. That would allow him to take his time and fiddle with the detail of the composition.

And take his time he did: he started on the project sometime in 1495 but didn't complete it until 1498. This exasperated the Dominican prior, who complained to the duke; summoned before his master, Leonardo explained that the painting was finished except for the face of Judas, for whom he was seeking a suitable model in the streets of Milan. Of course, he said, if the prior so desperately wanted the work to be completed, he could always use the prior's own face for Judas. This piece of humour appealed to the duke and got Leonardo off the hook; he was left in peace to finish at his own pace.

Leonardo is often criticised for using the oil and tempera technique, but this is probably unfair. The method itself was not invented by him, having been around since the 14th century. But it *was* risky, and he was not to know that the builders of the wall upon which he was painting had worked hastily, filling the walls with moisture-retaining rubble. This was to have a disastrous effect as the moisture stopped the paint from adhering properly to the surface; within a year it had begun to deteriorate. Over the centuries, it underwent several restorations, the last of which was completed in 1999, when the refectory was sealed from the outside world so that the picture could be preserved in a climate-controlled space.

Many great works of art have been reproduced so often that the original can be a disappointment when seen for the first time, and there can be few pictures that have been reproduced as often as this one. But when you are finally ushered through the double doors and into the refectory, it doesn't disappoint. Judging by the early copies that were painted some twenty-odd years after the original was completed, what we see today is indeed a pale shadow of what must have been an astonishingly vibrant image. Even so, what remains is compelling, and not in the least disappointing.

What strikes you immediately is the sense of drama that Leonardo imparts to the scene. Shock radiates out from the central figure of Christ as his revelation that one of them will betray him travels to each end of the table, those closest protesting their innocence with a passion you can almost feel, those further away expressing disbelief and doubt, while a very dark-skinned Judas seems to be almost disinterested in the whole affair. Then of course there is that enigmatically effeminate image of Saint John the Apostle that so excited the interest of Dan Brown in his novel *The Da Vinci Code*. Like Caravaggio a hundred years later, Leonardo achieves a realism of expression by reproducing the faces of real people he encountered in the streets of Milan, and this also contributes to the feeling you are actually there, in the room.

But all that is in the future: let's go back to the late 15th century. Duke Ludovico was becoming ever more extravagant, spending great sums of money on pageants, building projects, and the commissioning of art works like the *Last Supper*. This was not just a whim; rather, it was a deliberate policy designed to emphasise the legitimacy and permanence of his rule, a strategy deployed by most of the great spenders of the Italian

Renaissance. The difficulty of course was that all this spending had to be supported by increased taxes, which stored up resentments in the population that would inevitably come back to haunt the duke.

Leonardo, meanwhile, was probably oblivious to all these problems and continued to be a beneficiary of the ducal largesse. A half hour walk from the wonders of the Last Supper brings us to another reminder of the man's extraordinarily broad talents: the canals of Milan. The Italian word for a canal is *naviglio* and the district to which our perambulation has brought us is called Navigli (the plural of *naviglio*), since it is the place at which two canals, the Naviglio Grande and the Naviglio Pavese, connect in a large turning basin. The canals were originally built to connect the city with the Po and Ticino River systems to the south, and were essential to Milanese commerce.

The duke had conceived a grandiose scheme to extend the existing canal network to connect Milan with Lake Como, an extraordinary undertaking given the differences in altitude between the two places. So when Leonardo came along, he naturally gave him the task of researching the feasibility of such a thing. The canal was never built, but Leonardo's sketches of canal locks and tunnels can still be seen in the Navigli Museum. Today Navigli is a lively area where bars and restaurants line the canals, serving some of the most elaborate *aperitivo* spreads in Milan, and a lovely place to spend a lazy Sunday afternoon.

Then, sometime in 1489, the duke commissioned him to create the equestrian statue of his father, which was to be the largest such statue ever to be made, requiring more than seventy tons of bronze. As we have seen, he made an impressive clay model of the subject, but the statue itself was never to be completed, as the duke's hold on power faltered and slipped in the last decade of the fifteenth century. A series of ill-advised political manoeuvres precipitated what are now known to history as the Italian Wars, a long three-way struggle between France, Spain and the Holy Roman Empire to determine which of them would control the Italian peninsula. When the French king Louis XII decided to enforce his claim to the throne of Milan, duke Ludovico was thrown into panic. Locking himself inside the Castello Sforzesca, he diverted all his resources into preparing for the inevitable invasion, including requisitioning the seventy tons of bronze originally intended for Leonardo's *gran cavallo* to be melted down and made into cannons. Leonardo sensibly saw the writing on the wall and prepared to flee.

In the summer of 1499, the French invaded and, meeting little resistance from the Milanese, chased Sforza out of Milan, which they occupied in September. Leonardo was still there, and in fact remained in the city for three months, finally slipping away in December, accompanied by his twenty-year-old assistant (and probable lover), who went by the nickname 'Salai', which is approximately translated as 'rascal'. From all accounts the name was well deserved, though Salai was to remain devoted to his master for most of his life. As for the statue on which he had lavished so much work, it was used for target practice by the French crossbowmen and eventually smashed into pieces.

After a period of wandering from city to city, Leonardo found himself back in Florence in 1500, forty-eight years old and famous, but stony-broke. The Medici had by now been thrown out of Florence, and the city was under a new republican government; nevertheless, commissions soon arrived, and before long he was hard at work painting an altarpiece for the church of Santissima Annunziata. But he was restless and unhappy, and in 1502 he left Florence to join the new rising power in northern Italy, Cesare Borgia, who had offered him a job as his military engineer.

Quite why the artist, who frequently confided to his notebooks his disgust with war, chose to go and join the notoriously violent Borgia is something of a mystery, but he stayed with the warlord for over a year, coming back to Florence in 1503. This was the period when he began working on the Mona Lisa, and the designs for an enormous wall painting depicting the battle of Anghiari for the great hall of the Palazzo della Signoria. Typically, work on the latter was slow, and he was never to finish it, leaving Florence to return once more to Milan in 1506. Milan was still under French control, and Leonardo was to spend the rest of his life in the service of successive French kings, until he died in 1519 at the Chateau d'Amboise, in the arms, it was said, of the French king, Francois I.

Leonardo's life, like that of so many other artists in Italy during the Renaissance, was lived at the whim and behest of a series of powerful patrons, and his fortunes rose and fell with theirs. The dukes and princes of northern Italy were hardly more secure than the artists they employed, always one coup or invasion away from being ejected from their palaces and fortresses. Not surprisingly, while they had power they tried to project an image of permanence and wealth, and the commissioning of grandiose works of art was one of the tools they employed for that purpose. This is one explanation (among many) for the paradox that Harry Lime describes so eloquently.

\*

Art and power have not always been happy bedfellows, and many an artist has found a way to rebel, sometimes with great subtlety, and sometimes more overtly, against the demands placed upon them by their patrons. A famous face might be painted from an unflattering angle or placed in an incongruous position in a crowded fresco. The artist might put his own visage into the picture, sardonically looking out at the viewer as if to say he is only doing this for the money. Today, Leonardo would be described as a pacifist, and in his case he expressed his disgust for the way in which his talents were being used by designing a tank-like war machine that would never have worked, since its cogs would have caused it to spin on its axis.

One last diversion on our little tour of Milan shows that such subtle acts of rebellion are still being perpetrated on smug patrons today. The Milan stock exchange is housed in the grandiose Palazzo Mezzanotte (the name has nothing to do with midnight, but refers to its architect, Paolo Mezzanotte), which fronts onto a little square called the Piazza degli Affari. Right in the middle of the piazza stands a shocking sculpture of a huge five-metre-high hand, all of its fingers chopped off except the middle one, which is raised in the traditional insulting gesture.

The artist who produced this giggle-inducing work is Maurizio Cattelan, and its official name is L.O.V.E.—an acronym standing for *liberta, odio, vendetta,* and *eternita,* or 'freedom, hate, revenge, and eternity'. Ever since it was installed in 2010, Cattelan has refused to explain what his intentions might have been, saying merely that people could take what they liked from it. One interpretation is that it is an attack on fascism, the fingers having been severed from a hand that is giving the fascist salute outside a building that is one of the few remaining from the fascist era. But others have noted that the work was commissioned in 2008, when the financial crisis was at its height, and the sculpture is giving the middle finger to the financiers of the stock exchange.

But I think the better interpretation is that offered by our tour guide, who said to look more carefully: the back of the hand is facing *away* from the stock exchange, so perhaps it would be more accurate to say that the sculpture represents the financiers flipping the bird at the rest of Italy as they pocket their profits from government bailouts while applauding the imposition of austerity on everyone else. She also told us that the sculpture was disguised until the day it was actually unveiled, so that no-one could object until it was too late. In any event, it generated the predictable outrage, but has been standing there as an entertaining example of Italian humour ever since.

It also encapsulates, I think, Milan's rather cocky sense of individuality. That the statue was allowed to stand, despite its rather insulting gesture, speaks to a self-confidence that is typical of the city. 'We are big enough', it seems to say, 'that we can take such mockery in our stride.'

# Chapter 15

# Italy has a Riviera too

The Italian Riviera begins where the coast of Tuscany ends, a little south of the big naval city of La Spezia and runs all the way around the Gulf of Liguria until it eventually merges with the much more glamorous French Riviera near the town of Ventimiglia. Genoa is right in the middle of this arc of coast, and the Italian Riviera is considered to have two halves, depending on which side of Genoa it lies. The western stretch, centered on the town of Savona, is called the Riviera di Ponente, while the eastern bit that curves down until it meets the Tuscan coast is called the Riviera di Levante.

The eastern Riviera is very much the more upmarket of the two: where its western cousin is homely and laid-back, even a bit on the scruffy side, the Levante is the place where the rich and famous take their yachts to pop in and out of the famous harbours of places like Portofino, Santa Margherita Ligure, and Rapallo. Apart from these famous towns, tourists are also attracted to the famous villages of the Cinque Terre and the many other genteel resort towns that dot the coast, Chiavari, Sestri Levante, Moneglia, and many others.

Less by design than by accident, our first visit to this area was in May just a little before the peak summer season got into full swing. That meant that hotels had scaled back their charges from astronomically expensive to merely eye-watering, while the beaches and shops were still in getting-ready mode, and a good deal more laid-back than they would be later in the season. Our destination on this first visit was to be one of the Cinque Terre villages; *Cinque Terre* in Italian simply means "Five Lands" and refers to the five villages that are inserted into crevices along a rugged section of coastline.

For most of their long existence, the villages—in order from north to south: Monterosso al Mare, Vernazza, Corniglia, Manarola and Riomaggiore—were almost completely isolated. By land, they were accessible only by way of sketchy donkey trails leading through densely forested wilderness, so that the only realistic way of approaching them was from the sea. This made them a target for pirate raids, against whose depredations the towns built forbidding fortifications, but otherwise they were left in peace until the 19th century, when a railway line was built through a series of coastal tunnels, inaugurating the era of mass tourism. That long era of isolation gave the five villages a kind of mysterious, romantic appeal, so almost from the day the railway was finished the coast started to become a tourist attraction. Fortunately, the area was declared a UNESCO World Heritage site in 1997, which has no doubt been a saviour of sorts, preventing rampant over development of the kind to which the Italians are sadly addicted.

When we visited it was a little early for the tourist hordes that descend on the area in the summer months, but even so the train up from Florence was still pretty crowded. The three-hour journey took us down the valley of the Arno, and then north up the Tuscan coast to La Spezia, where we changed trains to the shuttle service that runs continuously to and from the five towns. We finally arrived in Monterosso at around 2 pm, joining the stumbling rush of people down several flights of stairs to emerge blinking in the sunshine onto the street; in front of us was a long sandy beach filled with colourful umbrellas, and the sparkling expanse of the Ligurian Sea.

The guidebooks had told us that Monterosso, the most westerly of the five towns, is the most frequented by tourists, not least because it is the only one to possess a substantial beach, running the full length of the bay. Unsurprisingly, many holidaymakers who come here just to soak up the sun and never visit any of the other towns. That makes some a bit sniffy about the place, but the fact that it is a substantial and easily accessible town means it is also an attractive base from which to explore the other four towns.

Monterosso actually has two parts, divided by the bulk of the Collina dei Frati Cappuccini, or hill of the Capuchins, a great rocky outcrop topped by the Capuchin convent that gives the hill its name (and yes, in case you are wondering, the coffee concoction was named for the Capuchin order, whose friars wear a white cassock and a brown hood). The original village, the old town, lies to the east of the hill, and the new town to the west. The railway station is in the new town, and our hotel, the Albergo Baia, was thankfully just a hundred metres or so along the waterfront from the station entrance.

There is a breed of hotel in Italy that hovers somewhere between two and three stars, comfortable enough in itself but not quite ever aspiring to heights of greatness in terms of service or facilities; the Baia is one of those. Built in 1911 as apartments and converted into a hotel after the second world war, its four stories stand right on the waterfront. The rooms are well appointed, and the public areas well kept; the staff are polite and helpful, though not effusive. They are presided over by a somewhat grumpy looking woman who we presumed was the owner; when she wasn't sitting out on the street having a cigarette, she was engaged in endless conversations with her employees, the kind that even without a word of Italian you can just tell they are all having a good old whinge together.

Almost from the minute we arrived, we could sense the faint ghost of Basil Fawlty lurking somewhere. For example, the lift, though perfectly functional, is reserved only for the movement of baggage, definitely not for the use of hotel guests, we were informed: we had to use the stairs. Though there is a big restaurant, it is only open for breakfast, which seemed to be a wasted opportunity, especially considering that it sports a splendid outside terrace facing onto the beach. Anything that involved moving food or drinks outside the confines of the hotel building also seemed to be a problem; though the hotel offers its guests an exclusive beach area, complete with umbrellas and sun lounges, it couldn't quite manage to organise food or drinks down there. And when we were meeting some new acquaintances for a drink before dinner, we were told that *we* could drink on the terrace, but our guests couldn't. You get the idea—it all seemed slightly comical without ever really being inconvenient or difficult.

It is true that there isn't a great deal to see in Monterosso, apart from the convent and the slightly bizarre fourteen-metre-high sculpture of Neptune that stands at the end of a little promontory just along the beach from our hotel, originally supporting the terrace of the Villa Pastine. But the old town is a pleasant place to wander around and sample the local restaurants, which at this season were not too crowded, while the calm waters of the bay are perfect for swimming (we did venture in one afternoon, though the water was still a little on the chilly side in May).

'Coming to the Cinque Terre and not hiking,' *Lonely Planet* says, 'is like sitting down for dinner in an Italian restaurant and eschewing the wine'. Of course, *Lonely Planet* does tend to cater to a young and physically active demographic, and we reasoned that those of us who are older are perfectly entitled to ignore this advice. Not that we are averse to exercise; it's just that a brisk stroll is more our speed than a serious hike.

But that phrase rang in our ears like a rebuke, and so we decided that we had to attempt at least one of the trails. There are many to choose from, but several of them are completely closed following the floods in 2011, and all of them are prone to periodic closures if there has been any rain. When we were there, the Blue Trail between Monterosso and Corniglia was open, and since this is generally considered the most accessible path, we decided we would at least do the first section, which would take us to Vernazza, the next town down the coast. Can't be too hard, we thought—a couple of hours walking, the park officials breezily told us, and you'll be sitting down for lunch.

What they didn't tell us is that the first part of the hike is more or less straight up. A short stretch of gently climbing path lulls you into a false sense of security, and then you are hit with a good forty minutes of climbing a series of flights of steps, each cunningly arranged—or so it seemed—to mislead you into thinking that *this* was the last flight before the path levelled out; arriving panting and red-faced at the top, you would turn a corner to be confronted, not with the nirvana of a flat stretch, but with yet more steps.

Our protesting minds kept whispering that we should just quit and go back down, but we managed to resist the temptation and soldiered on, admittedly with frequent stops get our breath, admire the view, and chat to the many others who were out that morning attempting the same feat. Though there were many experienced hikers who passed us, all properly kitted out and with determined, professional looks on their faces, there were also plenty who, like us, hadn't quite anticipated the challenges the trail would bring. There was one particular girl, American and very much on the large economy side with respect to physique, who had clearly been duped into making the attempt by her friends; she was entertainingly inventive in her curses for them and for the obstacles she was being forced to clamber over. But she did have pluck, I'll say that: she kept going and made it all the way to the end.

Eventually we found ourselves on a relatively flat section of the trail that clung rather perilously to the side of the terraced hill, closely planted with olive trees and vines, and here the astonishing view made it all worthwhile, and the pain of the climb was, if not forgotten, at least buried. As we looked back down on Monterosso, we marvelled at the toughness of the villagers who must have made this trek on a daily basis to get to their trees and vines in order to eke out a living, something that many still do, although these days there is a kind of simple funicular that carries them up.

The advent of mass tourism has also created opportunities of other kinds for the locals—including one old timer who, with the shrewdness of country people everywhere, had installed himself at a bend in the trail with a pile of oranges and lemons, and a small electric juicer plugged into a power point somewhere up in the trees. With this set-up, he was busy selling freshly made fruit juice to just about every tired and thirsty hiker who passed him, at a tidy €2 per cup. We reckoned he probably made a very nice little sum over the summer.

If there is a single one of the villages that can be considered iconic, it is Vernazza, which finally came into view conveniently close to lunchtime. Seen from above, it really is a pretty sight. The houses rise in pastel painted terraces that curl around the only really workable harbour of the five towns, overlooked and protected by the fortifications of the Castello Doria. After an equally steep—and at times just as trying—descent down the hillside, we found ourselves in a shadowed warren of narrow lanes, strung with the ubiquitous washing lines that seem to be a visible measure of the villagers' indifference to the tourist tide surging below their windows. Eventually we found our way out onto the busy, restaurant-lined waterfront.

The earliest records of Vernazza as a fortified town date back to 1080, and because it possessed one of the few naturally well protected harbours on the coast, it made an excellent base from which ships could venture out to deal with the pirates who plagued much of the Ligurian coast. It was a prosperous place for several hundred years, but by the middle of the seventeenth century was in decline, like the rest of the Cinque Terre villages. The construction of the Genoa-La Spezia railway revived its fortunes and ended the town's long isolation. Though there are no obvious signs of it today, in 2011 Vernazza was buried four metres deep in mud after torrential rains caused landslides. The town had to be evacuated and remained empty for many months while the clean-up took place.

While it would have been possible for us to continue walking along the trail, we felt we had done enough to legitimately claim our 'I've walked the Cinque Terre' t-shirts, and therefore had earned a leave pass to use the railway to visit the other villages. A short trip deposited us at Riomaggiore, the easternmost and largest of the five, which, with a population of a little over 1,500 souls, considers itself the capital of the Cinque Terre. From the railway station, the restaurant-lined main street snakes down through a slot-like canyon to the tiny harbour, barely big enough for the fishing boats to creep in and out. Rio does, however, boast a modern supermarket and a post office, which is probably the town's main justification for its claims to 'capital' status.

Apart from walking the trails and using the train, the other way to get between the villages of the Cinque Terre is by boat, and that's the option we chose the following day. In some ways a boat trip is a better way to get a sense of just how isolated these villages must have been before the trains arrived. As the ferry skips down the coast, all you can see is green-covered mountainous terrain that meets the sea in perpendicular cliffs, utterly wild and inaccessible, the only sign of habitation the occasional patch of vine-terraces.

Having passed Corniglia, which perches high above the coast and is the only one of the towns that has no port of any kind, our motor-launch slid into the tiny harbour at Manarola. Mind you, calling it a harbour is a serious exaggeration; it is not much more than a patch of water at the foot of the cliffs, protected only by a rough breakwater from the swells. Arriving and departing from here must have been a perilous business in the days when all maritime traffic relied on wind or human muscle. Fortunately, it offered no real challenge to our ferry's powerful diesels; we were smoothly disembarked and sent off to explore the village, which, with just 350 inhabitants, wasn't a big expedition.

*

Santa Margherita Ligure is a little over an hour up the coast from Monterosso by train, and together with its two glamorous neighbours, Rapallo and Portofino, it is the heart of the Italian Riviera, a place of dazzling white yachts and grand hotels. Our particular lodging place, The Continental, stood on the northern side of Santa Margherita's broad bay, just a short walk from the railway station (much to our relief). If the Hotel Baia was a fine example of an Italian family hotel at the lower end of the scale, the Continental represented the opposite end of that scale. Built in 1903, the hotel is a typical Art-Nouveau style building, three storeys high, its coffee-coloured facade punctured by two rows of full-length windows flanked by green shutters above a pillared portico decorated with the full complement of European flags snapping in the breeze. The place oozes class from the moment you arrive, that kind of smooth old-world Italian obsequiousness that is neither fawning nor offensive, just ineffably polite. Our room, when we got there after completing the usual preliminaries, was on the opposite side of the hotel, with a fine view across the bay from our own little private courtyard.

Sometimes when you travel, the hotel is the destination, a place to be enjoyed for itself rather than simply a place to lay your weary head after a day doing tourist things. The Continental is one such place, with its beautiful terrace, perfect for an afternoon Negroni, its fine restaurant staffed by waistcoated waiters and an unflappable maître-d', and its flower-filled gardens leading down to the private beach. It provided a perfect stage set for our little fantasy stay, and we did our best to make the most of it.

Santa Margherita sits at the north-eastern corner of a peninsula that pokes out into the Ligurian Sea. At the opposite end of the peninsula lies the most famous town of the Italian Riviera, Portofino, towards which we set out on foot early on our second morning, along a footpath that in the summer is painted as a kind of faux red carpet, rather kitsch but fun nevertheless. The path first follows a road that clings to the base of the cliffs, winds in and out of little bays, passes through the little village of Parragi, and finally climbs up through the forested hills until it emerges behind the great bulk of the Grand Hotel Splendido. From there, the path descends again, and you get your first view of the pretty multi-coloured facades of Portofino, once a tiny fishing village jammed into a slot in the coastline, and now the playground of the rich and famous.

You can sense how much money there is in Portofino the instant you walk into the town. Every inch of the place is manicured to perfection, every shop is a boutique, and even the inevitable tourist tat seems to be of a better quality. And of course, everyone is dressed to the nines in their very best Armani or Gucci gear as they settle in for lunch at prices capable of bankrupting small nations. Well, I exaggerate a little, but you get the idea. Certainly we were a little taken aback at paying the equivalent of $15 AU for a coffee!

Expensive Portofino might be, but it is also as sensually beautiful as its pictures suggest, the tall narrow facades of the buildings curving around the northern side of a little bay jammed full of small boats, diminutive cousins to the sumptuous yachts the size of small cruise ships that are snugged up against the quays, and the bulk of the tree-covered hill on the opposite side of the harbour, capped by a castle, the oddly-named Castello Brown.

It is a bit of a slog to walk up to the Castello, but well worth it for the iconic view across the harbour. The castle itself dates back to the fifteenth century, and batteries of guns placed there played a role in repelling an attack by famed Genoese admiral Andrea Doria in 1575. Abandoned in the first part of the nineteenth century, the remains were purchased in 1867 by Montague Yeats-Brown, then English consul at Genoa. Apparently, he had admired the site from the deck of his yacht, the *Black Tulip*; if you are a rich Englishman seeing something you like from the deck of your yacht, of course you buy it, in this case for the princely sum of 7,000 lira, and build your own villa on the site, complete with extensive gardens. I suppose we must be thankful that at least he did so with good taste and a respect for the integrity of the older structure.

As I said at the beginning of the chapter, we were visiting the Italian Riviera slightly out of season. But we did come back two years later at the height of summer, travelling down by boat from Genoa with stops at the impossibly cute little seaside village of Camogli and the isolated bay at San Fruttuoso, where a tenth-century abbey looks benignly down on frolicking beachgoers crowding the sand that fringes the tiny bay. Both places were absolutely throbbing with tourists, and the boat was full of passengers on its last leg around the peninsula into Portofino.

This being pre-COVID, when cruise ships were considered as symbols of affluent excess rather than floating petri dishes, we didn't pay any particular attention to a big MSC-lines ship moored in the bay, other than the usual fascination with her sheer size. The ferry slowed and cruised into the harbour, and as soon as we disembarked we realised there was something a bit different from our last visit, and it wasn't just that the waterfront and restaurants were much more crowded. As we walked along the quayside, restaurant after restaurant seemed to be filled with groups of men, laughing and drinking their mid-afternoon Negronis and Camparis. And not just ordinary men; virtually all of them, young and old, were coiffured, barbered, immaculately dressed, and in every other way obviously gay.

You have probably guessed why in about the space of time that it took to read the last two sentences: the cruise ship in the harbour was hosting a gay cruise whose passengers had disembarked for their obligatory shore excursion to Portofino. It was all rather fabulous and just a little intimidating to watch literally thousands of gay men colonize the place, albeit just for a few hours. Not that their presence seemed to bother the locals in the least, who were taking it all in their usual calm stride.

Gay or not, the crowd were no different from any other cruise ship invasion. They had presumably been ferried ashore first thing that morning, had spent the forenoon roaming about the town buying a few souvenirs and over-priced lunches, and by the time we arrived they were pretty well ready to get back to their pampered luxury back on board, having 'done' Portofino. Not that I want to be too condescending on this point: we have done cruises too and have followed much the same routine in port. At least in places like Portofino there is a genuine economic benefit for a small town, unlike the more dubious value added (or subtracted) in places like Venice, where the cruise ship industry seems to contribute to overtourism without offering much financial compensation.

All in all, we were glad to have had the chance to visit the Italian Riviera in both seasons, and we enjoyed its charms without reservation. What we really needed, though, was another couple of million dollars in the bank. That way we could have fitted right in with the glamorous jet set, gone to all the right restaurants, and spent lazy afternoons lounging on the sun deck of a friend's fabulous yacht. Instead, like most ordinary people, we had to content ourselves with looking on vicariously, and pretending. But it was fun, nevertheless, and we always had our glamorous hotel to come back to at the end of the day, where the staff could be relied on to treat us in the style to which we would like to become accustomed.

# Chapter 16

# Surprising Turin

Turin was something of an afterthought when we planned our odyssey (if an odyssey can, properly speaking, *be* planned). To the extent that we thought of Turin at all, the associations were cars and football, neither of which were subjects that got our pulses racing. So when we had an unexpected gap in the itinerary, our only thought was that, since we were in northern Italy, a couple of weeks there seemed as good a way as any of filling in some time. But after two weeks there it seemed absurd that we never had Turin on our list as a highlight to be anticipated with the same delight as Rome, Venice, or Florence.

Like most European cities, the historic centre of Turin is a lived-in place. Built on the original neat grid bequeathed by the urban planners who designed the Roman city of Augusta Taurinum, most of the city's apartments are contained in eighteenth and nineteenth century buildings of a uniform five stories in height, six if you count the mansard roofs pierced with dormer windows. Many apartments have full length, Venetian-shuttered doors opening onto balconies that overhang the street, and the apartment buildings are usually arranged around an internal courtyard, which means that even a small apartment like ours got an abundance of light and airflow.

The city is also dotted with many small open-air spaces, piazzas and gardens, and as you walk around Turin, you can hardly go more than a couple of blocks before you come across a delightful little square, planted with trees in a formal design, manicured lawns and a fountain in the middle, where kids are at play and parents chat, all overlooked by bustling cafes and restaurants. At first this feels like a very human-scale place.

But then it strikes you that Turin is very self-consciously a royal capital, full of imperial architecture and imposing ceremonial spaces. The granddaddy of them all is the vast piazza Vittorio Veneto, reputed to be the largest in Europe, something you can easily believe if you stand in the middle and contemplate the acres of open space that recede in every direction, the restaurant umbrellas clinging to its edges as if people are afraid to venture into the centre.

Less ostentatious but just as grand is piazza San Carlo, which, with its colonnaded porticoes and twin churches at one end, has a formal elegance that rivals Piazza San Marco in Venice. Long, straight Via Po connects Vittorio Veneto with the third of Turin's grand open spaces, the piazza Castello, rather more organic in layout, with the royal palace on one side, the opera house on another and plonked right in the middle the oddity of the Palazzo Madama, a baroque facade tacked onto the original four-square castle that gives the square its name.

Speaking of palaces, Turin is full of them, and they are as monumental as any in Europe. Palazzo Madama faces the huge royal palace across the square, today home to an extensive art collection, and the Palazzo Carignano, birthplace of Italy's first king and the home of Piedmont's first parliament, is now the museum of Italian unification. And a little out of town, the Savoyards developed their own version of Versailles, the Venaria Reale; this enormous palace complex is one of the largest royal residences in the world. It was abandoned after Napoleon's conquest of Piedmont and fell into complete decay, but an extraordinary €235 million restoration project funded by the EU has resulted in the reincarnation of a truly astounding royal residence.

Back in the centre of Turin, almost every piazza, big and small, is decorated with a statue of one member or another of the house of Savoy, the dynasty that spent nearly a thousand years ascending the royalty ladder from counts to dukes, and eventually to kings of a region that included at various times Sardinia and Sicily, as well as modern Piedmont and bits of France and Switzerland. The House of Savoy also provided all four kings of a unified Italy after 1861; on the whole they are a martial lot, usually portrayed astride a horse, waving a sword at invisible and presumably vanquished enemies, severe and determined expressions stamped on their features.

Taken together, all these characteristics—the wide boulevards, the grand architecture and public places, the uniformity of the apartment buildings—have led to the common characterisation of Turin as an Italian Paris. I can see that—although for me the presence of iron balconies overlooking the street also evokes Nice, or Madrid, or Barcelona—but it is still very much an Italian city, if one that is very self-satisfied. An English expatriate writer who we met who lives in Turin put it well: 'Turin has always been so rich that the Torinese don't actually care much what outsiders think of them. For example, if they speak English to you, it's not because they have to, but because they want to'.

And when they don't want to speak English, they won't. We had first-hand experience of that when, waiting for a table outside a crowded restaurant, we found ourselves gazumped by an Italian couple who snagged the seats we had been promised, and when I tried to protest this treatment in my very limited Italian to a head waiter whose English had been perfectly adequate when we arrived, he suddenly seemed unable to communicate with me at all and reverted to shrugging his shoulders and ushering us to an inside table (not what we wanted at all) with a disdain that would have done a Parisian proud.

*

There might be lots of statues to the Savoyard monarchs in Turin, but the Torinese whose name is most celebrated all over Italy was not a king at all. Camille Benso, Count Cavour, was the corpulent, wily prime minister of the kingdom of Piedmont who was one of the most powerful driving forces behind the nineteenth-century movement to unify the Italian peninsula. With the on-again off-again of his king, the Victor Emmanuel whose statue graces many a piazza in Italy, Cavour's natural environment was the coffee shops in Piazza San Carlo, where he would regularly be seen, wreathed in cigar smoke and arms waving, as he plotted and planned or a unification that many Italians suspected was really just a grand power grab by the Piedmontese.

They weren't far wrong, although the origins of the drive to unify Italy, the *Risorgimento*, or 'Resurgence', go way back to the Renaissance. After a convoluted series of civil wars, by the end of the eighteenth century the Austrian Habsburg emperors were in effective control of most of Italy. Then Napoleon came along and threw them out, creating the Kingdom of Italy, with himself as its monarch—a significant moment, since this was the first time since the days of the Roman Empire that Italy had been politically united.

The Congress of Vienna put an end to all that after Napoleon fell from power, and reinstated Habsburg rule over the Italian states. But the idea of an Italian kingdom didn't quite go away, thanks to the efforts of a group of intellectuals and political leaders known as the *Carboneria*, and in 1848 an insurrection started in a very Italian way: the people of Lombardy decided to stop smoking cigars and playing the lottery, thereby depriving the Austrians of the tax revenue those things generated. More serious disturbances followed in Sicily,

Tuscany, and Milan. After that, things start to get a bit complicated, so bear with me while I try to tell the story in as straightforward a way as I can.

The following year, the king of what was then called Sardinia-Piedmont, Carlo Alberto, decided that the time had come for his country to lead the campaign for unification by declaring war against Austria; this, the first War of Independence, was a disaster that led to a stalemate. But Cavour, who was by then prime minister, provided the leadership to keep the cause alive. A second war of independence was fought in 1849, with the assistance of Napoleon III, the emperor of the French (and nephew of the first Napoleon). At the battles of Magenta and Solferino their combined forces succeeded in humiliating the Austrians, and the Piedmontese annexed Lombardy, Tuscany, and the other small states of northern Italy.

Thus enlarged, Piedmont was now the dominant power in northern Italy. But the job of unification was far from complete: Venice and her hinterland were still under Austrian control, the pope controlled the centre of the country as he had since the Renaissance, and the Franco-Italian Bourbon kings ruled what was called the Kingdom of the Two Sicilies, controlling the whole southern half of the country.

The final phase kicked off in 1860, when Giuseppe Garibaldi led his red-shirted army to invade Sicily, landing at Marsala on the west coast and storming his way across the island; by September that year he had invaded the mainland and seized Naples itself. In March 1861 the kingdom of Italy was proclaimed, and Piedmontese king Vittorio Emanuele II became the first Italian king. It wasn't quite a complete kingdom, however: the Veneto was still controlled by Austria, and the pope refused to surrender control of Rome. When the 1866 Austro-Prussian war broke out, the new Italian kingdom opportunistically allied with the Prussians, and was rewarded with the possession of Venice when the Austrians lost. Finally, in

1870, the last domino fell when Rome capitulated to the forces of Garibaldi, and Italy was at last a united kingdom.

Through all of this, Count Cavour was the central political figure. A supremely talented wheeler and dealer, he skilfully manoeuvred the cause between the competing visions of the other intellectual and political leaders of the movement, some of whom wanted a unitary republic, while others were in favour of a looser federation. Though an aristocrat, he had liberal views but distrusted the extremists of the left, and in office he charted a course between the two. Avuncular and charming in public, he could be dictatorial in the exercise of power.

Yet until his final years, his aim was never the unification of Italy, which he frequently derided as a nonsensical idea. While he travelled to France and Britain, countries he greatly admired, in Italy he never went south of Pisa. The objective of all his machinations was to create an enlarged Piedmont controlling the whole of the north of the country, and he often applied the handbrake to those like Garibaldi who had wider aims. It was only after the revolutionaries had defeated the regime in Naples and pushed to the borders of Rome that he genuinely embraced the cause; alas, he never lived to see the final unification of the peninsula, dying just three months after he was appointed as Italy's first prime minister in 1861, aged just fifty, in his beloved city of Turin.

Turin, naturally enough, became the first capital of the new kingdom, though it only kept that status for a few years as the government migrated first to Florence (an event that caused riots in Turin) and then, after 1870, to Rome. But it was long enough to spur the development of the grand, imperial city we see today, and it is hardly surprising that one of the city's biggest museums is dedicated to the *Risorgimento*, housed in the vast Palazzo Carignano. Here, every step of the reunification is traced in great detail, sometimes excruciatingly so. Apart from Cavour, the other great figures of the movement loom large: Giuseppe Mazzini, who provided the intellectual leadership of the movement; Massimo d'Azeglio, Cavour's predecessor who convinced the king to accept parliamentary government; and of course the soldier-statesman Giuseppe Garibaldi. All of them came from Piedmont (Garibaldi came from Nice, which was then part of the Savoyard kingdom, and Mazzini was born in Genoa, which was absorbed into Piedmont in 1815), and all of their names are celebrated not just in Turin, but all over Italy, where they adorn countless streets and squares.

*

The Torinese enthusiasm for celebrating their history didn't end with unification. With the arrival of a new century came the wonders of industrialisation, and Turin rapidly developed as a manufacturing centre. Among other industries Fiat and Lancia initiated the development of one of the most successful automotive industries in the world, and just a little out of town, on the banks of the Po not far from the former Fiat factory, the triumphs of that industry are celebrated in the exuberant National Automobile Museum.

Neither of us could be described as car buffs, but we did feel we had to make the trek along the river to go and see this huge museum. It was well worth the effort, and I would defy anyone not to be entertained and charmed by this place, which takes the visitor through the history of the Italian car industry by way of a series of highly innovative and evocative displays, with the usual Italian flair for visual design. One example: you don't just get the Italian version of the Kombi van, standing alone among a bunch of other cars; instead, it is surrounded by a picnic basket, card table covered with a tablecloth and set for lunch (complete with a bottle of Chianti), a pair of tennis racquets, and a set of luggage cases from the era, covered in travel stickers. We half expected the owners of the van to emerge from somewhere and settle down for their afternoon's lunch in front of us!

The new century also heralded the arrival of another industry, the movies. The locus for the Italian industry might have been Rome, but it is Turin that possesses the best museum to Italian cinema, another place that exceeded our expectations. It is housed in the Mole Antonelliana, the national symbol of Turin whose image graces the Italian two cent coin. A 167-metre tower originally intended to be a synagogue, it was never used as a place of worship, but instead became the Risorgimento Museum, a role it filled until 1938. Today the Mole (pronounced 'Mol-*ay*') offers panoramic views across the city to the Alps from a platform reached via a glass elevator that is drawn up through the cavernous interior of the dome, providing a remarkable if vertiginous perspective on the museum below.

That museum, the Museo Nazionale del Cinema, is not so much a museum as a temple to the art form, with an emphasis, naturally enough, on Italy's contributions. Beautifully and imaginatively creative, the museum takes the visitor on a journey from the very earliest moving images dating back to the seventeenth century—a carousel of illustrated cards that gives a flickering illusion of movement when it is rotated at high speed—through to reproductions of the sets of some of Italy's most famous films. In three or four hours there, we didn't have a dull moment.

Italian exploits in another field, archaeology, are celebrated in another big museum, the Museo Egizio. Personally, I tend to find Egyptian museums a bit of a bore—endless rows of expressionless statues and acres of ancient pots—but this one is very different. Superbly curated, it is the largest collection of Egyptian artifacts outside Cairo. The 37,000-item collection is organised and presented in such a way as to give a real insight into everyday life in Egypt, as well as the usual mummies and statues. There is also a fascinating section that brings to life an Italian archaeological expedition to Egypt, complete with vehicles, tents and camp gear.

Needless to say, Turin has also collected a lot of art over the centuries, displayed in galleries big and small, and in the grand Savoyard palaces. There's an excellent modern art scene, too, focused on GAM, the huge Galleria Civica d'Arte Moderna e Contemporanea, with a huge permanent and rotating collection.

At any other time of year, visiting all these museums and galleries would have taken all of our time, and we had a fair go at seeing as many as we could. But it was the end of May, and the weather was warming up, so we also had to spend some time with the rest of the city's citizens, not to mention the thousands of students who come to Turin to study, enjoying the delights of the lovely Parco Valentino, which extends southwards along the banks of the River Po (the Po, incidentally, is Italy's longest river, rising in the Cottian Alps and flowing some 652 kilometres through Italy's richest agricultural region before emptying into the Adriatic near Venice). Apart from providing a great place to walk and maybe stop for a coffee or gelato at one of the little kiosks that line the riverbank, the park also hosts a quaint fake medieval village, complete with fake medieval villagers, which was quite fun to explore.

*

You might conclude, reading all of the above, that Turin is the perfect Italian city. Of course, it is not. What we saw was what most tourists see, a carefully constructed image of prosperity and elegance; what they don't see are the industrial suburbs with their miles of drab apartment blocks that lie beyond the Centro Storico, from which Turin gets its reputation as an industrial city. In this respect, Turin is no different from most other Italian urban centres; it is as if, after the war, there was a kind of devil's bargain struck with developers, who could do what they liked outside the historic core. Even so, Turin's reputation as an industrial city has been exaggerated, and we were genuinely surprised to find such a charming and attractive destination.

The last word for this chapter perhaps goes to our friend Rita Erlich, the Melbourne food writer, who said to us, long after we had returned, that she judges whether people really 'get' Italy by their reaction to Turin. I think we passed her test.

# Chapter 17

# The Lakes: Italy's Playground

The names of the series of lakes great and small that lie below the foothills of the Alps are well known to most: the big three, Como, Garda, Maggiore, and their smaller sisters Iseo, Varese, Lugano and Orta. They are places where the Italians of the north go to play, messing about in boats, swimming and sunbathing, paragliding and dashing across the water on jet-skis. Beautiful and rugged, their surrounding hills create a backdrop that is hard to rival anywhere for sheer beauty.

Of the three big lakes, Como is probably the most famous; certainly it is the most glamorous. Shaped like an upside-down letter Y, the lake has a surface area of some 150 square kilometres, and is about 150 metres deep. The town of Como sits at the bottom of the southwestern branch of the lake, and the more industrial centre of Lecco is at the bottom of the southeastern branch. At the junction of the three arms of the lake there are three of the most beautiful towns on the lake: Bellagio, which sits right on the junction, Menaggio, over on the western shore, and on the eastern side the little village of Varenna.

The latter was to be our destination for the first of our several encounters with lake Como, all the way back in 2004, when we travelled to Italy with our friends Russell and

Michael. After a week in Paris, we had caught the train to make the long journey across France and through the Alps to Milan, where we picked up a car to drive north. Since this was back in the days before every phone had a built-in satellite navigation system, we were dependant on the old-fashioned method of navigation: paper maps spread across the knees of a navigator in the right-hand seat of the car. Russell claimed the driver's seat, and Michael was to be our navigator. Meanwhile, Robert and I settled into the back seats and were thankful to have no responsibilities at all.

Of course, the inevitable happened. Though getting out of Milan is a fairly straightforward exercise, we managed to get confused and, temporarily at least, lost. That provoked an outburst of hysterics in the front of the car and necessitated a change of navigator (to me) in order to preserve a sullen peace for the rest of the drive. It usually takes about an hour and a half to get from Milan to Lake Como, but our little mishap cost us best part of an extra hour, and it was early evening by the time we arrived in Varenna, and checked into our accommodation, the Hotel Olivedo.

We were to become very fond of the Olivedo. A fairly typical family-run hotel, its yellow-painted liberty-style four stories stand right at the edge of the lake, immediately opposite the ferry terminal. At ground floor, there is a small reception area and the hotel restaurant, whose outside tables are protected from the sun by green blinds. Above, little balconies allow guests to watch the ferries come and go or just gaze across the still waters of the lake to the twinkling lights of Bellagio and Menaggio. Or, if they so choose, they can easily close the green shutters and retire to their well-appointed rooms and have an afternoon nap.

The proprietor of this establishment was a lady of indeterminate middle years named Laura, who ran the place with a quietly tyrannical efficiency, assisted by her mother, who was in her eighties and as sprightly as a woman half her age. Bespectacled and matronly, Laura possessed a sharp wit and tongue to match, and immediately dubbed us her 'fancy boys', an affectionate term she deployed with a flourish every evening when we sat down for dinner.

The dinner menu was fairly simple: a standard antipasto plate, followed by a soup or pasta (the menu offered only one of each), and finally a choice of veal, usually the crumbed veal cutlet called a Cotoletto Milanese, or fish. When we asked what kind of fish, we were laconically told it was 'lake fish'. Oh, and Tiramisu to finish. And that was it, accompanied of course by substantial volumes of cheap red or white wine. Simple, but always perfectly cooked and presented at the table with all the formality of a five-star restaurant.

As I said, the rooms were comfortable and quite spacious for a small hotel, though the building being tall and narrow we did have to climb several creaking flights of stairs to get to them. Posted on one of the landings of that central staircase was a curious sign that was clearly designed to fulfil the requirements common to every hotel in the world to provide instructions for the safety of their guests in the event of a fire. Usually this involves some floor plans and detailed directions to emergency exits and the like, but Laura had simplified things considerably. 'If there is a fire,' the sign read, 'you shout Laura! Laura! And I come running.' We giggled every time we saw this sign, not quite sure whether Laura was serious or just taking the piss.

The fact that the hotel was opposite the ferry terminal was to prove something of a blessing, since we made so much use of the ferries to get around. But it was also a constant source of free entertainment, as we sat in the restaurant having a drink and watching the knots of tourists waiting to get aboard the assorted vessels that ploughed their way on the triangular service between Varenna, , Bellagio and Menaggio. The routine was always the same: once arriving passengers had disembarked, a crew member would announce its next destination at the top of his voice, in a rather bored drawl, 'Men-agio! Bell-agio!'; this became the sound-track to our stay, as familiar as the frenzied cries of the gulls and the murmured splash of the water against the jetty.

Most of the ferries were workmanlike affairs, either the drive-on drive-off vehicular type, or straightforward passenger boats with an enclosed cabin and an open upper deck, although several times a day we were graced by the arrival of a fast hydrofoil that served the more distant destinations around the lake which would make a showy, splashy turn before slowing and settling back into the water; 'typically Italian' was the irresistible thought that came into our minds.

Of the big northern lakes, Como is the most spectacular; it is not as huge as Lake Garda, nor is it as varied as Lake Maggiore, but it does possess a more dramatic coastline, mile after mile of forested mountains that seem to drop precipitously into the water, only grudgingly allowing enough space for a single ribbon of road to cling to the shore. Getting around by ferry is almost the only sensible way to travel between the important places on the lake, and certainly the only way to get a glimpse of all those villas of the rich and famous for which Lake Como is renowned. Today, you can hop on a ferry across to Bellagio, the glamour-queen of this part of the lake and visit the Villa Serbelloni and the Villa Melzi d'Eril, then head across to Villa Carlotta to look at its gardens and a splendid collection of Canova sculptures, continue down the lake past the terraced splendours of Villa Balbianello and Villa d'Este at before finally alighting in Como.

All this concentrated glamour has inevitably attracted the modern-day equivalent of the wealthy aristocrats and industrialists who built all these villas: movie stars and other assorted celebrities. The most famous is probably actor George Clooney, but Madonna, Sylvester Stallone, Julian Lennon, Richard Branson and John Kerry have all owned houses on the lake's shores at various times. As a result of all this attention, everyone who comes to lake Como turns into a celebrity-spotter, an exercise that returns frequent false positives; when seen from a distance, any young-ish looking blond male accompanied by an equally blond beauty was magically transformed into Brad Pitt and Jennifer Anniston (this was 2004, remember).

After a day sampling the delights of the lake, we would return, sunburned and exhausted, for an aperitif on the terrace of the Olivedo while the sun dropped behind the mountains on the opposite side of the lake. Darkness fell with surprising speed until little was visible except the shimmering lights of Bellagio and Menaggio and the slow-moving masthead lights of the ferries as they made their patient rounds. Laura would drop by for a chat with her fancy boys, occasionally accompanied by her mother and their little dog, and if we weren't eating at the hotel that night, she would ply us with suggestions of other restaurants around Varenna, most of whose proprietors seemed to be related to her.

Though we were only there for a week, we became very fond of this little lakeside town, with its tiny church and traditional piazza, its unexpected views down the narrow lanes between rows of tall houses that framed a shimmering slither of lake, and its charming cafes perched along the shoreline, a perfect place from which to contemplate life from beneath a vine-covered pergola over a coffee and gelato.

As for the Olivedo, I am sure it is still there, and Laura is still welcoming guests with her lopsided and laconic smile. Certainly it was unchanged when we made a return visit a decade after our first acquaintance with the place, and very little had changed. The restaurant menu was a little more extensive, Laura's mother was semi-retired (though she was still doing the hotel's laundry), but otherwise it was exactly the same. Although Laura will no doubt retire someday, I fondly hope that whoever takes custody of the place won't change a thing.

*

Lake Garda, which is some 180 kilometres to the east of Lake Como, is the biggest freshwater lake in Italy, covering some 370 square kilometres, and because it is designated as Italy's emergency water supply catchment, very little industrial development has been allowed around its shores. For that reason it has become very popular with Italians as a holiday destination, who come here to take advantage of the mountain breezes to windsurf, or to take their kids to the sprawling Gardaland theme park near Peschiera del Garda at the southeastern corner of the lake.

Our visit to Like Garda was an excursion by train from Verona. The train deposited us at the pleasant little town of Desenzano, and from there we caught the first of many ferries, across to the lake's most emblematic town, Sirmione, which sits on a little peninsula jutting northward right in the middle of the southern shore. Occupying such a strategic position inevitably meant that over time this long narrow tongue of land would sprout fortifications, and the first thing you see as the ferry approaches is the rather fairy-tale Castello Scaligero, whose construction was started in 1277. The castle is a masterpiece of medieval military engineering, its formidable fortifications surrounded by moats providing protection to the equally fortified harbour beyond, from which the Scaliger fleet could control the lake. It was also a severe test for our knee-joints as we climbed to the top of the towers to enjoy the expansive views.

After a swim and a close encounter with some of the tamest swans I think I have ever seen, we rejoined the ferry for the next leg of our trip up the lake to the little town of Torri del Benaco. Our handsome young landlord in Verona had told us that

Torri was a nice and quiet spot, and a little off the beaten Lake Garda track, and as the ferry slid into a picture-perfect little semicircular harbour that sheltered a fleet of bobbing fishing boats, we congratulated ourselves for having taken his advice.

At some point, Torri must have been a place of some strategic significance, since the della Scala rulers of Verona built a substantial castle overlooking the port, one of several they erected up and down the lake. Only one wall of the original castle remains intact, but it must once have been a formidable fortification; today it provides a dramatic backdrop to the harbour, particularly at night when its old stones are floodlit. North of the harbour, the rest of the old town is strung out along the lake, squeezed between the main road and the *lungomare*, the broad pedestrian walkway lined with cafes and restaurants that follows the lake shore; in between the two is a pedestrianised street, Corso Dante Alighieri, which at the height of the summer season is filled with tourists and Italian families enjoying their *passeggiata*. Behind, wooded hills that hem the town against the lakeshore rise steeply to the town of Albisano, some two hundred metres above. All in all, as pretty a town as you could hope to see anywhere.

Torri is one of a dozen towns dotted around this vast lake, all devoted to meeting the needs of pleasure-seeking Italians coming north to escape the summer's heat and spend some time having fun on, in and above the water. Most are pleasant though undistinguished places, with little to see of any interest beyond the usual water-side activities. But there was one that I was particularly fascinated by, a place whose very name is evocative and which has a surprisingly important place in the long saga of Italy—the town of Salo.

With its population of 10,000 or so, Salo has had the usual chequered history, veering between subjugation by various overlords and brief periods of existence as an independent commune. But the most famous, or perhaps infamous, episode in that history was the two years during which it was the capital of the so-called Italian Social Republic, from 1943 to 1945.

In July 1943, the Grand Fascist Council overthrew and arrested their erstwhile leader, Benito Mussolini. By this stage the war was going pretty badly, as the humiliating rout of the Italian forces in North Africa was followed up by allied landings in Sicily. The dictator was imprisoned, and the new government began negotiations for an armistice; when that was secured, the Germans mounted a daring raid to extract Mussolini from his place of incarceration, annexed the northern half of the country, and installed him as the head of a new republic, the RSI, or *Republicca Sociale Italia*. Unable to return to Rome, which was too close to the advancing allied lines, the capital of the new government was established at Salo, and the RSI became known colloquially as the Salo Republic.

It must have been a rather surreal experience for the inhabitants of this quiet, elegant lakeside town when its *commune* was taken over as the seat of government and its graceful villas were co-opted as headquarters for the various departments of state. Self-important officials shuttled between them to meetings at which they occupied themselves designing new uniforms and preparing propaganda campaigns. The dictator himself meanwhile reviewed his personal guards and recorded bombastic speeches to be broadcast to an ever-diminishing audience of fascist faithful.

For it was in every respect a puppet government. Mussolini himself was kept under virtual house arrest; despite being nominally president and prime minister of the republic, his movements were controlled, and his communications were monitored by his German masters. Still, he tried to maintain the illusion that the RSI was the legitimate and independent government of Italy even as the allies pushed ever further north against bitter resistance from the Wehrmacht. Milan, he announced, would be the Italian Stalingrad; he himself would 'fight to the last Italian', though there were not all that many Italians still fighting as, deeply demoralised, they succumbed to the onslaught of the allies from the south.

At the end of April 1945, it was clear even to the delusional former *Duce* that the war was lost, and he fled from Salo, accompanied by his mistress, Clara Petracci. Their flight was to be a short one: just two days later they were identified and arrested by partisans at the village of Dongo, on Lake Como, taken to another village, Giulino de Mezzegra, where they were both executed. Their bodies were then taken to Milan, where they were hung upside-down from the canopy of an Esso petrol station.

The Salo Republic remains one of those historical footnotes that have a certain fascination to professional historians, but which are otherwise forgotten. Today there are desultory reminders of the republic's brief, flickering existence around the town—the odd plaque and a small museum—and in every other respect it is as if Salo has chosen to forget that it was once the capital of Italy (well, half of it, anyway). But the episode obviously did not completely disappear from the consciousness of post-war Italians. Several prominent leaders on the far-right of the political spectrum were associated with RSI in one way or another. And when in 1975 Pier Paolo Pasolini came to adapt the Marquis de Sade's *120 Days of Sodom*, he set it in the Republic of Salo, as did Roberto Begnini when he made *Life is Beautiful* in 1997. Clearly, this last glimmer of fascism still exercises its spell on the collective imagination.

\*

Long and sinuous Lake Maggiore has its head in Switzerland and its feet in Italy. Locarno, at the lake's northern end, is famous for its eponymous film festival, during which it is the very image of Swiss neatness, every street clean and tidy, and flowers everywhere, in pots, in planter boxes, and lining the little parks. Arona, at the southern end, possesses a lovely old town fronting the lake, and the usual Italian urban eyesore of a town behind. And between the two, about halfway up the lake on its western side is the town of Stresa, a town of genteel grand hotels.

As you drive in from neighbouring Baveno they are lined up along the lake shore, one after another, their very names proclaiming their grandeur: the Hotel Royal Stresa, the Grand Hotel Bristol, the Grand Hotel des Iles Borromees, and the Regina Palace. Every one of them fits the image of a European Grand Hotel, starting with the manicured lawns and artistically planted flower-beds, proceeding through the imposing entrance where a uniformed and gloved doorman sweeps open the brass-handled doors to admit you into the entrance foyer where guests are registered and their baggage dealt with by staff who are efficient and polite to a fault before going up the grand staircase to the luxury on the floors above,.

This, you instantly realise, is a place where the discreetly wealthy come to holiday. Stresa is not a town of glitz or overt, self-absorbed glamour. Rather, you have the sense that it has been welcoming well-heeled visitors for a very long time, and it doesn't see the need to make a fuss about it. And though mass tourism never takes no for an answer, the more modern hotels constructed after the war have, unusually for Italy, been built in a sympathetic style and sit comfortably alongside those built for the pleasure of the rich and privileged of the nineteenth century.

Our hotel, chosen to meet that mysterious combination of price and comfort which is unique to every traveller, was just such a 'modern' creation, if you can call a hotel built in 1954 modern. The Hotel Astoria stands between the Hotel Palma, a place of similar vintage, and the fine old pile of the Regina Palace. Set back a little from the street, it looks out to the lake across an expanse of lawn which in summer is dotted with guests comfortably sprawled on rattan lounges, taking in the sunshine. At ground level there is a glassed-in restaurant and every room on the five accommodation floors above has a balcony from which to contemplate the comings and goings on the lake.

One of the curiosities of this kind of Italian hotel is the presence of long-term residents, usually elderly people who either live in the hotel all year round or do so for the whole summer. The Astoria had its clutch of these, mostly immaculately turned-out old ladies who could be seen at any time of day enjoying an aperitif, playing cards, or just sitting and sharing gossip. And, as I discovered one morning at breakfast, they have privileges. Though the breakfast room was almost empty, when I planted myself at a particular table that I thought had a nice view across the lake, one of the waiters hurried over and informed me, *sotto voce*, that I could not sit there, because it was one of the tables informally reserved for 'one of the old ladies', though there was no sign that indicated that this was the case. But like any polite guest, I made no demur and shifted myself a couple of tables across to one with almost the same outlook.

Most of the old ladies, and the rather fewer old gentlemen, come from Milan, much as the wealthier set from that city have been doing for a century or more, no doubt attracted by the sunshine and gentle warmth afforded by the town's north-facing location. But tourists have also long been coming to Stresa to visit another man-made wonder—the Borromean Islands, which are clearly visible from the waterfront, and which at the peak of the tourist season are served by an endless convoy of boats that turn the placid waters of the lake into a scene reminiscent of the D-Day landings.

The islands are named after, and still belong to, the Borromeo family, who first came to prominence as merchants as far back as 1300 (the origin of their name, a corruption of 'Buon Romei' indicates they were originally from Rome). A hundred and fifty years later they were successful bankers who followed the well-worn path to nobility by marrying into a patrician family, becoming counts of Arona from 1446, counts of Peschiera in 1461, and Marquesses of Angera in 1623. In the process they built up their landholdings around Lake Maggiore, becoming so powerful that by the fifteenth century they were running a semi-independent state within the duchy of Milan, a status that was ended (as so many were) by the intervention of Napoleon in 1797. Though somewhat impoverished by this event, by 1916 they were still wealthy enough and important enough to be given the titles of Princes of Angera by the king of Italy.

Nor were their ambitions confined solely to the temporal sphere: between 1538 and 1881, they also managed to produce no less than seven cardinals, the most famous of whom, Carlo Borromei, was canonised in 1610; a huge statue of the saint now stands over the family's ancestral town of Arona, one arm extended in benediction. An austere and humourless man, he was a champion of the counter-Reformation, the catholic church's campaign to reassert itself after the ravages of the Lutheran-inspired insurrection against papal supremacy.

There are actually five islands dotted across this middle stretch of the lake, though only three are visited regularly today. The furthest and largest of them is Isola Madre, the site of the sixteenth century Palazzo Borromeo, beautiful in itself but also famous for its peacock-inhabited gardens designed in 'the English style' which seeks to create an ordered version of the countryside. Back closer to Stresa, Isola dei Pescatore ('Fishermen's Island') is the only one of the three that is inhabited all year round, though it only has twenty-five or so permanent residents; having neither monuments and nor gardens, the former fisher-families now mostly earn their income running small hotels, cute waterfront restaurants, and tourist shops catering to the endless stream of visitors.

But without doubt the most enchanting and spectacular of the three islands is Isola Bella. Its name is a cute play on words, not only meaning 'Beautiful Island', but also echoing the name of Isabella d'Adda, the wife of Carlo III Borromei, who in 1632 began the construction of a grand palazzo on what had been nothing more than a barren rock. The palazzo is indeed grand, but it is the gardens that are the real glory of the island. Inaugurated in 1671, they are an exquisite example of Italian Renaissance garden design, all symmetry and artfully designed perspective which reaches a crescendo in a baroque confection of niches and statues surrounding a pyramidal platform at the island's easternmost point. From here, there are wonderful views back to Stresa and the surrounding hills, and if you want a coffee with a view to die for, that can be had in the island's cafe, located in a turret on one corner of the pyramid.

Apart from the Isole Borromee, Lake Maggiore has many other attractions. Arona possesses one of the cutest waterfronts you will find anywhere; across the other side from the lake is the perfect Renaissance fortress, the Rocca di Angera; and if you can time your visit right, Locarno in film festival season is filled with the kind of buzz that only devotees of the silver screen can create. It's not surprising that when I am asked in casual conversations which of the Italian lakes that I like the best, I usually plump for Lago Maggiore. It is not as snobby as Como, nor as grand as Garda, but its towns and villages have a relaxed gentility about them that is very appealing. Still, that is a personal view, and I think Maggiore wins the competition only by the barest of whiskers. The question even splits our household, since Robert is more of a proponent of the sophistication of Lake Como. In any case, my message is: if you haven't been to the lakes, go! And if you have, I am happy to debate their pros and cons over a glass of prosecco any time you like.

# Chapter 18

# Bologna: Red, Clever and Fat

If nicknames are a mark of affection, Bologna must be beloved, for the city has no less than three monikers: *La Rossa* ('The Red'), *La Dotta* ('The Learned') and *La Grassa* ('The Fat'). And beloved Bologna certainly is: ask an Italian which is their favourite city, and many will nominate the attractive and uncomplicated capital of the vast province of Emilia-Romagna, that great swathe of flat land north of the Apennines through which the Po makes its steady way to the sea. Though a flourishing and diversified industrial centre, the city's heart is one of the largest historic centres in Europe, home to about a third of the million or so people who live in the greater Bologna area. Despite the considerable ravages of the second world war, careful restoration projects starting in the 1970's have left a city that is both functional and beautiful.

One source of one of Bologna's nicknames is apparent from the minute you step out of the train station, for red is the predominant colour of the buildings, in every shade from a near-pink to a deep terracotta, a colour preference that goes back to the middle-ages thanks to the use of local clays to make the bricks from which the city is built. At the city's heart is the appropriately named Piazza Maggiore, a noble square surrounded by the usual vast cathedral to the south, the Palazzo d'Accursio, the town hall, to the west, the equally commanding Palazzo del Podesta to the north, and a long colonnaded arcade on the remaining side, behind which lie the grid of narrow streets which were once the heart of the city's markets. Thus, the religious, temporal and mercantile face off against each other across the piazza, a configuration that, though hardly unique, seems particularly apt for a city whose history is one of constant oscillations between these three poles.

Absorbed into the Lombard kingdom after the end of the Byzantines in northern Italy, by the twelfth century Bologna was more or less autonomous under loose imperial rule and was a substantial mercantile centre of some ten thousand people. So many were the visitors to the city that the authorities ordered the construction of porticoes along the streets to provide them with shelter and a place to sleep; constructed initially of wood before they were eventually replaced by the stone arcades we see today, they had to be a minimum of six feet deep so as to enable a full-grown man to stretch out his full length. Though most modern visitors have access to much better quality sleeping options than their medieval counterparts, the colonnades still provide shelter from sun and rain for the Bolognese as they bustle about their daily business.

Life in medieval Bologna cannot have been entirely peaceful, however, if the existence of twenty or so fortified towers within the old city's boundaries is any indication. Estimates vary, but by the middle of the twelfth century it is thought that there were between eighty and a hundred such towers, each a robust fortified residence. Quite why they were constructed is something of a mystery, but Bologna was by now becoming a cockpit for the long-running struggle for supremacy between the pope and the Holy Roman Emperor, and it is possible that they were constructed to provide protection to the city's prominent families during the periodic conflicts that this rivalry provoked. Whatever the cause of this tower-building spree, by the middle of the thirteenth century the need for them seems to have passed, and they began to be demolished. Of the twenty that remain, the most famous are the two that stand at the end of Via Rizzoli, both leaning at rather surprisingly drunken angles, and which are now one of Bologna's most beloved symbols.

Our apartment in Bologna was also on Via Rizzoli, and it had a brilliant view across to Piazza Nettuno and the facade of another palazzo behind whose walls one of the more melancholy episodes of the long papal-imperial struggle was played out. Emperor Frederick II was one of the more extraordinary figures in the history of the empire; though heir to the German Hohenstaufen dynasty, he was born in sunny Sicily and grew up in that exotic brew of Christian-Islamic-Jewish culture and remained throughout his life more Italian than German at heart. Multilingual, a scholar as well as a soldier, Frederick had a very modern, secular outlook on life that put him at odds with a papacy bent on holy war against the Islamic infidel. He spent much of his thirty-year reign in conflict with various popes, who excommunicated him and pronounced him the Antichrist.

Though Frederick married three times and had seven legitimate heirs, he also had several mistresses who bore him a number of illegitimate children, one of whom was Enzo, the son of a rather obscure woman known only by her Christian name, Adelaide. Said to have a strong physical resemblance to his father, Enzo shared Frederick's love of culture and soon became the emperor's favourite child. Becoming king of Sardinia by marriage in 1238, he faithfully supported his father's wars against the papacy and the Lombard League (of which Bologna was a leading member), the alliance that the pope had assembled to resist him. In 1249, the thirty-year-old Enzo was captured in battle and brought to Bologna where he was imprisoned; his captivity lasted until his death, twenty-two years later, and he spent all those years behind the walls of the fine medieval palace that now bears his name, the Palazzo Re Enzo.

During all this time, the Bolognese commune was sturdily independent, but that independence was weakened by infighting among the city's leading families, which created an opportunity for the pope to impose his rule on the city. Various revolts over the following century failed to throw off the papal yoke, but eventually the Bentivoglio family, who curiously enough claimed descent from King Enzo, established themselves as the rulers of a state that was all but independent. Pope Julius II put an end to that in 1506, initiating a long period of clerical rule and economic decline as the city was neglected by successive popes and consigned to indifferent administrators more intent on extracting customs duties from the merchants than fostering economic growth.

After a brief interruption when Napoleon turned up in 1796 and incorporated Bologna into the Cisalpine Republic, the city fell back into clerical torpor after the Congress of Vienna restored the status quo. Unsurprisingly, the Bolognese voted enthusiastically to join the new Italian state in 1860, the shrewd capitalists among them recognising the opportunities that a national market would bring. They were right, and the city's fortunes improved dramatically as industrial development took off. Paradoxically though, this was also when the seeds were laid for the growth of a strong left-leaning political movement, and Bologna began to earn a second basis for its 'red' nickname.

The years 1919-1920 are known in Italian history as the *Biennio Rosso* (the 'Two Red Years'), when over a million industrial and agricultural workers engaged in more than 3,500 strikes, led by the newly formed Socialist party. The inevitable reaction came as the city's traditionally moderate elites turned in desperation to Mussolini and his new Fascist Party. After they came to national power in 1922, the new regime poured money and investment into Bologna, which became an industrial powerhouse in the inter-war years. Alas, that made the city vulnerable when the tide of the second world war turned, and the bombs began to fall, seriously damaging the historic centre.

After the armistice of 1943, Bologna became a centre for partisan resistance against the German occupiers, something that is commemorated with great poignancy on the walls of the Palazzo d'Accursio in the form of photos of the heartbreakingly young partisan patriots who were killed by the Germans during the occupation. Liberation and the end of the war saw a resumption of economic growth, but also the resurgence of socialist politics. From 1945 to 1999 the city returned to its red roots and elected a succession of communist and socialist mayors. Sadly, much of this period also coincided with the 'Years of Lead', when Italy was racked by spasms of political violence, of which the worst was the terrible bombing of the Bologna railway station by a neo-fascist group in August 1980, when 85 people were killed and another 200 injured.

With this history of stubborn, tenacious independence, it is no surprise that political activism is never far from the surface in modern Bologna. Mind you, the word 'protest' probably conveys entirely the wrong connotation for political activity in Italy, which usually resembles a particularly noisy street party, with lots of cheerful, chattering people chanting slogans that seem to be no more menacing than those shouted by the happy fans of a winning football team. Indeed, it is often hard to tell the difference between a political rally and a family festival. I remember once walking into a piazza in Florence to be confronted by a large crowd of people, mostly families, talking and eating and drinking while their children played on fairground rides specially set up for the occasion; most people were wearing red shirts, and some desultory attention was being paid to a speaker on a platform at one end of the piazza, which were the only clues that this was in fact a rally for the Communist Party of Italy!

*

Bologna is the home of the world's oldest university, which hosts some 82,000 students and nearly 3,000 academic staff, and it is this that earns it the second of its three nicknames—*La Dotta*, ('The Learned'). Students are everywhere, not just in the north-eastern quadrant of the historic centre where the university itself is located, but can be seen all over the city, filling the cafes and walking or cycling the streets. Compared to many other major Italian cities, Bologna often feels incredibly young.

Yet the university of Bologna itself claims to be the oldest in the world, founded in 1088. Its initial focus was on canon and secular law, and so it is no surprise to learn that Bologna University numbers no less than four popes among its alumni, and one saint (Carlo Borromei), while Dante Alighieri, Albrecht Durer, Petrarch, Torquato Tasso, and Umberto Ecco are among the artists and writers who have graduated from Bologna. In the twentieth century, Guglielmo Marconi, Pier Paolo Pasolini, and Romani Prodi all served on the university's faculty, and today it is still one of the most prestigious and important universities in the world, and certainly the leading Italian academic institution.

Unsurprisingly, wealthy and learned Bologna also hosts a vibrant artistic culture. There are of course the usual array of churches and chapels that are home to many fine frescoes, and there are several excellent traditional galleries that exhibit Gothic, Renaissance and Mannerist art. Local lads, the Carraci brothers Ludovico, Annibale and Agostino, were at the heart of the Bolognese School of painting in the sixteenth and seventeenth centuries, founding one of the country's first art academies in 1582.

But Bologna also has a very fine modern art gallery, called MAMBO (Museo d'Arte Moderna di Bologna), where we discovered the work of yet another local hero, Giorgio Morandi (1890-1964). Morandi never married, living with his sisters in an apartment in Bologna for his whole life. His oeuvre was still-life painting, mostly involving arrangements of various kinds of jars, vases and other containers, and landscape paintings of the countryside around Grizzana, a village outside Bologna where he built a summer house. His painting style is flat and modernist, and dominated by pastel colours, to my mind somewhat derivative but nevertheless distinctive in approach and subject matter.

Morandi exercised such a fascination on Robert's mind that he undertook one hot sunny day to go and make the pilgrimage to the country house, which is today decked out as a museum. Splendid idea, except that, as it turned out, the railway station was down in the valley, and the village of Grizzana was on top of a hill. No buses were in evidence, so he set off to walk to the village—two hours and all uphill. Then when he got there, the place seemed to be closed! Robert, however, is never deterred by such trivialities, and he interrupted some locals who were enjoying a lunch party in the garden outside their house to ask for their help (I might add that Robert's Italian which never did advance much beyond the rudimentary, was at this stage of our travels almost non-existent, so it must have been an amusing exchange).

Eventually, they helped him find the rather surprised curator of the museum, who opened it up and showed him round. The house has been left almost exactly as it was when the painter died in 1964, which Rob later told me was a rather strange and eerie experience. The bemused curator, who had probably never encountered a tourist as determined as Robert, drove him back to the station in a typically generous Italian gesture.

Most Italians are very attached to and proud of their place of origin, and of their local heroes, whether it be football players, artists, or musicians, and Bologna is no different. We got a sense of the emotional attachment they have to one of their high achievers when we went to an outdoor concert in the Piazza Maggiore. The performers were the orchestra of the Teatro Pubblico di Bologna (the city's opera company) conducted by their director Ezio Bosso, a rather remarkable man who suffered from a type of motor neurone disease. His physical frailty was obvious—the illness had paralysed him from the waist down, his fingers and wrists were swathed in bandages, and his speech was halting. Yet when those fingers touched the piano, and when he was directing the orchestra, he was transformed, the face projected on the huge screen was close to ecstasy, and the orchestra responded to produce beautiful, beautiful music. Watching all this was both moving and humbling, and it was clear from the reaction of the audience that all of Bologna was in love with him. Sadly, Bosso died in May 2020 from the complications of his illness.

\*

When they aren't studying or making good-natured mayhem in the streets, Bologna's students, like students everywhere, supplement their income by working in the city's restaurants and bars, where the source of its third nickname, *La Grassa* ('The Fat'), is proudly celebrated in a rich culinary tradition that draws on the agricultural wealth of the Po Valley. Via Pescherie Vecchie ('Old Fishmongers Street') is the central street of the old market quarter of Bologna, a little quadrilateral that is at the heart of the Bolognese food culture, filled with butchers, fishmongers, fruit and vegetable vendors, small cafes and smart restaurants. Wandering in and out of the shops in this area is guaranteed to enchant even the most jaded of gourmets, and unlike many such areas in other cities, it is clear that this is not just a tourist precinct, judging from the number of locals who throng the streets every day.

Food is as important to Italians as family and football, so it is no surprise to learn that every region has its culinary specialties to which the inhabitants are very attached and very determined to protect and promote. For example, navigating the pasta minefield involves a kind of linguistic gymnastics; thus, while most Italian pasta names end with the masculine plural suffixes *–ini, -elli, -illi, -etti,* the feminine plurals *-ine, -elle,* might be used to convey the sense of 'little'; or with *-oni,* meaning 'large'. Thus humble, regular spaghetti has its larger and smaller counterparts, *spaghettoni* and *spaghettini,* each served with particular variations of sauce according to rules that are as arcane as the laws of freemasonry—and to the outsider just as opaque.

A Bolognese example is *tortellini,* which is a meat-filled round pasta with a distinctive flap on one side, and which should not be confused with *tortelloni,* which has the same shape, but is considerably larger. But this is just the tip of the iceberg: in Bologna, *tortellini* are served floating in chicken broth, while *tortelloni* are usually filled with ricotta and spinach, not meat, and served with butter and sage. You don't want to confuse the two and suggesting that *tortelloni* might be served in broth is liable to cause an outbreak of headshaking among the matrons at the pasta shop.

Incidentally, there are some charming legends explaining the particular shape of *tortellini.* One, somewhat prosaic, says simply that *tortellini* was created by an unknown cook who moulded the pasta in the shape of the navel of a Bolognese woman. More fancifully, another story involves Lucrezia Borgia, the notorious (and very beautiful) daughter of pope Alexander VI. Apparently Lucrezia was travelling and arrived in the small town of Castelfranco Emilia, near Modena. The innkeeper was captivated by Lucrezia, and in the night, he couldn't help himself—he peeked through the keyhole into her room. But all he could see was her navel; undeterred, and in typical Italian fashion, he turned his desire into inspiration, making a new pasta in the shape of Lucrezia's navel in homage.

Of course, one can't talk about Bolognese cuisine without exploring its most famous and eponymous dish, *Spaghetti Bolognese*, shortened in Australia to 'Spag Bog' or 'Spag Bol'. In fact, this popular combination of spaghetti and a rich, meat and tomato sauce is only barely connected to Bologna. There are many stories about how it evolved, but the one I quite like goes like this: when, after the war, American GIs returned home after lengthy stints in the occupation forces in Italy, they naturally enough turned to their local Italian restaurateurs and asked them to replicate the meat and spaghetti meals they had encountered in Bologna. But most of those restaurateurs were migrants from southern Italy, where the tradition is for tomato-based sauces, and so they combined the two into the dish we know as Spaghetti Bolognese.

In Bologna, the nearest equivalent is in fact something quite different. Firstly, it is always served with tagliatelle, not spaghetti. Secondly, the sauce, or 'ragu', is heavily meat based (usually veal, sometimes veal and pork) with only a little tomato paste (and some purists argue that it should have no tomato paste at all). But the combination is delicious in its simplicity, as are so many of the best Italian recipes.

Food also draws the visitor to Bologna into the towns and cities of its surrounding region, the Romagna. From the city's functional railway station, it is a short trip to places like Modena (for the balsamic vinegar and amaretti, small almond-flavoured biscuits), Parma (for an endless variety of hams and parmesan cheese, often served together in a delicious combination), and Ravenna (famed for its asparagus). And if it had been Christmas, we could have found in Ferrara Pampepato di cioccolato, a cake made of cocoa, milk, honey, spices, almonds and lemon peel, then covered with candy-studded chocolate frosting. The produce from all these places finds its way into the regional capital, which tosses them together into a culinary salad of great variety and vitality, as befits una citta grassa.

For us, a month in Bologna proved as much an eye-opener as our fortnight in Turin. And like Turin, Bologna is a city whose charms are peculiarly Italian. When people think of Florence, or Rome, or Venice, or Naples, what inevitably comes into their mind is some iconic image—the Florentine Duomo, the Colosseum, the Grand Canal, Mount Vesuvius—but there is no similar symbol that leaps into the consciousness for Bologna. Instead, what visitors remember is a place that has a distinctive character, a warmth and enthusiasm that is suffused through the very buildings themselves, so that you come away feeling charmed and happy, as after a good meal in homely yet sophisticated surroundings.

## Chapter 19

# To Spoleto for a Festival

Umbria is the only region of Italy that is entirely landlocked, though it does boast the spectacular Lake Trasimeno, and it is most famous for the hill towns that decorate the ridges and promontories of the forested mountains that overlook the valley of the Tiber. The province's popularity has grown in recent decades as visitors and expatriates expanded their horizons beyond the manicured delights of Tuscany in search of what they thought of as a more 'genuine' Italian experience (whatever that means), and today it is probably as popular a destination as its neighbour to the west. Still, as one travels into Umbria from Tuscany, whether by train or car, there is a distinct sense of entering a different region: the fields and farms feel a little scruffier, there is more in the way of industry (mostly small-scale manufacturing and processing plants) and the landscape is more rugged and untamed.

Of all the Umbrian hill towns that we might have made a beeline to visit, Spoleto leapt out as being a must-see for reasons that are very specific to us as long-term residents of Melbourne. Way back in 1986, the famed Italian-American composer and conductor Gian Carlo Menotti was persuaded to let Melbourne join Spoleto and the American city of Charleston to stage what he then called 'The Festival of Three

Worlds'. The idea was that the arts program would migrate over the course of the year between the three cities, with Menotti as overall artistic director. The arrangement didn't last all that long—by 1990 the Melbourne leg of the trio had become the Melbourne International Festival of the Arts, and the other two cities reverted to being artistic twins, as the Festival of Two Worlds (*Due Monde* in Italian)—but this brief connection happened at a time when Robert was working at the Victorian State Opera; the opera company had of course participated in the festival, and so when we began planning our expedition, going to Spoleto for the festival was a must-do.

Arriving after a road trip down the Via Emilia, we dropped the car at the Hertz depot near the railway station and waited to be picked up by a driver that the owner of our apartment had organised. We were most impressed when a black Mercedes with the legend 'Spoleto Festival' emblazoned on its doors swept to a halt in front of us, and our driver, a big burly bloke named Carlo climbed out to help us with our luggage. How did they know we were in town for the festival? And how come we were being picked up in an official festival car? Alas, our excitement was premature: it turned out that Carlo was just doing a favour for our landlady.

Over our years in Italy, the business of finding and booking apartments always had an element of uncertainty about it no matter how hard we worked to research each place to make sure it would meet our requirements; we looked at photos until we were blue in the face, and we read and re-read the description until we could recite it in our sleep, but we were never quite sure until we arrived whether the accommodation would be a source of happiness or disappointment. In this case it was definitely the former—the apartment was much larger than the pictures had suggested, light and airy, with a full kitchen, study area, two bathrooms, plus a living room and a bedroom.

Absolute luxury. Best of all, it overlooked the Piazza del Mercato, the buzzy central square of Spoleto.

Now, this was a definite breach of my rules for choosing apartments. We had learned from hard experience that, appealing as it might be to be able to open a window and look out on a charming square filled with activity, the Italian habit of congregating and partying until late in the night—particularly during the summer—often meant sleeplessness for those of us following a more sedate schedule. In this case I didn't know that the apartment fronted the piazza, since the address was clearly shown on the map as being one street back: it just hadn't occurred to me that the front door might be at the back of the apartment, so to speak.

But this time having a perch over the piazza turned out not to be a problem, since the windows were double glazed and shut out virtually all the noise at night, and in any case the square was relatively quiet most of the time, at least until the festival got into full swing, which it definitely wasn't when we first arrived. In fact, the town was as quiet as a Mexican cantina at siesta-time, the air hot and drowsy despite our position on the top of a hill, and the streets virtually deserted. A short walk brought us to the tourist office, which was closed, with a hand-written sign saying that the festival box office has been moved down near the Opera Theatre (and it too was closed for lunch when we made our way there). Was there really a major arts festival about to start in a couple of days? It certainly didn't feel like it.

In the meantime, there was the old town to explore. Spoleto is not a big place: a couple of piazzas, a long pedestrianised main street that connects the restored Roman Theatre with the new-ish opera house named after Menotti, a very fine Duomo, and that's about it. In between, the town is crisscrossed by narrow lanes and passageways that wend their way up and down the hill, providing a workout for the legs, and if you're up for it another walk uphill brings you to the Rocca Albornoziana. This fortress was built for the rather militant Spanish cardinal Gil de Albornoz, who conducted two campaigns in the fourteenth century aimed at restoring papal influence in Umbria following years of insurrection. Having resisted many sieges over the years, the Rocca was turned into a jail in 1800 and used as such until the late 20th century; today it is a museum, though much of it was closed when we were there.

Our own corner of the town was focused on the Piazza del Mercato, once the forum of the original Roman town and then, in the Middle Ages, the site of Spoleto's main market, from which activity it derives its present name. An irregular oblong overlooked by apartments like ours, the piazza's most distinguished feature is the baroque facade of a former palazzo at the northern end of the square, complete with clock and fountain. The necessities of life are supplied by the well-stocked little *alimentari* (grocery store) and the *tabacchi*, while half a dozen restaurants of various types cater to locals and visitors alike. Though no full-scale market appeared while we were there, several itinerant fruit and vegetable sellers would set up shop every other day, which would have been handy if we knew what days they were going to appear; as it was, we either had to make do with what we could buy at the *alimentari* or make the trek down the hill to the big Tiger supermarket.

Living on the top of a hill is all very well, and when towns like Spoleto were built such sites offered important defensive advantages. But in our more settled and peaceful era, it soon became obvious that life would be much more comfortable down in the valley below, and after the war the practical-minded Spoletini began to desert the old town in favour of a new, modern town that quickly sprang up on every piece of flat ground that could be found at the base of Spoleto's rock. Pretty soon all the services were down there, which posed a challenge to those who were left behind, many of them aged and less agile than they might have been in their youth. The solution was simple: build an escalator to take people between the top and bottom of the hill. This minor engineering marvel, the *scala mobile*, carries residents up and down through long tunnels and deposits them at convenient points all the way up to the Rocca itself. Needless to say, once we discovered its existence we never felt the need to walk up the hill again.

Meanwhile, the festival was finally showing signs of arriving. Still, it didn't so much burst into life as creep into it. There was an official launch event of sorts, but when we got there it turned out to be a panel of folk who we presumed were the festival's management, making a series of speeches from behind a long table to a room packed with journalists. At an event like this in Australia, the tedium of listening to self-important speeches from self-important people would at least be rewarded with something to drink and eat; not so here—after the speeches were done, everyone just ambled off. And since the speeches were in Italian, we were none the wiser. But over the next few days, the presence of festival-goers and festival workers, the latter mostly youngsters identifiable by the badges dangling from lanyards around their necks, began to be more obvious.

One evening, having finished dinner, we were having a drink in one of the cafes on the piazza, and Robert started chatting with a young artist, a native of Spoleto, who goes by the very un-Italian sounding and rather improbable name of Ob Queberry (we instantly nicknamed him Obi-Wan). He had been commissioned by the city council to decorate the surface of the piazza with the various images that had been used in previous festivals.

Now, we had been a little curious about the fact that the Piazza del Mercato, instead of being paved or cobbled, was just covered in a layer of very roughly poured cement. Ob told us that the piazza had in fact always been cobbled, but a decision had been taken to pull all the cobbles up and re-lay them. However, the work had dragged on in the usual Italian way, and suddenly the authorities realised that unless they did something the piazza would just be a sea of mud by the time the festival got under way, which would not be a good look. So they decided to simply cover it in concrete, which would be broken up after the festival was over so that the cobbles could be be re-laid. Then someone in the city council realised that it would look pretty drab, and so young Ob was commissioned to brighten it all up with his brightly coloured murals.

The trouble was that the commission came a bit late, and so he was still hard at work painting his last mural the day before the festival started. That wasn't the end of it though; we ran into him the following evening and he was standing in what we came to know as his habitual posture—paintbrush in one hand and beer in the other, cigarette dangling from bearded mouth—looking perplexed. It seemed that the council had come up with another bright idea: he was to paint the words 'Spoleto 60 Festival' in gigantic letters right down the middle of the piazza. That might sound easy enough, but whichever bright spark thought of it hadn't figured on the fact that, though the piazza is notionally a pedestrian precinct, vehicular traffic is still allowed through; what is more, with the restaurants beginning to operate at full capacity, there were people everywhere crossing to and fro between bars and restaurants. And just to add another layer of difficulty, the weather was threatening rain.

Not for the first time, we learned one important fact: in Italy, every problem rapidly becomes a community project. In no time, Ob had gathered about him a gang of people, including his quite lively and somewhat madcap girlfriend (she described herself to us as being his 'sex-friend'!), all of whom were ready to wield brushes to get the job done. But given the less than propitious circumstances, the work couldn't start until midnight at least, when the traffic could be stopped and most of the restaurant patrons had gone off to bed. In the meantime, what else was there to do except drink, smoke, and talk?

As anyone who knows him would be aware, this kind of scenario is irresistible to Robert. In no time at all he had declared that he was going to help out, which also meant that we both had to stay the course with the partying Italians until the work could start—which it did, around one in the morning when most of the crowd had dispersed, and most of the rain had stopped. Ob then got to work carefully marking out the letters in chalk on the rough concrete surface, stopping regularly for a cigarette, a drink, and a chat with his various helpers, among whom Robert and I had both been given honorary membership. Finally, three hours later, this new addition to the temporary art scene was completed—including a very carefully inked "t" in the word 'Spoleto' painted by one Robert Gibbs, and we all went off to bed, worn out.

That might have been the end of the story, but there was more. A day or so later, poor long-suffering Ob told us that the council had decided that they didn't like the whole thing, and they had instead decided that he should paint it all over with a long strip of red that would run down the middle of the street, with the number sixty picked out in blue in the middle of it, as a kind of 'red carpet'. By now, the piazza was starting to get quite busy with festival patrons, so Ob was facing another late night to get the job done (and in the process bury Robert's contribution beneath a layer of thick red paint; ah well, fame in the art world is fleeting!). But Ob's bad luck didn't end there; he had only painted half of the carpet when a sudden downpour washed it away, leaving streaks of red running across the piazza and into the gutters. He was a persistent and patient young man, though, and he stuck with it. Finally, three days into the festival, it had its red carpet.

*

Though Gian Carlo Menotti died in 2007, his presence is still very powerful in Spoleto, particularly at festival time. That is hardly surprising, since he founded the festival way back in 1958, when the composer was at the height of his powers as a composer. Born near Lake Maggiore into the family of a coffee merchant, Menotti was a child prodigy and wrote his first opera at eleven years of age. Though he got his initial musical training in Milan, the death of his father prompted a crisis in the family business, and young Gian Carlo went with his mother to Colombia in an attempt to revive it; after that, his mother returned to Italy, but Menotti went to Philadelphia to study music at the Curtis School, where he met fellow students Leonard Bernstein and Samuel Barber. Menotti and Barber became lovers and musical collaborators, buying a house in upstate New York where they lived together for forty years, until Barber's death in 1981.

Menotti conceived the *Festival Dei Due Mondi* as a vehicle to compare and contrast the cultures of the old and new worlds, a cultural dichotomy within which he had lived most of his life. Spoleto was to represent the old world, and Charleston, in South Carolina, would represent the new, and Menotti would be the artistic director of both (quite how Melbourne would fit into this scheme was never quite clear—presumably we represented the even newer world). For quite a long time, this unique vision seemed to work, but in the 1990's ructions disturbed the artistic tranquillity when Menotti clashed with the board and management of the Charleston festival in a struggle for control that was appropriately operatic in scale and drama. Charleston decided to go its own way, and it was not until 2007 that any signs of a rapprochement emerged.

By now, Gian Carlo had died, and the festival in Spoleto was being run by his son, Francis Menotti, a former actor and figure skater who the composer had adopted in 1974. Francis had been artistic director of the festival for some years, during which time the festival's attendances and revenue declined; whatever affection the government of Spoleto might have had for the father was not extended to the son, and before long yet another coup was under way, and Francis was removed from his position, and replaced by veteran film director and composer Giorgio Ferrara, who continues to the run the festival to this day. Francis Menotti didn't go quietly: for years he maintained that the festival had been 'stolen' from him and his father, and he launched a series of legal challenges to try and wrest control of the festival back from the city, to no avail.

At the festival we attended in 2017, not a lot of this drama was immediately evident until we started talking to festival veterans and locals who have been involved with the festival for some time. One, a rather morose theatre technician, told us in no uncertain terms that the festival is but a shadow of its great days when Maestro Menotti was in charge. Not that he laid everything at the feet of the festival's management; the trouble was, he said, every hill town in Umbria has some kind of festival these days, whereas when Menotti was in charge Spoleto was unique.

Be that as it may, once the festival finally got under way, there was plenty to see and do. The operatic centrepiece was a very fine production of Mozart's last and probably most dramatic opera, *Don Giovanni*, which proved slightly problematic for us: we had left our booking run a bit late, and so the only seats we could get were in a box about three levels up with rather cramped sightlines, and though we had expected that there would be surtitles in English, in the event they were only in Italian, which made following the finer details of the plot a tad challenging. But none of that detracted too much from our enjoyment of a strong if fairly traditional production.

I made a fleeting reference earlier to a restored Roman theatre, and this was the venue for a remarkable homage to Maria

Callas, a dance production performed by a company assembled by Eleanor Abbagnato, a well-known and much-loved Italian ballerina. The first part of the production was a pastiche of dances set to recordings by *la Divina* herself of well-known Italian operatic arias and scenes, which was kind of cute but not as interesting as the second half, a re-reading of the plot of *Medea* (one of Callas' greatest roles) set to modern music.

There was plenty of other music on offer—we made it to most of a series of concerts put on by young performers from the Fiesole Music School, where we were blown away by the sheer virtuosity of these young players at the beginning of their careers, delivered in the simple, austere beauty of the tiny Romanesque Sant' Eufemia Church. The New World contribution to the festival was a concert showcasing music by Colombian classical composers, a tradition of which we had previously been unaware. And the biggest gala event of all was an outdoor concert staged in front of the floodlit facade of the Duomo, a Requiem for Orchestra and Choir, in memory of those who died in the 2016 Abruzzo earthquake.

In between festival performances we spent our time inspecting the very considerable array of visual art in the town's many galleries and dropping into the bars and restaurants on Piazza del Mercato where we would connect with various characters who either lived in Spoleto, or were there for the festival. In the course of a week, we met an American theatre director who had just retired there, complete with long grey ponytail; a charming American woman who has lived there for a decade, and who had some odd conspiracy theories that she was sure would make a great book or (better) a blockbuster film; a hyper-active young photographer, a native of Spoleto who thought his English was much better than it was, and as a consequence was harder to understand than most Italians with little English; an English couple who Rob literally hijacked for a drink; and an earnest young American singer and conductor who was spending a few days at the festival before going on to join in some musical endeavours in Arezzo.

And that is the enduring memory that we have of that first visit to Spoleto: convivial, a little eccentric, and wonderfully atmospheric. I have always felt that, when it comes to arts festivals, smaller cities and towns provide a much better stage than big, sprawling metropolises like Melbourne or Sydney; that's not to say we shouldn't have an arts festival, just that it is harder to create the sense of intimacy, the feeling that everyone is engaged with and immersed in the experience, that we felt in this small Umbrian hill town—even if its organisation was more than a little shambolic.

# Chapter 20

# The Hill Towns of Umbria

If there is a single testament to the turbulence of the Italian past, it is the presence, in almost every province, of so many fortified hill towns. They are everywhere, crowning steep bluffs, draped over ridges and promontories, or occupying rocky headlands thrusting into the sea. Built originally to provide a place of sanctuary and security against a hostile world, their occupants could carry on their domestic lives in safety, only sallying forth to tend their farms in the valleys below, trade, or defend their territory. After the day's work was done, they could return to the tranquillity of a community that turned its back, physically and emotionally, on the dangers beyond their walls and gates.

Today, once you have made your way up the hill and into the precincts of an Italian hill town, you find yourself in an enclosed world of tall buildings and narrow streets that open into the occasional piazza overlooked by the dazzling facade of its church. It is an inward-looking urban plan that deliberately shuts out any glimpse of the surrounding countryside; only when your wanderings take you down some street whose terminus lies at the town's edge, and your eyes are dazzled by the vistas across sun-dappled countryside hundreds of metres below, that you remember that this whole elaborate construction is actually fixed to the top of a crag. The rest of the time, the outside world might, quite literally, not exist. One can easily understand just how comforting such an environment must have been to the townsfolk during the troubled times of the medieval and early modern eras.

It has been postulated that Umbria has a particular concentration of hill towns because the entire province more or less went to sleep during the fifty or so years between the restoration of papal rule after the Congress of Vienna in 1815 and the final emasculation of the Papal States when Italy reunified. While the rest of Italy under its various regimes began to industrialise, prompting their populations to leave the cramped confines of their rock-girt villages in search of employment in the factories that were springing up in the valleys below, Umbria remained frozen in its agricultural state under a clerical rule that had no interest at all in fostering innovation and modernisation; it was only after the Risorgimento that large scale industrialisation came to the valleys of the province. The happy result for modern tourism is that Umbria is blessed with a multitude of handsome old towns that grace the skyline of virtually every significant hilltop, presiding benignly over the increasingly ugly urban sprawl below.

The grandest of all Umbria's hill towns is its capital, Perugia, though it is fair to say that the old *centro storico* is well on the way to being overwhelmed by the ever-spreading urban mess below. The prosaic, workaday train station at which we arrived from Spoleto is located in a nondescript zone of flats and offices below the long ridge upon which the old town has sat for at least twenty-three hundred years. From there the natty Minimetro, a driverless train system, whizzed us up through a series of long tunnels that took us to the upper terminus, some 480 metres above sea level. We emerged to behold what must be one of the most glorious vistas in Italy, the view across a Tiber valley drenched in late afternoon sunshine, towards the massive bulk of Monte Subasio, beneath whose tree-clothed slopes we could just make out the town of Assisi.

Perugia's layout is simplicity itself: two long main streets follow the ridge line, connecting the bastions of what was once the mighty Rocca Paolina at its southern end with the main piazza, now called the Piazza IV Novembre (the date in 1919 on which the armistice was signed between Italy and Austria-Hungary, bringing the hostilities of the First World War to an end, now celebrated in Italy as National Unity and Armed Forces Day). From these two arteries, smaller streets wend their way down the hillsides toward the newer parts of the city, or else end abruptly at the old ramparts, these days lined with cheerful bars filled with chattering students enjoying a drink while watching the Tiber valley sink slowly into darkness.

Like many places in Italy, you can trace Perugia's history just by walking around and looking at the buildings. Piazza IV November might have a name that celebrates a twentieth-century event, but all of the buildings that surround it belong to the medieval and renaissance periods, when Perugia was a proud and independent commune whose governors met in the Palazzo dei Priori. This grand four-story Gothic edifice was built in stages and took a hundred and fifty years to achieve an appearance that, like the Doge's Palace in Venice, manages to be both imposing and yet at the same time light and graceful.

Facing it across the piazza is the cathedral of San Lorenzo, where three popes were once buried (though their tombs were destroyed in the fourteenth century). Perugia was a frequent refuge for the papacy as their domains were roiled by civil strife and they had to flee Rome; in fact, over the course of the thirteenth century no less than five popes were elected in conclaves held in the adjoining Palazzo delle Canoniche. The Perugini were to spend the next two hundred years embroiled in the struggles between the pope and emperor, known to history as the Guelph-Ghibelline conflict, the long feud between the popes and the Holy Roman Emperors to determine who would control northern Italy. Always independently minded, the leaders of the *comune* sided with the Guelfi as much out of anti-German sentiment as out of any loyalty to the papacy itself, with whom they were often at odds.

Evidence of the grip that the popes eventually asserted over the town can be found at the other end of the city, at the Rocca Paolina. In 1540, pope Paul III stripped the city of its privileges, imposed direct rule, and commanded that a huge fortress be built that would dominate the city and place it under permanent subjection of a papal garrison. Sections of the Etruscan walls were demolished in the process, and many of the medieval streets were simply bricked over and turned into tunnels which can still be seen today. From this powerful strongpoint the papal governors ruled Perugia for the next two hundred and fifty years, until the Napoleonic interregnum from 1797 to 1815.

Today you can't see anything much of the Rocca Paolina except the fascinating underground tunnels and the massive bastions. After the papacy was finally kicked out in 1860, the Rocca was razed to create a platform upon which the new Republic of Italy was celebrated in the elegant Piazza d'Italia, a beautiful and peaceful square surrounded by Liberty-era buildings that now house the city's government. From here, you can do a bit more time-travelling by taking an escalator down into the tunnels created when the Rocca's builders covered the old medieval streets, now fascinating museum and gallery spaces housing monumental sculptures and galleries devoted to contemporary art. From there, a series of more recent tunnels and escalators deposit you at the bottom of the hill, and into the more modern part of the city that dates from the nineteenth century onward.

Perugia and its surrounding region participated in the economic shift after unification from an agricultural to an industrial economic base, a process that continued into the twentieth century. Many companies and industries have come and gone in that time, but one business has endured and become forever associated with the city of Perugia: the chocolate company Perugina. Almost everyone must at some time or another have eaten one of their *Baci* chocolates, with its characteristic hazelnut centre. As Robert discovered when he went on a tour of the Perugina factory, located about eight kilometres out of town in the sprawling industrial complex of Sant'Andrea delle Fratte, the origins of the business have a very Italian romantic twist.

The company was originally formed in 1907 by four partners, Francesco Buitoni, Annibale Spagnoli, Leone Ascoli and Francesco Andreani. But it was Annibale Spagnoli's wife Luisa who, in 1922, came up with the idea of putting a whole hazelnut in the centre of the chocolate; rather oddly, she called it a *cazzotto*, which in Italian means 'punch'. After a couple of years, the company's marketing director, Federico Seneca, had the brilliant insight that this name might not be the most effective marketing device, and suggested that the confection be renamed as *baci*, or 'kisses'. He is also credited with the idea of inserting little notes expressing romantic sentiments like *Meglio un bacio oggi che un gallina domani*, which translates to 'Better a kiss today than a hen tomorrow', *Se puoi baciar la padrona, non baciar la serva* ('If you can kiss the mistress, do not kiss the servant'), and *Un bacio senza barba e una zuppa senza sale* ('A beardless kiss is a soup without salt'). They are typically Italian tags, sentimental, earthy and humorous all at once.

Legend has it that Seneca's little love notes were inspired by Luisa's clandestine love affair with one of her husband's business partners, Francesco Buitoni, who used to communicate their love for each other in little notes hidden in packets of chocolate. Whatever the truth of that story, the notes themselves became famous, and in the twenties were virtually a cult object. There was even a competition created for them, and the Baci image found its way onto an early issue of postage stamps by the Italian Republic. The chocolates themselves went global and became an Italian marketing success story; Perugina is now the largest employer in Umbria, with over 30,000 workers. Eventually, of course, their very success brought them to the attention of the global food giant Nestle, who bought the company in 1988. But Perugina is still a proud brand and hosts hundreds of visitors each day who come to see the chocolate being made and drool over the world's biggest chocolate, which stands over two metres high and weighs nearly *six thousand* kilos!

\*

If Perugia is the secular heart of Umbria, Assisi, on the other side of the valley of the Tiber, must be its spiritual heart. It, too, is a hill town, built along a spur of Monte Subasio, and like Perugia people have been living here for thousands of years. But where Perugia's old town is surrounded by a great messy sprawl of urban development, Assisi floats above the valley floor, seeming quite separated from the modern life roaring along the freeway below, an ethereal vision that could disappear into the mist at any moment.

Still, once you get up there the town seems solid enough, and the geography of the place follows the familiar pattern for hill towns, a long street following the spine of the hill, opening out at the end to a startling expanse of green turf separating the town proper from the precinct of the massive Basilica of St Francis. This very beautiful building hangs on the end of the promontory like the prow of a great ship, thrusting into the empty air above the sheer drop below. It is this complex, of course, that gives Assisi its special place in the world, indelibly and forever associated with the Catholic saint, Francesco d'Assisi.

I'll get back to Saint Francis in a moment, for unlike most visitors he was not the principal reason we visited Assisi for the first time. Rather, the motive for visiting Assisi was to catch up with an old chum from Melbourne, Jan Elliott, who has been spending her northern winters in Assisi for many years. That might seem eccentric to those of us who habitually try and escape Melbourne's often dismal winters, but Jan likes it the other way around, preferring the cold weather and finding summers uncomfortable.

Each year she rents the same little apartment in a narrow street at the eastern end of the town, not far from the main bus terminus in Piazza Matteotti. She stays for six months, occupying herself learning Italian and hanging out with a little group of expatriates from various parts of the globe who have made Assisi their permanent home. One of these is an American lady of indeterminate years who we came think of as 'the Cat Lady', because of her weakness for the local stray cats, which she could never resist feeding and taking into her home. Another, with whom we became firm friends, is a gentleman, then in his late eighties, named Roy.

Roy has lived in Assisi for many decades, after a working career with organisations such as the BBC which allowed him the opportunity to travel extensively. As a lifelong devout Catholic, Assisi was an appealing place to retire. Buying the under-croft of a house at the eastern end of the town which had been used to house a family's livestock, he proceeded to convert it into a small two-roomed apartment, where he has lived a relatively ascetic life ever since. Ascetic does not, in this instance at least, mean poor. The apartment might be small, but it has a little terrace that affords brilliant views across the valley and up towards the massive Rocca Maggiore, the papal fortress that dominates the town (constructed, incidentally, by the same fighting cardinal Albornoz who built the castle at Spoleto). And inside, Roy possesses a remarkable collection of medieval manuscripts, icons and furniture that he has collected over the years.

A sprightly and impish character, he enlivens his retired life by conducting tours of Assisi and other nearby towns, and is a wealth of knowledge on many subjects, particularly those related to Christianity and the church. And it takes almost no prompting to get him to recite in some detail the story of Saint Francis; I have to confess that I felt some misgivings as he launched into the tale, being more than a little cynical about the whole saint thing, but in this case Roy's often amusing way of telling the story got my attention, as did the story itself, which is indeed fascinating.

Let me tell the tale in my words, and hope that Roy finds them as compelling as his own version of the story. Born in 1181 or 1182 and baptised as Giovanni di Pietro di Bernardone, the future saint was the son of an Assisi silk merchant; his father Pietro was in France on business when the son was born, and on his return he took to calling him 'Francesco', perhaps because of his enthusiasm for all things French. The family was wealthy, and the young Francesco grew up, as you might expect, into an indulged, high-spirited young man who loved music, fine clothes and partying. It does seem, though, that even then he had a tender heart and a feeling for the poor: the story is told that, approached by a beggar while conducting a sale on behalf of his father, he abandoned his wares and ran after the poor man, giving him everything he had in his pockets (much to the annoyance of his parent).

The fact that Francis gave up all worldly trappings in favour of a life of poverty is well known, but this did not seem to happen all at once: rather, it was a series of transformative steps. First, after a period spent as a soldier on various campaigns against neighbouring Perugia, he grew disillusioned with his former life. Then he went to Rome on a pilgrimage, joining the beggars in St Paul's, wandered for a while in search of spiritual enlightenment, ending up back near Assisi. His father was less than thrilled by his son's turn towards the spiritual life, and Francis hid out in some caves for a while, trying to avoid him; alas, eventually he had to return home.

What followed was a series of escalations that might be familiar to any modern parent dealing with a strong-willed teenager. First Pietro gave his son a sound thrashing and locked him up in a storeroom. Francis simply waited until his father was away on business and then escaped from his confinement. Any chance of peace between father and son was shattered when Pietro decided to institute legal proceedings and have his son disinherited, presumably hoping to intimidate him into compliance. But the young man knew how to respond to this piece of blackmail: in the middle of the court proceedings, he dramatically renounced both father and patrimony.

Now committed to his life of poverty, Francis began preaching (something for which he had no license), exhorting anyone who would listen to take up a a life of peace, penitence, and brotherly love. Within a year he had eleven followers; from this core he went on to found a new religious order, whose principal rule was simplicity itself: 'To follow the teachings of our Lord Jesus Christ and to walk in his footsteps'. A little reluctantly, the pope decided to endorse the Franciscan order, and after that his movement grew quickly, acquiring adherents and inspiring other orders, such as the Poor Clares and the Brothers and Sisters of Penance.

Francis spent the rest of his life trying to imitate Christ as best he could and carry on his work. Though he spent most of his life in Italy, he did make some trips elsewhere in Europe, most notably to join the Fifth Crusade, and there are intriguing but improbable stories about Francis debating with Saladin's nephew, the great Egyptian Sultan Al-Kamil. Back in Italy, he had to intervene in the affairs of his own order, which had grown to the point where his simple precepts were no longer sufficient to regulate its activities effectively; that done, he withdrew from affairs and resumed his life of wandering poverty. In 1224 he experienced a vision of a six-winged angel on a cross, and received the stigmata. Two years later he died, suffering among other things from the effects of trachoma. Pope Gregory IX pronounced Francis a saint in 1228, and in 1230 he was buried in what is now the lower church of the basilica of Saint Francis, in Assisi, where he lies to this day.

In the skilled storytelling hands of our friend Roy, accompanied by quantities of red wine consumed in the environment of his rather cave-like apartment, the story of Saint Francis emerged as a tale that was both fascinating and inspiring, even to a religious cynic like me. Like Mahatma Gandhi, that other mendicant preacher from a different religion and another continent, he uplifted and galvanised others by the power of his example, refusing to be distracted by worldliness in any of its forms. One imagines that he must have possessed, as Gandhi did, some degree of cunning and insight into the motivations of his fellow men and women. It seems improbable that he was quite as simple a soul as Zeffirelli made him out to be in his hagiographic biopic *Brother Sun, Sister Moon*, but even so he must have been a genuinely saintly man, perhaps one of the few who genuinely deserve that appellation.

Today there is something of a St Francis industry in Assisi. Religious tourists flock to the place on package tours to be shown around the town and be given tours of the wonders of the basilica by brown-clad monks. Even Roy has a small part in this industry, leading small tours if the city. But compared to the sightseeing frenzies one witnesses in Venice and Florence, the tourism here is all rather decorous and subdued. It is as if Francis' character has somehow managed to seep into the stones of his birthplace, which does feel like a genuinely spiritual place.

The surprisingly peaceful main square, prosaically named the Piazza Comune, retains its medieval appearance, as do the long main streets that run along the top of the ridge. The simple brown stone facades of the houses are brightened up by pots of flowers hanging outside the windows, and are only occasionally interrupted by discreet little shops and restaurants. Even the great basilica that has been raised over his tomb is fundamentally simple in design, floating ethereally over the valley below, part of the landscape and yet detached from it. Inside, the greatest painters of the Renaissance—Giotto, Cimabue, Lorenzetti, Cavallini—were inspired to decorate the walls with beautifully luminous images commemorating the saint's life. The simple design of the basilica, without any side aisles or private chapels, allows the visitor to contemplate the story without distraction.

\*

Umbria is one of the most charming regions of Italy, and its days as the half-forgotten little sister of glamorous Tuscany are rapidly receding into the past as more and more tourists discover its charms. As well as Spoleto, Perugia and Assisi, the province boasts many other spectacularly-sited towns and villages— Spello, where they take flowers very seriously, Trevi, whose streets spiral down from the church of Sant'Emiliano, and dizzyingly elevated Todi, to name some of the more famous. And if you have had enough of toiling up hills and traipsing in and out of churches, Lake Trasimeno isn't far away, with its pretty lakeside hamlets of Passignano and Castiglione del Lago and its tranquil waters, perfect for swimming, boating or just enjoying a long lunch at a restaurant enjoying the views.

But for us, our time in Umbria also marked the end of our time in the northern part of the country during that first year of travelling. Though we didn't know it at the time, we were to return to the north for further explorations, but for now we were headed for a different world—the mysterious south.

# Chapter 21

# Welcome to the South

The term Italians almost universally use when they talk of the south is the *mezzogiorno*, which literally means 'midday'. This might seem an odd way to describe half of the country, but it has its origins in the days of the various maritime republics (think Venice, Genoa, Pisa, Amalfi). Before the days of the compass, seafarers gave names to the winds coming from different directions to help them describe their routes: *vento di tramontana* (the wind from the north); *vento di ponente* (the wind from the west); *vento di levante* (the wind from the east); and *vento di mezzogiorno* (the wind from the south). For some reason, this way of describing the south stuck, and persisted into the modern age, but truncated simply to *mezzogiorno*. Still, like many Italian terms, it does manage to convey a great many shades of meaning in the one word: heat, somnolence, the laziness of eternal summer, and a kind of offhand but benign derision.

The south of Italy is a place defined by preconceptions. As mysterious as Africa, dominated by organised crime, the fearsome *'Ndranghetta* and the *Cosa Nostra*, populated by indolent and ignorant peasants, deeply conservative and backwards, barbarous of habit. Or a place of sunny beaches and spectacular coastlines, a holiday maker's paradise, of romantic hilltop villages and spectacular castles, unique cuisine, and friendly old-fashioned hospitality. You pays your money and takes your pick, as the saying goes, from a whole menu of biases.

There was a 2010 movie called *Benvenuti al Sud*, or 'Welcome to the South', which plays on both sides of these prejudices for its comedy. Alberto, the postmaster of a small town in the northwest, attempts to carry out a prank which he hopes will get him transferred to Milan, where he can escape his domineering wife. But it all goes wrong, and instead he is sent off to Castellabate, a small village near Naples; when she learns of the transfer, his wife buys him a flak jacket, and he loads his car up with what he thinks are necessities for survival in the south—mousetraps, super-strength sunscreen, even a fire extinguisher. But when he gets there, he finds that, though the people of Castellabate are impossible to understand, and their customs odd, they are friendly and honest, confounding his expectations. It is one of those endearing cinematic confections that the Italians make with great ease, simultaneously celebrating Italian oddities while poking fun at their own prejudices.

As we made the five-hour drive from Perugia to Vieste, the first stop on our tour of the south which would eventually take in Puglia, Naples and Sicily, I wondered whether we would also find the south as strange as Alberto found Castellabate. We had only been to southern Italy once before, in 2004 , when we went down to the Calabrian seaside town of Tropea.. Having got there after an absurdly long train journey all the way from Milan, followed by a confused drive from the train station at Lamezia Terme, we got to our pre-booked hotel, rapidly decided that staying there would be a mistake (it had all the charm of a Butlins holiday camp and seemed to be populated entirely by very large and very naked German tourists who were arrayed in all their glory around the pool), checked back out drove back into the Tropea to look for an alternative.

Unfortunately for us, we had managed to arrive in the central piazza of Tropea in the middle of the afternoon siesta period. The place was as desolate and deserted as the main street of a town in a Spaghetti Western at high noon, and the natives seemed just as unfriendly. Eventually we mustered up enough Italian between us to extract the information from the newsagent that the local tourist office would be open at three, and they would be able to help. We found some way of amusing ourselves for a bit and eventually made our way back to the little piazza, now completely transformed and buzzing with tourists. A very pleasant young lady at the tourist office placed us in the hands of a young fellow named Alberto, who conducted us to a comfortable little apartment right in the middle of town. Amusingly, Alberto's mother was summoned to deal with this unexpected booking, shedding her Armani outfit as she climbed the stairs, donning gloves to give the joint a quick dust and make the beds. She gave us a somewhat odd look when we asked that they be made up as *letti matrimoniali*, or double beds.

Despite the confused start, we ended up having a quite wonderful time in Tropea, which is a gem of a town crowning a crag overlooking the Tyrrhenian Sea, and which is very popular with the Italians, who flock there in the summer for the food, sun and sand. We did all of that, eating and drinking and loitering on the beach for a few days, before hiring a car and making an epic drive all the way down to Reggio and across the straits to Sicily, stopping for lunch in Taormina before driving all the way back.

And what impressions had we been left with from this, our only previous sally into the south? Well, the people were undeniably friendly, particularly when they learned we were Australians; many of them had relatives back in our home country, though they were usually hopelessly confused about Australia's geography and found our attempts to explain the country's size just incomprehensible. The food we remembered as being good but not especially clever; the landscape as being brown and rocky for the most part; and the railway stations scruffy and on the dilapidated side.

Tropea is in Calabria, but this time our venture south was heading to the other side of the Italian boot, the province of Puglia. Our first destination was Vieste, on the Gargano Peninsula, which if you look at the map is a kind of bulge that might, to stretch the footwear analogy a little further, pass for a spur hanging just above the heel of the boot. From here down to the south-eastern tip of the boot, the stiletto if you like, is the province of Puglia, or in its Anglicised form, Apulia. Four million people live in Puglia, in a landscape that has been shaped over the millennia by a climate characterised by hot, dry summers and short, wet winters.

In the north of Italy the land is rounded and manicured; in the south it is rugged, wild, unkempt. We were travelling in midsummer, and a sun that was merely hot in the north had become oppressive and malevolent, beating everything into submission during the hottest hours of the afternoon. The afternoon siesta in such conditions is an absolute necessity, not merely a quaint local custom, and the towns that we passed through during the afternoon—were shuttered at street level, as much a ghost town as any in the Old West. They were not on the whole attractive visually—conglomerations of square, boxy apartment buildings, painted in white or in bright pastels, their flat roofs covered in a profusion of TV aerials. These are buildings designed to defend against the harshness of the outside world, providing a refuge until it is comfortable to go out and meet friends for the evening *passegiata*.

Yet for us this landscape had an odd sense of familiarity. Robert and I both grew up on Adelaide's northern plains, which are flat, dry, and hot as Hades in summer. As we passed through the flat lands of northern Puglia, we suddenly understood what so many Italian migrants must have felt on arriving in Adelaide: it was a landscape that had many echoes of the places they had left behind, and in no time at all they settled down to create market gardens, grow grapes and olives, and build their homes in the style they were accustomed to here in Puglia, white boxes adorned with pillared balconies (which we Anglo-Saxons, with the careless ignorant harshness of youth, used to deride as 'wog houses').

Leaving the plains behind, we were treated to spectacular coastal views as we ascended the mountainous plateau of the Gargano Peninsula, following its periphery around to our first southern destination, the port and resort town of Vieste. The town embraces a deep bay, on the southern side of which is a dramatic peninsula, where the steep and narrow streets of the *centro storico* climb up from the harbour towards the glowering fortress that was built to control this strategic point on the coast; on the other side is the so-called 'new' town, though it actually dates back to the eighteenth century.

Wandering through this part of Vieste on our first afternoon, it was immediately apparent that this was an area that is definitely not gussied up for tourists. The stone-paved streets are laid out on a rigid grid pattern that is angled to catch the sea breeze and are just as narrow as their counterparts across the bay, but instead of tripping over a carefully prepared display of souvenirs, you are more likely to bump into someone's washing, left to dry in the street. The houses themselves are unadorned cubes sporting iron-railed balconies whose neglected-looking flower boxes have to compete with yet more washing. Modern life has been visibly grafted onto the older structures in the form of exposed power and phone cables looping across the streets and the forest of TV aerials and satellite dishes covering the roofs. At ground level there are great patches of grey where the inexorable efforts of the salt-laden wind have caused the white plaster to fall from the walls; the occupants, it seems, are either too indifferent or too poor to make the necessary repairs.

During the heat of the day, the streets are deserted, the population either at work or sheltering in the cool shadowed interiors of their houses. But the street is the theatre of life for the Italians of the south as much as it is for their counterparts in Florence or Milan. By late afternoon groups of young boys have come home from school and are playing football anywhere that there is an open space, watched over with a tolerant eye by their *nonna* and assorted other relatives who have planted a few kitchen chairs out on the street to sit and enjoy a gossip in the cool of the sea-breeze that wafts up from the harbour. Tourists are few, and as we wandered by in our fairly aimless exploration they watched us approach with mild curiosity, breaking into a smile and giving us a nod as we offered a cheery *buona sera*. Later, these elderly residents would gather in the triangular piazza that separates the old and new towns for another round of gossip with their friends and relatives in a social ritual that is as old as the town itself.

The *centro storico*, over on the other side of the bay, could not be more different. From the long narrow point of the peninsula, three pedestrianised streets run up the hill, lined by perfectly restored houses. Each has its little shop at ground level flogging souvenirs and culinary specialties, their displays spilling out onto streets filled with tourists having a casual browse on their way to dinner. As the sun disappears and the streetlights come on, the atmosphere is one of carefree jollity, typical of any resort town in peak season. The act of shopping might even lead to purchasing, but for most this is incidental to the real mission of the evening: finding somewhere to eat at one of the restaurants that line the edge of the rocky bluff that falls away to the sea below, affording romantic views of the town and the sun setting on the sea beyond as they tuck into their *orecchiette con cima di rape* (orecchiette, the local ear-shaped pasta, with turnip tops—much more delicious than it sounds!).

Looming above the town is the Castello Svevo Aragonese. This massive fortress dates back to around 1060 when it was built by the Normans during their remarkable campaign of conquest in southern Italy. 'The Normans? From Normandy?' Robert queried me when I mentioned this fact over dinner. 'A bit far from home, weren't they?' The answer to which question is a bit complicated, but worth retelling, since the Norman presence in southern Italy is one of the keys to the whole story of the Italian south.

Every Englishman knows that in 1066 the powerful duke William of Normandy crossed the channel and defeated the Saxon king Harold to make himself king of England; so seminal was this event that the entire history of the English monarchy is dated from the conquest, and the generations of Anglo-Saxon history were all but wiped from English consciousness (how many Britons today can name more than one or two of the Anglo-Saxon monarchs who ruled England for two hundred years?). The Norman impact on southern Italy was just as dramatic, and was to have the same long-lasting effects, though the conquest itself was less dramatic and considerably more nuanced than its rather brutal English counterpart.

Whereas the invasion of England was undertaken as a matter of state policy, the subjugation of the southern half of the Italian peninsula was entirely driven by one remarkable family, the Hautevilles. The patriarch of the clan, Tancred de Hauteville, was a minor Norman lord, possessing not much more than a castle and its surrounding lands. He did not have much money, but what he did possess in abundance was sons—he had twelve of them, and obviously his patrimony was never going to be enough to keep them in comfort. The usual solution to this dilemma was for younger sons to make their own way in the world by hiring themselves out as mercenaries, and this the younger Hautevilles proceeded to do. But where most Norman families offered their services the duke of Normandy the Hauteville boys headed south to the sunny climes of Italy.

There, they found a world riven by conflicts, between the last remnants of the Byzantine empire and the scraps of the Lombard kingdoms, between pope and emperor, and between Italians and Arabs. These were perfect conditions for mercenaries, and the eldest two sons, William and Drogo, soon became major players in the endless little wars that were being fought out for control of the regions of Apulia, Calabria and Campania. But it was land that made a man rich in those days, and instead of taking their money and going home, they shrewdly sought payment in the form of feudal landholdings. Eventually they amassed so much land that William was recognised as Count of Apulia by his feudal overlord, Guaimar IV of Salerno, and the Norman foothold was established.

After William's death, various of his brothers inherited the county in succession, and by 1057 they had united it with Calabria, and the counts of Auplia now became dukes. This set the stage for the greatest of all the Hauteville brothers, Robert 'Guiscard' (the sobriquet variously means 'the Resourceful', 'the Cunning', 'the Wily', 'the Fox', or 'the Weasel': I suppose you picked your option depending on your view of his character). He was Tancred's sixth son, and he had arrived in Italy in 1047, accompanied by his youngest brother Roger. A big and energetic man, he soon achieved pre-eminence among the Norman lordlings and after he succeeded as duke of Apulia he set about a campaign to oust the Saracens from Sicily, and At his death in 1085 Robert was master all of southern Italy

Though the Norman empire was destined to fade from the stage of history within a century, the long term consequences of their conquest were profound. When they arrived in the south, the whole region was a patchwork of statelets at war with each other; by the time they had finished they had created a single unified feudal state that was to remain essentially intact for the next seven hundred years, in contrast to the chaos in northern Italy. We came across aspects of this legacy over and over again as we made our way southwards and then back up to Naples.

\*

Our itinerary after Vieste took us to the coastal towns of Barletta, with its magnificent castle built by Emperor Frederick II (a descendant of Robert Guiscard's youngest brother Roger), and the regional capital, Bari, a bustling port city with a crumbling yet charming labyrinth of an old town, and yet another of Frederick's castles. Then we went inland to base ourselves for a few days in the town of Martina Franca, pretty much in the middle of the fertile plateau called the Salento.

Martina Franca was one of those places whose charms you discover by accident. We could have stayed in any one of several famous towns in this part of Puglia, but I chose Martina Franca only because it is very central to the Salento area. But we had good vibes about the place the minute we arrived at our hotel, the rather grand Park Hotel San Michele. Set in a tract of parkland, it was one of those delightfully quaint Italian hotels where lunch is served on a vine-covered terrace by white-jacketed waiters, under the haughtily critical eye of a small population of ancient Italians of both sexes who seemed to be permanent residents of the place. And, most wonderfully since it was the height of summer, there was a swimming pool!

Having lunched and swum, we went off to explore the old town, a few hundred metres' walk away. The city's heart is the semicircular Piazza Maria Immacolata, beneath whose arched arcades the cafes and restaurants were in full swing; having already eaten, we did no more than have a drink at little bar run by an excitable young man named Christian. After that, we went for a stroll. It being a Friday, one of the main thoroughfares was blocked off and turned into a giant street-market whose stalls were lit by a series of elaborate illuminated arches spanning the road, one every fifty or so metres. As the sun went down and the evening's temperature crept down with it, the crowd became ever jollier as they made their chattering way past the stalls and food hawkers.

Our way back home took us past a church, outside which a big crowd had gathered trying to peer inside to where a society wedding was taking place, and then to the grand piazza outside the vast ducal palace, where lots of young people had gathered to chat and drink in the way of young people everywhere. There was, it transpired, an opera festival under way in Martina Franca, performances for which are held in the courtyard of the palace. Robert found out somehow that they were rehearsing the festival's centrepiece, Vivaldi's *Orlando Furioso*, that very evening. Nothing would do but that we should wheedle our way inside, despite the fact that the rehearsal was ostensibly closed, and have a gander at proceedings.

As I said, I had chosen Martina Franca as a base because it is central to the rest of the Salento plateau, and over the next few days we went off to visit some of the most famous towns in the area. The Salento is dotted with unique, conical-roofed houses called *trulli*. Basically a drystone hut, it is commonly believed that they developed as a tax evasion measure: because of high taxation on property, the people of this part of Puglia built dry stone wall constructions so that they could be dismantled quickly whenever tax inspectors were in the area. It is a story that seems vaguely improbable but is so good that one wants to believe it.

The greatest concentration of *trulli* houses can be found in the town of Alberobello, where there is a whole hillside covered with them; from a distance the slate cone-shaped roofs with mysterious symbols painted on the slate indicating the name of the architect perched, look for all the world like some kind of bizarre witches' convention. Unfortunately, it is also a huge tourist-trap, and the place swarms with coach loads who come to wander through the narrow streets, take pictures and buy souvenirs. Much more charming is the laid-back town of Locorotondo, which, though there is barely a *trulli* in sight within the town, affords great views across a countryside dotted with them. Its dazzlingly whitewashed town centre is a delight to wander through, and unlike Alberobello it doesn't feel like it has become a museum town.

Further south, our next stop was a place we had wanted to see since watching another of those amusing Italian films, *Mine Vagante*, or 'Loose Canons', in which the second son of a pasta factory owner decides to come out as a gay man to his parents, only to be thwarted when his elder brother does the same; so great is the parental shock that the second son decides to stay in the closet after all, a plan that goes awry when a trio of rather camp friends arrive to stay, with the inevitable consequences. Quite apart from the joy of the story, one of the film's attractions was the setting, the town of Lecce, which is known as 'the Florence of the South'. This is probably a bit unjust to both cities, since Lecce is actually quite unique, and the only similarity is that both have a rich architectural heritage and a well-preserved, unified appearance. Lecce owes its fame to a remarkable burst of building in the 1630's which left it with an extensive legacy of baroque religious and secular architecture, all built out of the local limestone.

Our final stopping place was the coastal town of Otranto, right down on the south-eastern coast of Puglia. An important port since Roman times, Otranto's old town sits on a peninsula and is almost entirely surrounded by impressive fortifications that connect it to the equally formidable castle. These days it is used for the much more pacific purpose of hosting art exhibitions; when we were there, it had an excellent exhibition featuring one of Caravaggio's masterpieces as the focus for a collection of southern Italian followers of the great master.

Otranto was also the site of one of the more horrific episodes in Italian history. At the height of summer in 1480, a huge fleet of 128 Ottoman ships appeared over the horizon carrying an army of over 20,000 men. Their commander, Gedik Ahmed Pasha, had been ordered by Sultan Mehmet II to invade Italy; landing near Otranto they quickly laid siege to town and castle, and on August 11th they launched their final and successful assault. In the ensuing carnage, nearly 20,000 men, women and children were either killed or enslaved. Eight hundred survivors were offered a choice between death and converting to Islam; tradition says they defiantly chose the former, and were all beheaded outside the city on August 14th, Assumption eve. The so-called Martyrs of Otranto were canonised, and their remains buried in Otranto Cathedral.

The history of most of the coastal cities and towns of Puglia is one of constant threat of attack, from the Ottomans, from the ever-expanding and acquisitive Venetians, from the Spanish in their never-ending quest to dominate the Italian peninsula, and from the plain old pirates who infested the waters of the Adriatic. It's not surprising that places like Monopoli, Gallipoli and Taranto were surrounded by formidable walls and protected on the seaward side by mighty citadels; today they form a picturesque backdrop to harbours crowded with pleasure craft and fishing boats, but it is not difficult to imagine panicked townspeople swarming across the bridges to find safe haven behind their walls in the face of a raid by Albanian pirates or a Spanish invasion force.

Otranto was a thoroughly restful place to park ourselves after a fairly rapid tour through Puglia, and we enjoyed plenty of time lolling about on the beach or wandering the laneways of the old town. But the best thing was entirely symbolic: we made a day trip down to the town of Santa Maria di Leuca, and there made our way to a rocky point upon which we took photos of ourselves standing at the very southernmost point of the heel of the Italian boot.

\*

Unlike postmaster Alberto, we didn't feel the need for a flak jacket before venturing down to Puglia, but like him we encountered cheerful, friendly and welcoming people, many of whom had the same affinity for Australians as their Calabrian cousins, and a landscape of austere beauty that served as a backdrop to some of the most charming and laid-back towns in Italy.

The south *is* different, though, even if some of the differences are subtle. Naturally, Puglia has a version of pasta that it claims as its own (orecchiette, little ear-shaped pieces of pasta), with the usual suite of rules about the sauces with which it can be served. Compared to the north the landscape is harsh and stony; yet at the same time Puglia is a massive food producer whose crops include wheat, tomatoes, zucchini, broccoli, bell peppers, potatoes, spinach, eggplants, cauliflower, fennel, endive, chickpeas, lentils, beans, and cheese. And let's not forget olives: Puglia is the largest producer of this Italian staple in the country. Farming here tends to be on an industrial scale, something familiar to Australians but quite different from the smaller holdings typical in the north.

Even so, Puglia is poorer—much poorer—than, say, Tuscany: that much was obvious in the decayed urban infrastructure, the general scruffiness, and the poor (non-existent, almost) public transport systems. There are almost no really large cities, except for Taranto and Bari, and its small, intimate towns have a sense of being anchored in the earth, unchanging and eternal. Mind you, the ever-restless travel industry is beginning to discover places like Monopoli and Gallipoli, and you can sense that the time will come when they too have to struggle against the feckless tides of creative destruction that seem to be an inescapable characteristic of mass tourism.

As we boarded the train in Taranto, we felt that after nearly three weeks we had finally left the north behind and were ready to tackle another place that would challenge our senses and give us another perspective on the south—Naples.

# Chapter 22

# Naples: It's Complicated

You cannot arrive in Naples and not be shocked. A city unlike any other in Italy, it is raucous, confusing, dispiriting, energetic, infuriatingly grubby, sun-baked and spectacularly beautiful, all at once. The minute you emerge from the railway station, you are confronted with a swirling stew of people of every ethnicity, coming and going or trying to make a living selling trinkets and tat. The traffic is intense, impatient and noisy, and in the heat of summer the cars contribute mightily to the miasma of pollution that blankets the city. It feels more like Africa than Italy, an impression heightened by the concentration of immigrants from that continent living and working in the area surrounding the station.

Yet the city is undeniably charismatic, with its sparkling bay dotted with islands, the dramatic backdrop of Mount Vesuvius, stern castles speaking to a long feudal history, magnificent eighteenth-century palaces, labyrinthine old town streets, and extraordinary vistas that open up at the most unexpected moments. 'See Naples and die', the saying goes (origin unknown, but quoted approvingly by Goethe), meaning that having seen it one can die in peace knowing that no other sight will ever match its beauty. At the same time, it is without doubt the dirtiest city in Italy. Naples has long had a problem with garbage collection and disposal, and though several people told us that things were improving and are much better than they were, it was still very disturbing to see a corner of the street outside our apartment turned into an impromptu rubbish tip, piled with bags of garbage mingled with all sorts of hard rubbish—beaten up old refrigerators, beds, sofas, all sorts of things. And I have never seen so many cigarette butts on the streets anywhere in Italy; smokers casually flick their butts on the ground without a thought, and certainly with no visible sign of guilt!

The Neapolitans themselves are for the most part warm and friendly, though there is often an initial reserve that must be penetrated first. They are welcoming of tourists and will happily give directions and provide assistance, working harder than most Italians to overcome the language barriers. Yet at the same time they can and will fleece you, without the smile ever leaving their face. This doesn't seem malicious, it's just the way their world works—if you can casually rip an extra €20 out of a customer's pocket because they are easily confused by your rapid Italian, well, why wouldn't you? And if you get caught out, if the customer pushes back against your chiselling, a rueful smile and a shrug will restore goodwill, no trouble at all.

More unnerving is the presence of quite brazen pickpockets. Once, on a crowded train down to Pompeii, a man casually slipped his hand into Robert's pocket, obviously in search of a wallet; when Rob noticed what was going on and gave him a glare, the man just shrugged and moved further down the train, not in the least abashed. On another occasion, we were treated to some amusing comedy when catching a bus back home from the Capodimonte museum: recognising that we were tourists, an English-speaking Neapolitan lady pointed out another passenger, a man, and told us to be careful of him, as he was a well-known thief. Once aboard, another lady enlivened the trip down the hill by trying to communicate the same information with a series of wordless grimaces and gestures clearly intended to warn us to keep an eye on our valuables. Everyone on the bus except us, it seemed, was aware of this fellow's proclivities.

For Italians, rules are always a matter for interpretation. It's not that they wilfully break them, it's more that they subject them to a kind of critical analysis before deciding whether they should be obeyed. Does that stop sign really apply to me right here and right now? After all, there are no vehicles to be seen in any direction, and no police to issue me a fine, so no harm done if I ignore it. Nowhere is that philosophy more prevalent than in Naples. In the oldest part of town, for instance, the fact that the streets are notionally pedestrianised is cheerfully ignored by the youngsters on their Vespas, who weave nonchalantly in and out between ambling tourists so neatly that you hardly realise they are there before they have gone, disappearing up some side street. It might be against the rules, but hey, if I can get from A to B and no-one gets hurt, does it matter that I've broken some by-law?

As a result, the centre of Naples feels anarchic. In the very oldest part of a very old city (Naples is one of the oldest continuously inhabited urban areas in the world), the streets are narrow canyons between five- and six-story buildings, in shadow much of the day, something for which shopkeepers and tourists alike are thankful in the heat of summer. Above, air-conditioning units cling like limpets to graffiti covered walls, sheets hang from washing lines strung between the buildings, and windows are covered by ingeniously designed shutters called *persiani* whose four panels can be adjusted into a variety of configurations designed to keep out heat but admit light. Below, pedestrians pick their way between rows of tables and chairs from the cafes and restaurants that encroach onto the already limited street space, while waiters tout loudly for business, armed with nothing but a cheeky Neapolitan grin from which a cigarette invariably dangles in one corner.

Emerging from the cramped confinement of the streets, you might find yourself suddenly and unexpectedly on an open piazza, graced by a church and filled with yet more restaurants and cafes sheltering from the sun under their umbrellas. Or you might come across one of those mad Neapolitan markets where you can buy almost anything if you are prepared to pick your way through the merchandise piled up willy-nilly on makeshift tables while being harangued mercilessly by villainous-looking vendors whose fundamental philosophy is that any trick is fair in the pursuit of making a buck. It is colourful, boisterous, more than a little intimidating, but at the same time fascinating. These markets do not exist for tourists, though tourists find them irresistible; rather, for a great many Napolitani this is where they do their everyday shopping for food and clothes and almost every other kind of household item.

If the only part of Naples you had ever experienced was the heady stew of the old town and the adjoining Spanish Quarter (so named because in the sixteenth century, when Naples was directly ruled by the Spanish, their garrison troops were housed there, on the slopes below Castel Sant Elmo), you would think that it was basically a pretty grubby sort of place. But if you head up onto the heights of Vomero hill or follow the bay westward to the suburbs of Chiaia and Posillipo, you soon find yourself in a more genteel environment of elegant streets lined with graceful nineteenth century apartment buildings, pleasant shops and cafes. From their windows and balconies (used for planting flowers, not hanging out the washing) the well-heeled citizens who live in these areas compete for the most enchanting views across the bay.

For it is nature, more than the built environment, that most defines Naples and gives it its well-deserved reputation for astonishing beauty. The city lies draped like a many-hued cloak across the bones of a breathtaking landscape, tumbling down the hills and trailing its edges into the sparkling blue waters of an enormous bay, dominated by the massive conical bulk of Mount Vesuvius and enclosed to the south by the distant tangled ridges of the Sorrento Peninsula. Hanging like jewelled pendants from the bay's extremities are the islands—Procida, Ischia, and above all Capri—which have been playgrounds for the rich since Roman times. No wonder the Napolitani flock in their thousands on warm evenings to amble along the *lungomare*, the broad pedestrian terrace that runs along the shore, and take in the view as the sun descends into the west, gradually turning the sea from blue to purple and transforming the distant islands into mysterious silhouettes.

*

One supposes that this setting must have seemed just as gorgeous to the early Greek settlers who arrived in the sixth century BCE and founded the town of Neapolis between the shores of the bay and the bulk of Mount Vesuvius. What is now the old town of Naples follows the simple grid of the ancient city, which soon grew to become one of the leading cities of Magna Graecia as the Romans called the cities of the Greek diaspora. Founding nearly ninety cities over several hundred years, the Greeks brought their civic culture to Sicily and southern part of the Italian peninsula. In the process they civilised the uncouth Latins and Romans, who adopted many of their customs and language.

Neapolis was one of the first of the Greek cities to fall to the Romans, in 327 BCE, and their new masters adorned the city with fine new buildings, and created t vast villas and extensive gardens around the shores of the bay where they could take their vacations from the rigours of Roman city life. Not that Roman Neapolis and its surrounding towns were entirely given over to pleasure: they were bustling, important centres of trade first and foremost, and the bay was filled with fat-bellied ships hauling cargoes from Sicily, North Africa, Egypt, Spain, and even far-off Britain.

The peace of the city was rudely disturbed at about 1:00 pm one day in October 79 CE, when without warning Mount Vesuvius erupted, spewing pumice and ash far into the air. For the next two days the citizens of Neapolis watched as a huge cloud hung over the mountains, the earth shook with tremors, and people as far away as Misenum, on the far western edge of the bay, fled in terror of this unexpected phenomenon. By the time the eruption ended, the nearby cities of Pompeii and Herculaneum had been buried in ash and lava, though Neapolis itself was mostly untouched.

Pompeii today is, of course, one of the greatest archaeological sites in the world, an almost complete Roman city preserved beneath the layers of ash and mud, and visiting it is a profoundly moving experience. Knowing how popular the site is, we made the effort to get up early in the morning and catch the rickety old Circumvesuviana train down there so that we could be at the gates at opening time; that was well worth the effort, because tourist buses generally don't arrive until ten-ish, and that meant we had at least an hour in which we could explore in relative tranquillity.

The site itself sits on what looks like a plateau, but was in fact the original shoreline. After the rather frenzied process of buying tickets you enter the city through what would have been a water gate; that takes you up past the remains of the basilica (the principal place of government and justice) and into the city's heart, the forum. In its day, this broad open space would have been lined on either side by colonnades and surrounded by temples dedicated to Apollo, Jove, and the late Emperor Vespasian. Over in one corner was the ancient food market, and on another the town's granaries stood. In short, the forum, like its modern successor the piazza, was the place where government, trade and religion all intersected.

It is when you go beyond these monumental spaces and wander into the maze of streets and lanes that run off to the east of the city's heart that the fate of Pompeii becomes more poignant. The walls of houses still stand to at least one story high for the most part, and in many places they retain their full two-story height. Here and there ancient Latin graffiti has survived, carefully preserved under plastic, and we are told that almost all of the walls in ancient times would have been so decorated. The messages that these ancient taggers scrawled on every available surface could be extraordinarily explicit: 'Weep, you girls. My penis has given you up. Now it penetrates men from behind', says one on the wall of what was probably a brothel. An official announces that the food in the house of a certain Cuspius Pansa is poison, while on a wall next to an inn, someone complained that 'you sell us water and keep the good wine for yourself' (some things never change, it seems). And the last word on this subject probably goes to the chap who wrote on a wall of the forum 'O walls, you have held up so much tedious graffiti that I am amazed you have not already collapsed in ruin!'

Ancient Romans of the more common sort didn't eat at home very much, preferring to grab a meal on the go from one of the many food shops that can be found on almost every corner of Pompeii. The counter tops of many are still intact, containing built-in bowls that were heated from underneath, in which hot food was prepared and kept; half close your eyes and you can imagine a throng of chattering workmen, their clothes dusty and their faces streaked with sweat, congregating around the bar exchanging gossip and insulting the hardworking bar owner while they consume a hasty meal in their short lunch break.

The wealthier citizens, on the other hand, took their meals in the dining room of their house, surrounded by brightly painted scenes of town and country, and served by deferential household slaves. Though the houses of the rich were often quite grand, they were usually inconspicuous from the street, entered from a plain door that gave access to a series of enclosed courtyards around which the principal rooms of the house were arranged. Pompeii has many examples of such houses, and the biggest of them, the House of the Faun, must have been very luxurious indeed. Built around two colonnaded gardens, it covers nearly three thousand square metres (more or less a whole Pompeian city block), had its own private bath house, and was decorated with beautiful mosaics, the most famous of which portrays Alexander the Great confronting Darius III at the battle of Issos; the original of this work is now in the Naples Archaeological Museum, though a copy can be seen at the house itself.

Wandering in and out of the houses and public buildings, and even just walking down the streets with their deep cartwheel grooves and stepping stones to allow the citizens to cross the road without getting their feet wet when it rained, you cannot fail to sense the ghostly presence of the twenty thousand souls who lived here. They might have glanced up at the peak of the mountain that had stood there time out of mind, never imagining that the city's destruction would come at its hands. The explosion released the energy of a hundred thousand Hiroshimas and buried the city in six metres of ash. Contrary to popular imagination, the eruption didn't kill everyone—only about 1,100 bodies have been found, and it is thought that the bulk of the population were able to get out of the city over the course of the two-day eruption. Even so the twisted casts of those who didn't make it are still quite chilling to behold.

The other famous site associated with the eruption is the town of Herculaneum. A little further around the bay of Naples from Pompeii, it was buried under about twenty metres of ash. Though the town was a substantial one, only a part of it has been excavated, most of the rest still sitting untouched in the soil beneath the rather unlovely Neapolitan suburb or Ercolano. What is visible is much smaller than Pompeii and much easier to get around; it is also rather more intact than its more famous sister, so you get a much more intimate look at the life of ancient Romans. We had been tempted to skip Herculaneum, but on the whole I'm glad we didn't.

*

After the fall of the Roman Empire, Neapolitan history followed the same course as most of the peninsula: after a period of barbarian and then Byzantine rule, an independent duchy of Naples emerged, was tossed back and forth between various powers intent on controlling Italy, until the Normans united it with Sicily in a configuration that was to endure on and off until the nineteenth century, though its story went through many twists and turns.

But by the eighteenth-century Naples was a wealthy and sophisticated capital, the second largest city in Europe with a population of more than 250,000 inhabitants, whose kings ruled over one of the most extensive and unified territories in Europe. Like so many others, we were dazzled by the sheer opulence of the royal palaces in the capital and the expansive magnificence of the Versailles-like country estate that the monarchy built for itself at Caserta.

The popular version of Italian history is that the south was backward, feudal, and poor, just waiting to be brought into the modern age by the industrialised civilisation of the north. After all, the Kingdom of Naples fell like a ripe plum before Garibaldi's armies, and the benighted poor voted by huge majorities to abandon their king and join the new Italian state.

But as is so often the case in history, the truth is a little more complicated.

It true that the wealth of the Neapolitan kingdom stood on somewhat shaky foundations. While the northern half of the country pursued industrialisation and modernisation, the Kingdom of the Two Sicilies, as it became known, seemed stuck in a feudal time-warp. The aristocracy owned most of the land which they managed through vast estates called *latifondi*, whose tenants paid sufficient rent to keep their owners in luxury while relieving them of the necessity of investing in any economic development of their assets. Great swathes of land were poorly cultivated by peasant farmers living in a state of near poverty while their landlords lolled about in Naples and Palermo attending soirees and balls.

Perhaps it is unsurprising that visitors to the kingdom came away with an impression of sloth and squalor and could not help but note the wide gulf between the somnolent poverty of the countryside and the splendour of the cities. The ruling Bourbons (a distant branch of the famous French royal family) were derided as the corrupt monarchs presiding over the worst-governed territory in Italy—though it was acknowledged that things were better than in the neighbouring Papal States, where the church's neglect of its secular responsibilities was near-total.

Yet this picture is at least a little misleading. The Bourbons, Charles VII and his son Ferdinand IV were, it is true, rather rustic in character. Charles preferred hunting to the complexities of economic management or law-making, and Ferdinand's earthy manners earned him the nickname *il rei lazzarone*, because he empathised with the city's underclass (known as the *lazzaroni*) and—horror of horrors—he enjoyed eating his *maccheroni* with his fingers like any ordinary peasant. But in fact both were that rarity, enlightened despots. They encouraged learning in the cities and chose intelligent and capable advisers to govern in their name, who pursued liberal social policies, oversaw a doubling in the kingdom's revenue and a decrease in taxation. Under their regime, Naples evolved into one of the great capitals of Europe.

And not everyone was condemnatory. Goethe, for example, thought that Naples was 'a happy country', where everyone lived in a state of 'intoxicated self-forgetfulness'. For such a teeming city, where life was frequently precarious, the murder rate was low, and instances of public drunkenness rare. Eighteenth century Naples was raucous but not much given to riot, and the most challenging scourge that a visitor might have to deal with was the ever-present army of pickpockets—some things never change, it seems. Above all it was a cosmopolitan place, which the French writer Stendhal thought was the only Italian city that had 'the true makings of a capital'; this rather condescending judgement ignored the fact that it had been one for over six hundred years, and of the only state in the peninsula whose borders had not been subject to rearrangement after every European or Italian war at that.

In the patriotic version of Italian history, all this was swept away by Garibaldi and his revolutionary heroes, when they landed at Marsala in 1860. Deterministic historians since have tended to see the end of the Bourbon regime as inevitable, given the corrupted state of the government; in fact the regime was not particularly unpopular, and probably less than one in twenty Neapolitans were in favour of unification with the north.

But that wasn't going to stop Cavour and his Piedmontese king, Victor Emmanuel. First, he tried to foment a 'spontaneous' uprising in Naples—unsuccessfully, since the sensible Neapolitans decided to wait upon events rather than lead them. Then plebiscites were arranged in both Sicily and Naples promising both states autonomy provided they agreed to be annexed by Piedmont; the question was a weighted one, leaving the people with the delusion that, though they might be absorbed into a new Italian kingdom, life would go on much as before. In the end there were large majorities in favour of annexation, though the ballots were clearly rigged in Sicily, which reported a 99% approval rate. Francis II, the last ruler of the Bourbon line, surrendered and abdicated in February 1861, and the Kingdom of the Two Sicilies was no more.

The new Italian monarchy behaved with considerable insensitivity and arrogance, spiriting off the bulk of the Bourbons' wealth to Turin, imposing taxes to pay for the Piedmontese national debt, and imposing doctrinaire free trade policies that deeply damaged southern agriculture and industry. In the process, far from creating the unified country that they were seeking, these policies entrenched a north-south divide that persists to this day and is a factor in modern Italian politics. Matteo Salvini's *partito liga* was, after all, originally called the '*northern* league', and it was built on northern prejudices against the mores of the slovenly south.

One might have expected that such a history would cast a shadow over the attitudes of southern Italians, and particularly the Neapolitans. After all, it was their treasure that had in a manner of speaking been stolen, and they who were reduced to mendicant status in the name of progress. But there is little sign of resentment among a people for whom simply getting on with life is much more important; Salvini and his allies might rail against the failings of the south, but you get the feeling that the south—Naples, anyway—couldn't care less.

The German poet and frequent visitor much admired what the Neapolitans call *l'arte di arrangiarsi* (literally 'the art of getting by'), and it is a spirit that seems alive and well in Naples. For the most part, southern Italians accept that northerners will never understand them, and that is okay. There are more important things to do, like making enough money to live a good life, enjoying the balmy nights along the *lungomare*, haggling down to the last cent in the markets, taking your girl on the back of your Vespa for a ride up to admire the view from St Elmo, critically listening to a cracked tenor singing the syrupy lyrics to an age-old Neapolitan song on a street corner in the old town, meeting up with your friends for a coffee and a *sfogliatella*, or just hanging out on the street watching the world go by. In short, life.

That enthusiasm for the joys of ordinary everyday life seems to suffuse Neapolitan art. Only a Neapolitan could have turned a ride up Mount Vesuvius on the new funicular railway into a jaunty love song, while the city's unofficial anthem must surely be '*O Sole Mio*', the opening line of which translates to 'What a beautiful thing is a sunny day!' Neapolitan composer Ruggiero Leoncavallo won fame for writing an opera about a tragic love triangle in a troupe of touring clowns, and Giovanni Verga wrote a short story about the passions and superstitions of a country village, *Cavalleria Rusticana*, (or 'Rustic Chivalry') which the young Milanese composer Pietro Mascagni turned into a brilliant exposition of the art of *verismo* opera. In the world of painting, Michelangelo Merisi da Caravaggio, though himself a northerner, created some his greatest masterpieces during his turbulent sojourn in Naples, and in so doing changed the very course of art. Have a closer look at the men and women that he and his followers inserted into the traditional religious stories: they are earthy, real people—in short, Neapolitans.

The celebration of everyday life isn't confined to high art, either. One of the most charming Neapolitan traditions is that of the Presepe, the making of elaborate nativity scenes (the literal translation of the word is 'crib'). Still popular today, these gorgeous and intricately detailed tableaux were all the rage in the eighteenth century, and you can see fine examples in several Neapolitan museums. The holy family was usually placed at the centre of scenes in which dozens and sometimes hundreds of figures made of terracotta or wood or even papier-mache are depicted eating and drinking, buying and selling, dancing and singing. The detail is exquisite: the figures are dressed immaculately, the food on the tables looks delicious enough to eat, and each face has its own individual character. Creating these tableaux demanded the highest level of artistic craftsmanship, skills that are preserved today in the forty or so active workshops located in the neighbourhood of San Gregorio Armeno, who produce an astonishing seventy thousand figures each year to meet the demand of Neapolitans wanting them for their home *presepe*.

Naples is, at every level, a complicated place, full of paradoxes. It takes your breath away, exasperates you, inspires you, defeats you, and excites you, all at once. Nothing is quite as it seems on the surface, and I venture to guess that not even the Napolitani themselves really understand the place. But one thing is for sure: they all love it. In our month-long stay, I lost count of the number of times that some local just had to tell us why Naples is the best city in the world, without an ounce of irony or self-deprecation. And you know what? Perhaps they are right.

# Chapter 23

# Palermo: Normans, the Mafia, and a Leopard

I have been in love with the idea of sea travel ever since the day in 1967 that my ten-year-old self stood on tiptoes at the rail of the promenade deck of the MV *Castel Felice*, watching the coast of the Isle of Wight slip by as we steamed past, bound for Australia with my family aboard. Of course, air travel, so much faster and more convenient, has long displaced ships as the principal means of moving people around the world, and so the opportunities to experience the slow joys of travelling on the water have been limited over the years to the occasional cruise holiday. Still, when we came to consider how we might make our way to our next destination, the island of Sicily, doing it by ferry seemed like a fun proposition, and so, after the usual hours of online research, we booked ourselves on the GNV ferry service from Naples to Palermo.

Travelling by ferry, we discovered, is not *quite* the same glamorous experience as joining a cruise ship. To begin with, there are no fancy terminals manned by obsequious staff to shepherd you through the boarding process. Instead, we arrived at Naples ferry terminal, where, having obtained our boarding tickets from a little ticket office hidden away in one of half a dozen nondescript buildings lining the wharf, we and about twenty other passengers were left standing in the hot sun for an hour or so, prevented by a friendly but uncommunicative security guard from entering the dock while a seemingly endless stream of cars and trucks drove out. The scheduled departure time of 11:00 am for our ferry, the *GNV Cristal*, had long gone before we were finally allowed to walk aboard through the cavernous vehicle bay and make our way to our cabin, a dinky little affair with a couple of bunks and a tiny bathroom.

To our considerable surprise, we and the others with whom we had been waiting were the ferry's only passengers on this leg—and, astonishingly given that it was the height of summer, there were no cars or trucks at all being loaded, so we had barely got ourselves settled before the ship was under way and beginning the passage out of the Bay of Naples, past the towering rock of Capri and into the open sea. It is a ten-hour journey from Naples to Palermo, enough time to watch the passing scenery from deserted decks as the coastline gradually receded into the distance, have a coffee and a sandwich lunch in the bar, and retire for a couple of hours to the cabin to watch a movie or two on the laptop and have a nap. By the time we had emerged for dinner in the buffet restaurant (one of two options aboard, the other being a proper table-service restaurant which looked decidedly empty when we went past), the *Cristal* was well within sight of the Sicilian coast.

As the sun surrendered its last grip on the day, we were sliding gently into the harbour. Leaning on the rail of the main deck, we were treated to a spectacularly beautiful panorama as the ship turned in a circle to ease into her berth. To the north, the immense massif of Monte Pellegrino was outlined in a luminous corona as the sun set behind it; the ring of hills that surround Palermo to the west and south had dissolved into barely visible inky shadows, below which the lights of the city blinked and shimmered in the warmth of the night. Along the shore we could just pick out the ruins of an old fortress, a *palazzo* or two, church domes and spires, all half seen behind the yellow glare of the dockyard lights.

Disembarkation procedures were just as informal as the embarkation process back in Naples, and after a few minutes we found ourselves standing on a dark crowded wharf, trying to work out what to do next. As we and our fellow passengers were leaving the port area to begin the vain search for a taxi, we were confronted with a mass of cars and trucks of every description coming in the opposite direction, queuing up to board the Tunis-bound ferry that was docked on the other side of the wharf. Most of the cars were crammed full of personal effects; one was not only full inside but piled another four or five feet high on the roof with stuff, leaving barely enough room for the driver. They were immigrants who were returning home, and for the first time we had a sense of the scale of the human tide that washes back and forth across these waters, finding its locus in Sicily.

Having worked our way clear of this tangle, we started the fifteen-minute walk to our apartment, following the directions helpfully provided by Mister Google, through darkened back streets that were jammed with parked cars and lined with ugly concrete apartment buildings overlooking deserted streets. Eventually we found our apartment and were greeted by our very solicitous AirBNB host, Mari. Though the apartment was probably one of the best we have rented—two bedrooms, two bathrooms, even two living rooms—our unglamorous arrival had left us a little apprehensive, and we went to bed wondering quite what kind of city in which we had arrived.

We needn't have worried. When we woke up the next morning and took stock of our surroundings, we realised that, more by good luck than good judgement, the apartment we had found was located in one of Palermo's nicer areas. Politeama is that part of Palermo north of the city centre built in the years after unification. It is laid out in the fashionably tidy grid pattern, whose main street is the leafy via della Liberta, lined with art-deco apartment buildings and boutiques displaying their upmarket wares. At the southern end of the suburb is a wide piazza, dominated by the grand Teatro Politeama Garibaldi. Beyond the piazza, the main street has a series of name changes until it emerges as the pedestrianised Via Macqueda outside the city's equally grand opera house, the Teatro Massimo, reputed to be Italy's oldest (and the setting for the final scenes of *The Godfather III*).

The theatre is a kind of dividing point between the gentility of Politeama and the more tangled, anarchic streets of the old town. This area dates back to Arabic times, and is arranged into four quarters around the focal point of an octagonal piazza called the Quatro Cantii It is here that, if you wander off the main streets into the tangle of narrow lanes, you encounter the more earthy world of workaday Palermo, where the building facades are dilapidated and crumbling, the balconies rusted, and the washing flaps above your head in the slight breeze that does little to diminish the summer heat. Vendors ply their various trades in lively street markets that snake their way through the winding back streets, and little piazzas play host to cafes and restaurants whose main customers are local Palermitani, not tourists.

\*

Given the natural advantages of its sheltered bay, it is hardly surprising to learn that the Palermo region has been inhabited since prehistoric times, though it was the arrival of Phoenicians from the eastern Mediterranean in 734 BCE that really kicked off the history of the city, when they built a colony there, which they called Ziz. Renamed as Panormos by the Greeks, it became an important city in Magna Graecia, and flourished through the Roman period, when fertile and productive Sicily was the empire's granary. The Byzantines then ruled for several hundred years, before Sicily and Palermo fell to the great Arab expansion of the eighth and ninth centuries.

This is where Sicilian history gets interesting, and the influences that created a unique culture begin to emerge. Nowhere else in Italy was subjected to such a sustained period of Arabic influence. For two and a half centuries, Palermo was the capital of the Emirate of Sicily, one of the great civilisations of the Mediterranean basin, and Palermo competed with Cordoba and Cairo for the splendour of its buildings and the importance of its trade. Arab traveller Ibn Jubair visited the city, and wrote that:

*'The capital...contains all the real and imagined beauty that anyone could wish. Splendour and grace adorn the piazzas and the countryside; the streets and highways are wide, and the eye is dazzled by the beauty of its situation. It is a city full of marvels, with buildings similar to those of Córdoba, built of limestone. A permanent stream of water from four springs runs through the city, and there are so many mosques that they are impossible to count. The eye is dazzled by all this splendour.'*

Like the Arabic rulers of southern Spain, the Arab Emirs of Sicily were tolerant of the Christian and Jewish populations they had displaced, for the most part allowing them to live and worship as they always had, though subject to some restrictions and taxes that encouraged the natives to convert to Islam. No doubt such conversions were the price that the more practical-minded were prepared to pay, as much for financial advantage as out of any genuine religious conviction. In the Emirs' courts, scientific and cultural learning flourished, preserving western knowledge of Greek culture until the rest of Italy was ready to re-embrace it, and making their own unique contributions in the fields of mathematics and astronomy.

Then, in the eleventh century, the Normans turned up and overturned everything. Roger de Hauteville, the twenty-six-year-old younger brother of Robert Guiscard, was the leading light in their joint expedition to Sicily, and when they captured Palermo in 1072 Robert invested his brother with the title Count of Sicily, though it would take almost another two decades before the Arabs were finally defeated and expelled from the island.

The Great Count, as Roger was known, turned out to be as enlightened a ruler as the emirs he had deposed, allowing his Muslim subjects their mosques and freedom of trade. Roger died in 1101, and for the next decade the county was ruled by a regent for his two sons, one of those capable but unacknowledged women who appear from time to time in pre-modern history, Adelaide del Vasto. The youngest son, another Roger, came of age in 1112, and began his personal rule as Count of Sicily. Ambitious and politically astute, he eventually made himself master not only of Sicily, but of all the Hauteville possessions in Calabria and Apulia as well. In 1130 he supported the successful candidate in a disputed election for the papacy, for which his reward was a crown when pope anointed him king Roger II of Sicily.

Sicily entered now on yet another golden age, as over the next decade Roger II consolidated his hold on the kingdom and presided over a glittering multi-ethnic court, in which Muslim scholars debated with Greek theologians, an Englishman named Thomas Brun served as a senior government minister and had a secretary named Othman, and the great geographer Muhammad al-Idrisi created the world maps that Vasco da Gama and Christopher Columbus were to use centuries later. When Roger died in 1154, he was one of the greatest kings in Europe.

Unsurprisingly, Norman building can be seen all over Palermo. The grandest pile of all is the Palazzo dei Normanni, the oldest royal residence in Europe, which the Normans adapted from the original palace built by the Emirs. They developed a complex of residential and administrative buildings linked by courtyards, gardens, and enclosed galleries, mimicking the Arabic style. Its most famous room, and the highlight of any visit, is Roger II's glistening Capella Palatina, which is a riot of gold mosaic. The palace is still the seat of the city's government, which gives it a lived-in feel quite different from most museums.

Not far from the palace stands the striking pile of the Castello Zisa, begun by William I (Roger's son, known as William the Bad) and completed by *his* son, another William (William the Good! Neither nickname seems to have been well-deserved). Conceived as a summer residence and today used as a museum, it is a fine example of Norman-Moorish architecture, with all the square solidity of a fortress enlivened by the grace-notes of Arabic decoration.

Multi-ethnic and religiously tolerant Sicily may have been, but that didn't stop the Norman kings from building some fine Christian churches. Along the coast from Palermo, beneath the towering rock of seaside Cefalù, Roger II ordered the construction of a fine church, where he and his wife were to be buried. And out at Monreale, in what was then the countryside, William II took just four years to build a huge cathedral, over a hundred metres long, probably the greatest of all the Norman churches in Sicily. Back in Palermo, less grand and easy to overlook is the little Church of San Cataldo, built in 1154 in an intriguing blend of Norman and Moorish styles with its three blue domes and austere Romanesque interior, an invitingly cool place in which to escape the Palermitan heat for a few minutes.

Just up the street is the massive Norman-Baroque cathedral. Begun in 1185 by the interestingly named Walter Ophamil (an Anglo-Norman who was known in England as Walter of the Mill—one can imagine the twelfth century Palermitani puzzling over the name and finally settling on this crude phonetic

# Chapter 24

# Afterword

The travels described in this book took place between 2017 and 2019; now, three-quarters of the way through 2021, it seems as though they passed in another world. When Covid-19 emerged in Milan and Lombardy in February 2020 we had been back in Australia for several months, and as the crisis in Italy evolved and spread across Europe and the world it was hard to watch the news reports that showed familiar Italian cities under siege in scenes that would all too soon become familiar here in Australia. For a people for whom the weekly family gathering has the status of an inviolable ritual, being forced to bunker down in their apartments for weeks and months at a time must have been particularly hard to bear.

We also saw, of course, extraordinary outpourings of emotion. Who can forget the scenes of people singing Verdi's great hymn *Va pensiero* from their balconies? Endlessly inventive, they improvised and make the best of things, a characteristically Italian way of dealing with problems. And, also characteristically Italian, they frequently flouted the rules, thus prolonging the crisis: Covid-19 brought out the very best and very worst of Italian behaviour.

Watching all this from afar, and then coping with our own outbreaks, it took a while to understand that it will be a long time before we are able to go back to Italy and revisit our old haunts. Even at the time of writing, when Europe is just begin-

tion seems impossible to stamp out and the Mafia's influence in the south seems ineradicable. There is often a dispiriting sense that changing anything is difficult, if not impossible, an attitude that puzzles Americans and Australians, people addicted to change.

Despite all this, the Italians have managed to create an economic miracle out of the ashes of the second world war, and the country is today still an economic powerhouse within Europe. It provides universal education and good quality healthcare to its citizens, and is generous to those who have suffered misfortune, including the refugees and economic immigrants who wash up on its shores looking for a better life. Italy is a compassionate country that has not lost its soul to self-interest and the demands of the dollar. Much of that can be attributed to the soft-heartedness of the Italian people, who, though they can be harsh in their judgements and unsubtle in delivering them, still have a great deal of natural empathy. It comes, I think, from the fact that family is at the heart of Italian social life: for them, a refugee is not an economic problem or a threat, he or she is a father, a mother, a brother or a sister.

It was a privilege to be able to live among the Italians for a period of time and absorb at least a little of their ethos. It is my fond hope that this book will have communicated something of the nature of that ethos, perhaps encouraged those familiar with Italy to see it in a new way, and inspired those who have never been to think about visiting. Above all, I hope my words have been entertaining. If I have achieved any of those things, I am well content.

past of the Italian peninsula offers enough dramatic and illuminating stories to inspire dozens of novels.

'Italy,' nineteenth-century statesman Claus von Metternich once wrote, 'is only a geographical expression.' It was a self-interested statement, since at the time he was trying his best to stamp out any idea of Italian unification; ever since, the Italian people have done their best to refute this idea, promoting assiduously the symbols of their country and naming every other street and piazza after the heroes of the *risorgimento*. But you can't quite eradicate a thousand years of separateness in a mere hundred and fifty years, and the citizens of every region, city and village still give their first loyalty to their local community. And so Italy is a place that is much more diverse than you expect it to be. All Italians aren't just Italians: they are Piedmontese, Neapolitans, Tuscans, Florentines, Romans, Palermitans, Genoese.

That diversity of outlook and pride in their local place is a value that much of western society has discarded in favour of cookie-cutter efficiency. In Australia, in America, in Britain, we crave uniformity, we expect every supermarket to look the same and offer the same range of goods regardless of the season, and we are happy to give our custom to shops that are mere representatives of some chain or another. But Italians haven't entirely given in to the forces of global homogeneity: for them, the preservation of local customs and local businesses takes primacy over the mirage of efficiency that globalisation offers. It is admirable, and beguiling.

The more I think about it, the more the idea of *la dolce vita* pops back into my mind. The Italians simply know how to live well, and that skill seems to permeate every aspect of life in Italy. Not that their life is perfect; neither is their country. But what life or country ever is? Italy's politics suffers a degree of dysfunctionality that at times borders on the bizarre, the slowness and idiocy of the Italian bureaucracy is legendary, corrupto Naples. The station is an antique dating back to 1866, and was used in—you guessed it—the third of the *Godfather* films. The train was of course impossibly late, so much so that we had to make a mad dash by taxi at the other end to be the last passengers to board our ferry.

\*

And so, having finally made our way to the southernmost province of Italy, we come to the end of this tour through the regions and cities of one of the most charming and interesting countries in Europe, if not the world, and it is time to sum things up. Yet I find myself, after expending my energy on all these words, struggling to do so. That is perhaps not surprising: so much has been said and written about Italy that the idea that I might be able to find something original to say seems faintly absurd.

So let me instead use someone else's words. 'Italy', wrote Russian poet Anna Akhmatova, 'is a dream that keeps returning for the rest of your life.' That perfectly sums things up for me. I find myself over and over again remembering the taste of a gelato in Naples, the awe-inspiring interior of the cathedral in Florence, the flash of sun on water in the harbour at Vernazza, the softness of the hills of Tuscany, the almost painful sunlight of the south. These little visions appear, just like dreams, at all sorts of odd moments, and they seem to be beckoning me back, irresistibly. The damned place has got in my blood, and I'll never get it out.

What is it that so fascinates? Everyone who loves Italy will have their own answer to that, coloured by preferences and experiences. Of course, I start from the history, which is omnipresent, there in the very stones of the streets and buildings, the carved symbols and coats of arms hanging over the gateways, the historically costumed parades that express Italians' pride in their past. I knew almost nothing of Italy's history before our long sojourn there, but I discovered that the chaotic

campaign: a rather sterile concrete monument marks the spot. Marsala once boasted a beautiful baroque town centre, but sadly it was badly damaged during the second world war, and much of the newly rebuilt city is rather charmless. Still, we managed a decent lunch and a glass or two of Marsala's most famous product, the sweet wine that bears its name.

This wine has been produced in the area time out of mind, but it took an Englishman to popularise it. In 1773, English trader John Woodhouse landed in Marsala and recognised that the local fortified wine had a similar taste to the Spanish sherry that was then very popular in England (not surprising, since both are made using a similar process). Woodhouse promptly began mass production and commercialisation, and the region never looked back. Today, Marsala is more often used in cooking outside Italy, but in Sicily it is popular as an aperitif, served between the first and second courses of a meal, or as a standalone drink accompanied by aged parmesan or gorgonzola cheese.

The final leg of our visit to Sicily took us to the other end of the island, to the famous town of Taormina. This is yet another of those fairy-tale places, perched on a long ridge of land high above the Straits of Messina, beautifully preserved and rather hopelessly overrun by tourists in the summer. The town's most famous sight is the massive and perfectly preserved Greek theatre, occupying a natural amphitheatre at one end of the town and still used for performances of opera and dance. Equally impressive is the view of Mount Etna from the Piazza IX Aprile; we kept hoping that the famously active volcano would offer us at least a gentle demonstration of its power, but alas the most we got were a few wisps of smoke one afternoon.

In a fitting end to our time in Sicily, we found ourselves standing on the platform of Taormina's train station waiting for the train that would take us to Catania and our ferry back

spent travelling with her former husband, then a senior Australian politician.

Chris and Dorothy were also our companions on various excursions beyond Palermo. One memorable visit took us to the mountain-top town of Erice. There was a story behind this, and as so often it started with one of Robert's obsessions. Long ago, someone had given him a book entitled Bitter Almonds, the story of a young girl named Maria Grammatico who was sent with her sister to the nunnery of San Carlo, in Erice. There, she learned to make handcrafted pastries and marzipan confections that the nuns sold to customers through a grilled window. The book is part memoir, part recipe book, but the salient point that got Robert's imagination was the fact that Maria now runs a pastry shop in Erice. So nothing would do but that we should go and visit.

Hiring a car, we drove the hundred or so kilometres through the Sicilian countryside until we arrived at the base of an enormous great rock towering some seven hundred metres above us. A few minutes' winding drive and we arrived at the car park just outside the town. Needless to say, the views across the plain towards the town of Trapani, surrounded by its saltpans glistening in the morning sun, were truly spectacular. But we weren't there for the view: we were on a mission to find sister Maria and her *pasticceria*. It didn't take long to find it, have a coffee and some marzipan treats, after which Robert just had to have his photo taken with Maria herself (she is a sprightly nonagenarian who seemed slightly bemused at this enthusiastic Australian with his minimal Italian who chatted determinedly at her as the photo was being taken).

Not wanting to waste the day's hire of the car, we decided to keep going and head for Marsala for lunch. Marsala is at the extreme western end of Sicily, and is famous for two things: Garibaldi and wine. It was here that the great liberator landed with his thousand men on 11$^{th}$ May 1860 to begin his Sicilian

ings. And with all that money sloshing around, the Mafia re-emerged as enablers and corrupters, helped by their mates in the civil administration, and transformed themselves in the process from rural thugs to a sophisticated urban criminal organisation.

The horrors that the Sicilian Mafia have inflicted up and down the length of Italy as they resisted efforts to bring them under control are well known. But they were opposed by brave Sicilians such as magistrates Giovanni Falconi and Paolo Borsellino, determined to rid their beloved island of this scourge. Both men were assassinated, but they inspired many others to follow them, and gradually the Mafia were worn down; today most of their leaders are in gaol, and though the Mafia's hand is detected everywhere in the endemic low-level corruption that still afflicts Palermo, their influence is nowhere near as total as it once was.

Still, the knowledge of that recent violent history lodges somewhere in the back of the mind of any visitor to Palermo, and certainly we had felt a mild twinge of apprehension as we walked down the landing ramp from the ferry on that hot night. But whatever residual anxiety we felt had disappeared within a few days, driven out by the excitement of discovering this complex, fascinating city. Like so many other places in Italy, Palermo soon joined the 'must visit again' list.

*

Our arrival in Palermo had coincided with the arrival of two Aussie friends, Chris and Dorothy. Neither would be happy with me if I didn't immediately make it clear that they are *not* a couple, simply friends who had been travelling together in North Africa. They had disembarked from one of those massive ferries that trundle back and forth between Sicily and Tunis, after what they described, politely, as a 'challenging' trip. Chris is an old friend, but Dorothy we had not met before; she soon endeared herself to us with her funny tales from a life

for the thieves and a fee from the victims. And from this protection racket was born the uniquely Sicilian scourge of the Mafia.

The Mafia were mostly a rural phenomenon during the early years after unification, but they proved difficult to defeat for a weak and under-resourced police force; ironically, it was the advent of an even greater expert in the gentle arts of thuggery, Benito Mussolini, that led to the Mafia being pretty well suppressed. The *Duce* saw them as a threat to his power and was ruthless in carrying out a war against them that left the various clans exhausted and forced deeply underground by 1929.

But irony is piled on irony in Sicilian history, and the modern-day resurgence of the Mafia is often put down to the successful allied campaign to liberate Sicily in 1943. Most of the island's civil institutions had been destroyed, and the Americans set about creating a new civil administration from scratch. In their haste to do so, few background checks were made and many of their appointments turned out to be Mafiosi, cunningly disguised as anti-fascist dissidents and anti-communist patriots. Not for the last time, American carelessness and naivete was to have far-reaching consequences.

In the course of their efforts to dislodge the German and Italian forces from the island, the allies had bombed Palermo heavily, all but destroying the port and surrounding areas; nearly eight decades later you can still see devastated buildings that have never been demolished or restored. That meant there was a lot of rebuilding to be done. Then, after the war was finally over, rural immigrants flooded into Palermo, and the city's population grew by a hundred thousand people.

To house all these new residents, it was decided to expand the city to the north in a massive construction boom that became known as 'the sack of Palermo', because developers were allowed to run wild, ignoring building codes and tearing down old palazzi and villas to make way for shoddy apartment build-

Mafia-related corruption still seems to be endemic if the stories we were told are to be believed.

But where did the Mafia spring from? They are seen as a modern phenomenon, but in fact their roots go all the way back to the fifteenth century. By this time, the Sicilians had lost their independence through a series of dynastic twists and turns, and were no more than a province of Spain, ruled by a series of viceroys. But vice-regal authority was weak, so they bought loyalty by handing out lucrative government positions and grants of land to the local nobility, who steadily enriched themselves by developing vast estates in the countryside. New towns and villages were founded that were populated by bringing landless labourers from the cities, and growing vast crops of wheat for export.

Something curious was happening out in that countryside which was to have a profound impact on the future of Sicily, and as so often in Italian history Napoleon was its unwitting instigator. Land reforms instituted under his brief rule as king of Italy forced many of the feudal barons to sell off much of their land to settle their debts (and finance the pleasures of their lifestyle in Palermo). As a result, by the time Garibaldi landed with his thousand troops at Marsala in 1860 the number of landowners had swelled from two thousand to twenty thousand.

That meant that there were more disputes that needed settling, more contracts that needed enforcing, more transactions that needed oversight, and more properties that needed protecting. At the same time, the feudal armies through which the aristocracy had hitherto enforced their will were disbanded, and policing functions were handed over to the newly created Italian state. However, there weren't enough trained policemen to do the job properly, so the landlords recruited young men into informal armed companies to hunt down thieves and negotiate the return of stolen property, in exchange for a pardon

Lampedusa lived and worked, converting part of it into the suite of apartments where Glenn and Giovanni have been staying for so many years. Gioacchino himself has also had a storied career as an artistic director, musicologist and writer.

So it was particularly moving when Nicola generously offered to give us a tour of the apartments in the palazzo, where we could see the library in which Lampedusa worked, and, in a glass case, look at the handwritten original draft of The Leopard, lines of neat script on yellow paper, not a line crossed out or amended; next to it was the typed-up version and the original first edition printed book. Nicoletta read for us the first few paragraphs, in English since all of us except Giovanni were native English speakers, and we even met, very briefly, the duke himself, who was fossicking around in the kitchen for something as we passed through. Interestingly, Gioacchino was given a fictional treatment in a novel by Canadian author Stephen Price in his biographical novel *Lampedusa*, which was published in 2019; as I read it, back in Melbourne, I wondered what the duke might have thought of the character that Price invented for him.

*

Modern Palermo's reputation has been shaped more by the Mafia than the glittering worlds of the Norman kings and their aristocratic successors. More than any other city in Italy, Palermo has suffered the ravages of this multi-limbed organisation of criminals and standover merchants, and has paid the price in blood of trying to win what seems a never ending war against their domination of the political and economic life of Sicily. While the worst of the outrages committed by the *Cosa Nostra* seem to have receded into history, the organisation itself has not disappeared, and its presence looms large in the imagination, if not the daily life, of most Palermitani. Rightly or wrongly, they are blamed for most of the city's ills, and

us to meet her and have a look at the palazzo, we jumped at the chance.

The charming and vivacious woman who introduced herself with a smile simply as 'Nicoletta' was indeed Nicoletta Lanza Tomasi, and her proper title is the Duchess of Palma, a title acquired when she married her husband, Gioacchino Lanza Tomasi, a scholarly expert on opera—and is the adoptive son of Giuseppe Tomasi di Lampedusa.

The palazzo in which we stood had been built at the end of the seventeenth century. By 1728 it had been converted into a religious university, quaintly named the Imperial College for the Education of Young Aristocrats, but when the college closed down forty years later the building was bought by Giuseppe Amato, Prince of Galati; he unified what had been a jumble of facades facing the sea, and created the terrace and the ballroom.

In 1849, the palazzo was bought by Prince Giulio Fabrizio Tomasi di Lampedusa; Giuseppe Tomasi was Prince Giulio's great-grandson, and he was brought up in the Palazzo Lampedusa, the family's main house in Palermo. That house was destroyed by allied bombs (it has in fact only recently been restored), driving Giuseppe into a long bout of depression, and forcing him to move to what is now the palazzo Lanza Tomasi. In 1954, in an attempt to combat his condition, he set out to write the manuscript that became *The Leopard*, using his great-grandfather as the model for the novel's central character, Prince Fabrizio. Diagnosed with lung cancer in 1957, he died the same year, his masterwork still unpublished.

Some years before his death, he had met and befriended a group of young intellectuals, among whom was a distant cousin, Gioacchino Lanza; in 1957 he adopted the young man, who succeeded to his title as duke of Palma di Montechiaro when the writer died. Since then Gioacchino and Nicoletta have worked to restore and preserve that palazzo where

is an eternal Sicily underneath that is impervious to change; perhaps this is hardly surprising for an island that has absorbed wave after wave of conquerors, taken what it wanted from them, and then eventually turned them into Sicilians.

It is a beautifully written book, languorous in pace and deeply evocative of time and place, but Lampedusa was unable to find a publisher for it before he died (one publisher told him it was 'unpublishable'). Even when it did finally find its way into print it was controversial, attacked by conservatives because they thought it portrayed the aristocracy as decadent, by the left because of its criticism of unification, and by the communists because Lampedusa adopted a decidedly non-Marxist view of the Sicilian working classes. Yet eventually it won great critical acclaim, and became a classic of Italian literature, winning the Strega Prize in 1959. And of course in 1963 Luchino Visconti made a fine film of the book, starring Burt Lancaster.

Having read the book many years ago, and of course having seen the film, Robert and I were both very excited when, through newly made friends, we had the chance to see the very place where Lampedusa wrote it. In Florence we had made the acquaintance of Glenn and Giovanni, the former an English art teacher and artist, the latter his partner and a native of Sicily; Glenn had just retired, and they had moved permanently to Palermo from London just a week or so before our arrival, where they were in the process of moving into their newly renovated apartment.

Over previous years before they made their permanent move, whenever they visited Palermo they stayed at an apartment complex in the Palazzo Lanza Tomasi, owned and managed by a lady who Glenn simply referred to as 'the Duchess'. At first, we thought this was either an affectation on his part, or perhaps a kind of nickname, but Glenn was insistent that she was a real, actual duchess; we were more than a little intrigued by this, and when Glenn suggested he could arrange for

ning to achieve some semblance of normality after the horrific ravages of the virus, the prospect of walking across the Ponte Vecchio or taking a *vaporetto* down the Grand Canal still seems to be an elusive prospect. We have all learned that Covid-19 makes fools of planners, and so like every Australian all we can do is dream and wait.

But Italy continues to exercise its fascination and attraction, and I have no doubt that the moment we are able to do so we will be booking that long flight and experiencing once again the thrill of landing in Rome or Milan, enjoying a pasta and glass of wine in a sunny piazza somewhere, and stimulating our intellects with visits to the great art galleries.

Born in Hertfordshire, England, Anthony R. Wildman migrated to Australia with his family in 1967. He grew up and was educated in South Australia, where he acquired a degree in history and politics from the University of Adelaide, which was the start of a lifelong fascination with both subjects.

After a career in business that saw him working in the oil industry, banking and finance, business services and management consulting, Anthony has embarked on a new phase of his life as a writer and novelist.

Though his long-term home is in Melbourne, Australia, where he lives with his partner Robert, he has journeyed extensively throughout Europe, Asia and America, satisfying his love of travel and new experiences.

**Also by Anthony R. Wildman:**

*What News on the Rialto? - The Lost Years of William Shakespeare*

*The Diplomat of Florence - A Novel of Machiavelli and the Borgias*

www.ingramcontent.com/pod-product-compliance
Lightning Source LLC
Chambersburg PA
CBHW050306010526
44107CB00055B/2127